"Immigration stands as the metric of whether or not America embraces social justice in the twenty-first century. In *Welcoming the Stranger* Jenny Yang and Matt Soerens contextualize the narrative of an issue that requires analysis and discussion not from the extremes of political ideology but rather from a platform of truth, justice, and compassion. Jenny and Matt equip us with the necessary acumen to reconcile Romans 13, the rule of law, with Leviticus 19, treating the alien as one of our own. Accordingly, the universal Christian symbol is the cross. The cross is both vertical and horizontal, redemption and transformation, conviction and compassion. This book will challenge us to meet at the point of convergence, the great intersect, where John 3:16 meets Luke 4, immigration via a biblical worldview."

Samuel Rodriguez, president, National Hispanic Christian Leadership Conference

"Drawing from their experience in the trenches, Soerens and Yang challenge their readers to move beyond the all-too-contentious and simplistic debate and think critically and biblically about what it means to love our immigrant neighbors. Clearly written and theologically informed, *Welcoming the Stranger* combines evocative stories of real people and the complexities of their lives with lucid explanations of immigration policy. Soerens and Yang's book offers balanced yet impassioned analysis that is so rare but so essential to help Christians bring their faith to bear on this vexing policy issue."

Amy Black, professor of political science at Wheaton College, author of *Honoring God in Red or Blue*

"Every Christian leader seeking an informed, biblical response to this urgent issue should read this book."

Bill Hybels and Lynne Hybels, cofounders of Willow Creek Community Church

"Justice, compassion, and truth are too often missing from the immigration debate in this country. *Welcoming the Stranger* provides all three with comprehensive information on every aspect of the current problem, its roots and commonsense solutions. Every Christian seeking an informed response to this critical issue should read this book."

Jim Wallis, president, Sojourners

"Here is a book for every Christian and every church leadership team interested in one of the greatest mercy/justice issues of our time: how will the church care for immigrants in our midst? The authors write with sensitivity concerning the volatile emotions on all sides of the debates as they offer essential information designed to help us formulate responses to this very complex issue. *Welcoming the Stranger* inspired me to expand my heart of compassion and take action."
Paul Borthwick, author of *Great Commission, Great Compassion*

"My friends Jenny Yang and Matthew Soerens have done the church a service by pointing our attention to the biblical expectation that we should care well for the stranger among us. Rather than reducing this conversation down to talking points, they have provided a thorough, researched, and biblical examination of a topic that's often hotly contested. I would encourage you to take the time to read and consider the explanations they offer. I think you'll find it practical as you attempt to live out a Christian calling in a challenging culture."
Micah Fries, senior pastor at Brainerd Baptist Church, Chattanooga, Tennessee

"This work by Yang and Soerens is vital for our time as it maps out a pathway of hospitality for those who are seriously seeking a biblical response to issues of immigration. Confusion abounds as we wrestle with issues that are extremely complex with no simple solutions. Opposing voices are polarizing, leaving Christians in need of a guide that helps us reflect Christ well to a world that is watching. This is that guide!"
Carla Sunberg, general superintendent, Church of the Nazarene

"*Welcoming the Stranger* has become a widely read explanation of a biblical response to immigration. It's refreshing to read Christian authors address a global crisis in a decidedly Christlike manner. Soerens and Yang lead the reader through a logical argument for a compassionate policy shift on this volatile topic. I can genuinely say after reading this book that maybe there is hope that the church will once again welcome the stranger."
Reid Ribble, former member of Congress representing Wisconsin's eighth congressional district

MATTHEW SOERENS & JENNY YANG

WELCOMING THE STRANGER

REVISED AND EXPANDED

JUSTICE,
COMPASSION
& TRUTH IN THE
IMMIGRATION DEBATE

IVP Books

An imprint of InterVarsity Press
Downers Grove, Illinois

InterVarsity Press
P.O. Box 1400, Downers Grove, IL 60515-1426
ivpress.com
email@ivpress.com

Second edition ©2018 by Matthew Soerens and Jenny Yang
First edition ©2009 by Matthew Soerens and Jenny Hwang

InterVarsity Press® is the book-publishing division of InterVarsity Christian Fellowship/USA®, a movement of
students and faculty active on campus at hundreds of universities, colleges, and schools of nursing in the United
States of America, and a member movement of the International Fellowship of Evangelical Students. For
information about local and regional activities, visit intervarsity.org.

All Scripture quotations, unless otherwise indicated, are taken from The Holy Bible, New International Version®,
NIV®. Copyright © 1973, 1978, 1984, 2011 by Biblica, Inc.™ Used by permission of Zondervan. All rights
reserved worldwide. www.zondervan.com. The "NIV" and "New International Version" are trademarks registered
in the United States Patent and Trademark Office by Biblica, Inc.™

While any stories in this book are true, some names and identifying information may have been changed to protect
the privacy of individuals.

Cover design: David Fassett
Interior design: Jeanna Wiggins
Cover images: watercolor strokes: © Ani_Ka / DigitalVision Vectors / Getty Images
                old shipping label: © ariellebw / iStock / Getty Images Plus
                traveler with suitcase: © fcscafeine / iStock / Getty Images Plus

ISBN 978-0-8308-4539-2 (print)
ISBN 978-0-8308-8555-8 (digital)

Printed in the United States of America ♾

Library of Congress Cataloging-in-Publication Data
A catalog record for this book is available from the Library of Congress.

P	22	21	20	19	18	17	16	15	14	13	12	11	10	9	8	7	6	5	4	3	2	1
Y	36	35	34	33	32	31	30	29	28	27	26	25	24	23	22	21	20	19	18			

TO OUR PARENTS,

Dave and Jane Soerens and

Byong-tak and Jong-hye Hwang,

with love and gratitude

CONTENTS

FOREWORD

Leith Anderson

NEW **Y**ORK **RABBI** **TAUGHT** **ME** **A** **LESSON** I had never before heard. He said that there is no Old Testament commandment to love your parents, husband, wife, or children. There are only three commands: to love the Lord your God, love your neighbor, and love the alien in the land. Deuteronomy 10:19 gives this third commandment to love and explains why: you were once aliens yourselves.

My mother was an alien in America. Her father died early in the last century of pernicious anemia, a disease that most of us have never heard of and that would easily be treated today. My widowed grandmother couldn't support herself and three daughters (all under six years old), so she moved back in with her parents. Nearly twenty years later she met and married an American and moved to the United States. But my mother had to stay behind because of US immigration laws and quotas. Unlike her younger sisters, my mother was an adult, and immigration was harder for her. She waited a year or two and then received a visa as a domestic worker, sailing across the North Atlantic to New York and to her new country.

When I was a little boy I went with my mother to the post office every January, where she was required by law to register as an alien. On our family vacations to Canada, she always waited for us on the US side of the border out of fear there might be problems returning if she left the country. Eventually she became an American citizen.

She lived to be almost one hundred years old, spending the last seven years of her life in a nursing home in Boca Raton, Florida, where much of the staff was foreign born. The hallway buzz ranged from Haitian Creole to Jamaican English. Her physician was from Southeast Asia. They loved my mother. They gave her care I could not provide. They were kind and gracious. These immigrant caregivers prayed for her, quoted the Bible, and sang hymns. They were the best of believers.

As my mother's final hours counted down, they came to her room in a steady stream. Some came to see her on their days off. Because my mother outlived most of her friends, these who were not native born became my mother's final friends.

I love these immigrants. I need these immigrants.

You see, every immigrant story is a personal story. Behind the statistics and politics are stories of mothers and fathers, sons and daughters, husbands and wives. There are millions of stories that vary as much as race, nationality, gender, and faith.

When you read about all the complexity of immigration and think about what needs to be done, remember God's commandment in Deuteronomy 10:19 and love the immigrants.

ONE

THE IMMIGRATION DILEMMA

Some [Christians] on either side of this debate insist that this issue is not complex. For them, it is simply a matter of legality or justice for the poor. . . . But denying the complexity of this issue is both intellectually wrong and practically unhelpful. If we aren't willing to deal with the intricacy of this issue, we won't ever be able to make headway in solving it.

MARK D. ROBERTS, EVANGELICAL PASTOR, PROFESSOR, AND AUTHOR

NEARLY EVERYONE SEEMS TO AGREE that we have an immigration problem in the United States. The exact nature of the problem, though, is heatedly disputed. From one perspective, our nation is facing an unprecedented invasion of "illegal aliens," who violate our laws upon entry and then become a drain on social services and public education systems, depress wages and displace native-born American workers, and then contribute to increases in poverty, crime rates, and even terrorism. A campaign flier for candidates for the Carpentersville, Illinois, city council some years ago expresses the frustrations of many Americans:

Are you tired of waiting to pay for your groceries while Illegal Aliens pay with food stamps and then go outside and get in a $40,000 car? Are you tired of paying taxes when Illegal Aliens pay NONE!

Are you tired of reading that another Illegal Alien was arrested for drug dealing?

Are you tired of having to punch 1 for English?

Are you tired of seeing multiple families in our homes?

Are you tired of not being able to use Carpenter Park on the weekend, because it is over run by Illegal Aliens?

Are you tired of seeing the Mexican Flag flown above our Flag?[1]

Others see the current state of immigration as a problem for very different reasons. They see millions of people who have, usually for economic reasons, accepted displacement from their home countries to pursue a better life for themselves and their families in the United States, just as generations of immigrants have done before them. Tragically, from this perspective, these people are not welcomed into our society, but are scapegoated and forced into a shadowy existence by broken immigration laws, even though they contribute to our nation's economy by performing a host of jobs, most of which few native-born Americans would be willing to do. Undocumented immigrant Elvira Arellano spent a year living inside a Methodist church in Chicago in an ultimately unsuccessful attempt to avoid deportation that would separate her from her eight-year-old, US-citizen son. She became something of a spokesperson for this perspective:

> Out of fear and hatred of an enemy you cannot find you have set out to destroy our lives and our families. As you knocked on my door, you are knocking on thousands of doors, ripping mothers and fathers away from their terrified children. You have a list of . . . Social Security no-match numbers, and you are following that list as if we were terrorists and criminals instead of workers with families. You are denying us work and the seniority and benefits we have earned, and you are taking the property we have saved for and bought.[2]

From either of these perspectives, the immigration dilemma seems frustratingly simple. As both sides rail against the other, and against the government, where Congress has proposed competing bills but has yet to pass into law any substantial changes in immigration policy, we are left with the status quo—essentially the same status quo we faced a decade ago when we wrote the first edition of this book: an estimated eleven million people with no valid immigration status living and, usually, working in the United States. After the presidential campaign of 2016, in which immigration became a central issue, the debate over how to respond to immigrants in the country illegally seems more polarized than ever.

Since the first edition of *Welcoming the Stranger*, another category of "stranger" has become particularly controversial: refugees, who have long come to the United States *with* legal status at the invitation of our federal government, have joined immigrants *without* legal status as a uniquely suspect category of "foreigner" in the minds of many Americans. As with the debate over illegal immigration, the refugee debate seems frustratingly simple to those on either side: to some, it is foolhardy to admit anyone into our country from nations plagued by terrorism, lest we welcome terrorists themselves. To others, welcoming the persecuted and oppressed is an unqualified good, integral to our national character. The two sides have a hard time understanding the other, as evidenced by harsh words shared over social media and even over family dinners and church potlucks.

Less vocal in these immigration debates are the many who suspect that immigration is actually a complicated, nuanced issue. Partisans of a particular policy position are apt to view the issue as very simple—right versus wrong, us versus them.

Yet, as political scientist Amy Black notes, it is these "easy" issues that often prove the most complex and the hardest to resolve since our presumptions keep us from hearing the other side.[3] Within this debate, a growing middle recognizes this is not a simple issue. They want a more thoughtful, informed understanding of the issues than offered by the two-minute screaming matches by advocates of differing perspectives on cable news channels and talk radio.

Those of us who seek to follow Christ, in particular, face a challenge in sorting through the rhetoric to understand how we can reflect God's justice as well as his love and compassion in designing a national immigration policy, and in the ways we relate individually to the immigrants in our communities. On first glance at the issue, we recognize that immigrants are people made in God's image who should be treated with respect; at the same time, we believe God has instituted the government and the laws that it puts into place for a reason, and that as Christians we are generally bound to submit to the rule of law. Many are left conflicted, unsure of what our faith requires of us on this pressing issue.

Through the work of World Relief, the Christian ministry where we both work that serves refugees and other immigrants throughout the United States, we might find ourselves on a regular basis in a church, speaking with people about issues of immigration and citizenship, or in a congressperson's office, talking with staffers about the need to fix the immigration system. Sometimes we speak in Spanish or with translation in Lithuanian, Arabic, or Cantonese to an audience of immigrants eager to naturalize or fearful of what a newly announced immigration-enforcement policy will mean for them and their families. Other times we are speaking in front of a predominantly nonimmigrant church group, answering questions about immigration policy. When we are in front of an audience of nonimmigrant evangelicals or before congressional staffers who are helping our political leaders form immigration policy, we find that many are asking the same questions we have often asked ourselves. This book seeks to address some of the most common questions and misconceptions that we and other Christians have wrestled with as we consider the immigration "problem."

This book is written out of our own personal experiences with this dilemma, tracing through much of the investigation our own questions have led us to in seeking to understand immigration policy—and, more important, immigrants themselves—through the lens of our faith. While it would be disingenuous to pretend that we do not have strong opinions about how we (as individuals, as the church, and as a society) should approach this issue, our foremost interest is not to convince you of the virtue of any particular piece of legislation. Rather, we hope this book will encourage our sisters and brothers to take a step back from the rhetoric and combine a basic understanding of how immigration works, and has worked in the United States, with a biblical worldview. We do not believe there is one Christian prescription to solve the immigration issue (though there may be decidedly un-Christian ways to view the issue), and there is plenty of space within the church for charitable disagreement on issues such as this.

LEARNING THROUGH RELATIONSHIPS

More than just a policy question, immigration is also personal to each of us, because of the many immigrants we have come to know. These relationships have transformed our own perspectives. Each immigrant, and each nonimmigrant affected by immigration, has a distinct story that cannot be summarized by abstract statistics or polling data.

I (Matthew) have been particularly marked by getting to know some of my neighbors, first in a diverse apartment complex with neighbors from more than twenty nations, now in a neighborhood where most households are of Mexican origin.

My first friend in the apartment complex where I lived for many years is Jean.[4] He is now in college in a suburb of Chicago, but he was born in Rwanda shortly before genocide broke out in that small East African country in 1994. He fled with his family to Tanzania, then to the Congo, and then finally to Zambia, where he lived for nearly a decade. In 2005, Jean and his family were accepted by the US government as refugees to be resettled in the United States. With the help of churches, volunteers, the Rwandese community already in the United States, and World Relief, they have made a new life for themselves step by step. When I met them, Jean's mother and father were working hard in difficult, low-paying jobs at all hours of the day and night to pay the bills and even to pay the US government back for their seven transatlantic airline tickets. Jean was less concerned with his family's finances than about fitting in at his school, mastering American English (his fifth language, which he was concerned he spoke with an accent) and finding a lawn-mowing job for the summer. He was tired of sharing a bedroom with his four sisters and often mentioned what he missed of Africa, but he was thankful to be safe.

Another neighbor, Elena, had a very different story. She came to the United States from Mexico in 1990 at age twenty-six, crossing the border illegally with the expensive assistance of a *coyote* (a people smuggler), hoping to find a job that would let her make ends meet—something she could not find in Mexico. She has now lived and worked here for more than a quarter century, is involved in her church (a Catholic parish that has nearly as many people in its Spanish-language masses each weekend as in its English masses), has married and divorced in the United States, and raised two children on a limited income. She speaks enough English to work the drive-through at the fast food restaurant across the street, but she is not fluent and often came by to ask for help reading a letter in English from her children's school; she often also brought delicious enchiladas or *chilaquiles*. (I gained forty pounds as her neighbor for eight years, for which I think she is partially responsible.)

Elena is very proud that her children speak English but sometimes laments their reluctance to speak Spanish. She prays for a legalization of some sort, or that her US-born children will eventually be able to help her get a green card. She notes the small amount of assistance that the African refugees like Jean's family receive from the government, for which she is ineligible, even though she too struggles to support her family. Still, she is happy to be here. "I live better here than in Mexico," she told me shortly after I met her. "Here, nothing lacks"—an astonishing statement, given that she sometimes fell behind on the rent payments for the modest one-bedroom apartment that she shared with three others in her family, could not afford a car, and had no health insurance—"I have work. In Mexico, there is no work."

Two doors down from Elena lived an African American family who moved from a rough neighborhood on the west side of Chicago, seeking to avoid the gang violence there. The mother, Serena, worked at a fast food restaurant while preparing to take the GED high school equivalency exam. She got along fine with her neighbors—she even gave Elena's daughter a ride to school on rainy days—but she told me she did not think it was right that the Mexican immigrants come illegally and take jobs when her husband was out of work. She too notices the help that the African refugees receive from churches and wonders why something like that is not available for someone who was born in this country.

Living in relationships with immigrants, refugees, and other low-income people has forced us to grapple with the question of what it means for us, as followers of Christ, to love our neighbors as we love ourselves. It has also awakened us to the ethically complex questions of immigration and refugee policy—who do we let in, what do we do with those who came in even though our government did not allow them in, and what effect will our policies have on those already here and struggling to get by? Of course, our attempts to address these questions have been shaped by our own personal journeys.

MATTHEW'S STORY

I grew up in an evangelical home with parents who were (and are) committed to their faith in Jesus Christ. We attended a nondenominational evangelical church where politics were seldom if ever mentioned. I suspect, though, that a survey would have shown that a large majority of my congregation, including my family and me, identified with a generally conservative political stance—particularly on issues such as abortion or religious liberty, but also probably on issues of immigration policy. I had little exposure to immigrants growing up in the small city of Neenah, Wisconsin. While Hmong people from Laos had been resettled in neighboring towns, I never interacted with them. There were a few Mexican and Asian immigrants in my town, but almost everyone in my elementary school was descended from white immigrants from Europe at least two or three generations back, if not more. My own ancestors came from Holland in the mid-1800s, long enough ago that the immigrant experience felt removed from my reality; what I knew about immigrants and immigration I knew primarily from television. As I relocated to the Chicago area for college, I realized that refugees and other immigrants were all around me, yet I still did not know them.

Ironically, I began to think a lot more about US immigration while outside the United States. I spent a summer living and volunteering in San José, Costa Rica. There I played sports, tutored, and led Bible studies in a community of immigrants from Nicaragua. Much like Mexicans and Central Americans who go north to find a better economic situation in the United States, hundreds of thousands of Nicaraguans have gone south, both legally and illegally, to take advantage of a more vibrant economy in Costa Rica—and like immigrants in the United States, Nicaraguans in Costa Rica are not always warmly welcomed. In fact, most Costa Ricans would never set foot in the neighborhood where I was volunteering because of its reputation for poverty and violence. I was startled to hear the crude ways in which some Costa Ricans, even committed Christians, scapegoated the hard-working Nicaraguan immigrants, many who had become my friends, for all the country's ills—and then God convicted me that I'd harbored similar attitudes toward immigrants in the United States that I'd never bothered to know personally.

I returned to Central America a few years later, where I worked with a local organization affiliated with World Relief, *Pueblos en Acción Comunitaria*, as they sought to help farmers in rural Nicaragua raise their incomes by providing small loans. In my time there, I saw firsthand the extreme poverty and chronic unemployment that motivate many people to emigrate. Particularly when lured by promises and rumors (true or untrue) of generous salaries and unparalleled opportunity in the United States, many of the people I met hoped one day to find a better life in another country for their families, even if that meant going *mojado* (literally, wet—as in having crossed the Río Grande River illegally). Seeing the conditions in which many Nicaraguans live—for some, on less than $1 per day—I could hardly blame them for entertaining this option.

When I returned to the United States, I accepted a job with World Relief's office in the suburbs of Chicago, where I was able to use my Spanish language skills to partner with churches to assist immigrants in integrating into our society. In the process I have gotten to know many immigrants, heard their stories, and begun to understand why they left their home countries for the United States. My specific job description as an immigration legal counselor allowed me to learn a great deal about our country's immigration laws, exposing my own previous ignorance: much of what I believed about immigration was inaccurate.

On graduation from college, I also decided to move into the diverse apartment complex where Jean, Elena, and Serena lived. My move was based, at least in part, on a desire to understand who my new neighbors were, to try to love them as myself (though I have not always done this well), and to share with them the grace and love I have experienced in Christ. Within that apartment complex, located in a well-to-do suburb of Chicago, I had neighbors born in Mexico, Sudan, Somalia, Rwanda, Burundi, Sierra Leone, Burma, Vietnam, and India, among other countries, as well as some Caucasians (like myself) and African Americans whose ancestors came to this country decades or centuries ago. Being a part of this community allowed me to put human faces on the immigration dilemma and has led me deeper into questions of how I ought to think about and act on the immigration "problem."

When that apartment complex was bought by a new company and converted into "luxury apartments" that few of my immigrant neighbors could afford, my wife and I moved to Aurora, Illinois, to a neighborhood where the vast majority of our neighbors are Mexican immigrants or their families. Worshiping in a Spanish-speaking church, we have witnessed the fear on many of our neighbors' faces as a US presidential election rife with anti-immigrant rhetoric gave way to a new administration that many of my neighbors feared would disrupt their lives and livelihoods.

Since the publication of the first edition of this book, my role with World Relief has shifted as well. Most of my job is now focused on engaging local churches, whose leaders are wrestling with the biblical, legal, and political complexities of immigration. While there is fear in many immigrant congregations, I also frequently encounter fear among native-born Christians, some of whom are concerned that a growing immigrant population could harm their economic prospects, endanger their safety, or simply change the culture around them to such a point that they no longer recognize it. Those fears, on all sides, have been heightened after a political season in which immigration has played a more central role than ever in my lifetime. My challenge is to help these diverse groups of Christ-followers understand the other's perspective and recognize the opportunity that immigration presents for the church in the United States if we respond out of biblically informed convictions, rather than fear.

JENNY'S STORY

I grew up in a Christian home where both of my parents were immigrants from South Korea. My older brother and I were born in Philadelphia a few years after my parents immigrated to the United States.

My dad has one of the most amazing stories of resilience and strength of any immigrant I have ever met. His grandfather and father owned a large, well-regarded newspaper in Korea in the early 1900s. Through this company a love for journalism grew in my family. During the Korean War of 1950, the communist forces invaded Korea and proceeded to kill all the media personnel first. My grandfather was killed during the war, and my father, still an infant, was left with his mother, who eventually became sick and died when he was ten years old. My father was an orphan and extremely poor in a country where rice and spare portions of vegetables were the meals of the day, and where a single pair of shoes with holes was supposed to last you years through the winter snow and summer heat. My grandmother, however, was a Christian. (Many Koreans were being brought to faith by American missionaries who were entering Korea in large numbers at the time.) Her faith in God led my father to also accept Jesus Christ as his Savior at a young age. His faith in God sustained him through his parents' death and as he lived with his uncle, who was also poor and struggled to support my father through school.

In order to support himself my father tutored his fellow classmates and helped the teacher after school. He eventually became president of his class in high school. Having loved cars all throughout his childhood, he applied for a grant to go to Japan to visit the car manufacturing factories there. He received the grant and went to tour the Japanese car manufacturing facilities, which deepened his love for cars. Upon his return, he wrote a report for the company that employed him. My dad learned how to fix cars in his local neighborhood and eventually entered a national car-repair competition and won first place. One of the judges during the competition noticed my father and asked him if he would like to go with him to the United States. My father's dream since he was a young child was to go to the United States, a land where the "streets were paved with gold" and there was an abundance of food and opportunity to pursue his dreams. In Korea, he didn't really have a place he could call home, and it would have been extremely difficult for him to climb up in society.

He readily accepted and landed in the United States with the dream of one day opening up his own business. He started working for Volkswagen and then for the Ford Motor Company as a mechanic, then went back to

Korea for a few years, where he met my mother. They married and immigrated to the United States. Through hard work and the grace of God, my father fulfilled his lifelong dream by eventually owning his own auto mechanic shop. Life in the United States was not as easy as he thought, however. When he first immigrated to the United States, he went to the supermarket and bought a can of breadcrumbs with a picture of fried chicken on the front. He was so ecstatic because he did not know fried chicken was so cheap and easy to eat! He hurriedly went home and eagerly opened the can, only to peer in and see bread crumbs staring back at him. He saved money, ate fast food, and lived in a small apartment. He also regularly attended church and found a sense of community there. While life was not easy, he was always grateful to God for the opportunity to immigrate to the United States, and he did everything he could to express his thanks by raising his children to love God, serving in the church, and giving back to his community.

My father has a deep, abiding love of this country grounded in the opportunities he was given when he first arrived. During his citizenship interview, the interviewing officer commended my father for his hard work ethic and his easy grasp of English, saying he was a model immigrant and that the United States was proud to have people like him here. My father has never missed a day of work and uses his auto mechanic services to help those in need in the community. He still loves journalism and writes frequently for the local Korean newspaper, and he is a well-respected leader in his church and among his friends.

While my father's immigrant experience is a story I share often with friends and colleagues, I also grew up in the United States having to form my identity as a full American, born and bred in this country, yet with a cultural background and appearance distinct from the dominant culture. I was not an immigrant myself but grew up in an immigrant home where the hardships my parents endured to "make it" in this country formed my personal identity and my faith in Christ. Growing up as a minority, I wondered whether people would ever think of me as an American without having my appearance predispose them to think I was a "foreigner." In fact, in order to fit in, I didn't want to learn the Korean language growing up and struggled with whether to be proud of my Korean heritage. Even though I speak English fluently, love American football, and have been educated here, people are surprised sometimes that I can speak English as well as I can, and they have often asked me, "Where are you *really* from?"

The political debate over immigration in the United States was not something I paid particular attention to until later in life. While in college, I had studied migration issues at a macrolevel and always had a general interest in immigration due to my background. When I studied and worked in Madrid, Spain, I realized that immigration affects not just the United States but other industrialized countries too as their populations age and as migrants take jobs traditionally occupied by their native workforce.

Soon after college, I started working at World Relief on advocacy for refugee and immigration issues. I had my own reservations and initial misgivings about why the system was so broken in the first place and how it had come to this point. My advocacy work in Washington, DC, dispelled much of the misinformation I had previously believed.

More important, my work exposed me to the human side of the story. Stories of undocumented immigrants softened my heart and mind to investigate the issue further. Living in Baltimore, I knew that a growing immigrant population there was challenging the traditional ideas and expectations of what the city should "look like," and I knew this issue was affecting not just Baltimore but communities all across America and throughout the world. As I studied immigration I realized more and more how outdated laws and policies create confusion and pain, and that the church could play a vital role by bringing to light the human aspects of an issue mired in numbers and politics.

In the course of writing the first edition of this book, I also realized that questions of legal status had actually always been closer to me than I realized, but sometimes unmentioned. At one point I went back to my home church outside of Philadelphia to seek prayer from my former youth pastor. As I explained the topic of this book, my pastor mentioned that there were several undocumented Korean immigrant youth in the congregation whose lack of legal status had made it impossible for them to reenter the United States if they were to participate in a missions trip to Mexico like the one I had been a part of as a high schooler. To accommodate these undocumented youth, the church's short-term youth mission trips now go to cities within the United States rather than leaving the country.

Immigration issues and immigrants themselves are not going to go away. If the church does not respond now, it will eventually have to respond in one way or another. Will our response be one that we can look back on a century later and say we were proud to have taken? We must, as God's stewards, respond in a way that is based on facts and reflects God's justice and compassion. World Relief's position in the immigration debate grew out of its work with immigrants in the United States, and it was through this position that I grew to have a deeper understanding of the issue beyond the rhetoric. Since the first edition of the book, I have become more passionate that the church's position on immigration will define its witness to a hurt and broken world.

CHARTING THE COURSE

Through this book, we will attempt to put a human face on the immigration issue by introducing you to a number of immigrants. It is easy to forget, when talking about a complex issue like immigration, rife with competing statistics used liberally by both sides of the debate, that we are essentially talking about human beings, each one made in God's image. C. S. Lewis reminds us that each human being—the foreign born certainly not excluded—is an immortal being with a destiny much greater than this life alone, and in this sense is "the holiest object presented to your senses."[5] Our faith prohibits us from seeing any person as anything less than human and therefore sacred.

The terminology we use in English to refer to foreigners is quite unhelpful for keeping the uniqueness and sacredness of humanity in our minds. According to the dictionary, in the language of our immigration laws and even some older translations of the Bible, it is entirely proper to refer to a person from another country as an *alien*, and no disrespect is inherently intended. Yet the fact that the term is now more commonly used to describe an extraterrestrial means that our minds go to Hollywood-induced images of three-headed green Martians when we hear about aliens, not to human beings with families and faith, made in God's image just like ourselves.

We also prefer not to use the term *illegal* as a noun, as in "an illegal." We do not deny that it is illegal to enter the United States without a valid visa and inspection, nor do we condone any illegal activity. However, while entry without inspection (or overstaying a temporary visa) is an illegal activity, this does not define the person's identity. Many of us have broken a law at one time or another (we can both confess to having sped down the highway on more than one occasion), but if a single (or even, in the case of our speeding, repeated) act were to define our identity, we would probably all be "illegals." Such terminology, in common usage, lumps immigrants— whose entering or overstaying unlawfully usually does not require any malicious intent—with criminals like murderers, rapists, and kidnappers. It is too easy to dehumanize such immigrants when we lump them with such unsavory characters.[6] So, rather than referring to people as illegal aliens, we have generally opted to refer to people as undocumented immigrants throughout this text.

Chapter two will, we hope, help us recapture the human element of the immigration dilemma, focusing on who immigrants and refugees are, why they come to our country, and how they are received when they get here. We particularly focus on the roughly eleven million people who have no legal right to be present, as they, even more than immigrants who are here legally, bear most of the ill will stirred up by the immigration debate, and are probably the most likely to be dismissed as different from ourselves. A few of the stories we convey here are updated versions of stories we wrote about in the first edition of this book; several others are new.

In chapter three we present a concise history of our nation's immigration history—from the earliest settlers entering at Ellis Island to the new waves of immigrants that began to reach our shores after the last major immigration reform was passed in 1965. We cannot adequately understand the current situation without understanding what has occurred in the past. In particular, we want to look at where our churches have been on this complex issue—which, as it does today, has always stirred passions.

In chapter four, drawing on Matthew's experience as an immigration legal practitioner, we explain our current immigration legal system—one that is quite complex, and that can be difficult to understand even for those who work with it day to day. A basic understanding of how our immigration laws work (and do not work) today is crucial if we are to understand why so many people have come to the United States illegally.

Chapter five takes a step back and examines immigration from a biblical and theological perspective, reviewing the many immigrants in Scripture and what the Bible has to say about interacting with immigrants. While we will, of course, not find a specific prescription for US immigration policy spelled out in the Bible, we can certainly identify principles that help us ascertain how God would have us, as followers of Christ, address this complex topic. Above all, we suggest that the ethic of loving our neighbor—including the immigrant—is central to God's desire for us as we wrestle with this issue.

In chapter six, we address many of the most common concerns about immigration—both legal and illegal—including those from a Christian perspective. While some of these security, economic, cultural, and political concerns are the same critiques that have long dominated the immigration debate, several others have become more prominent in the current political moment.

Chapter seven considers the impact of immigration on our country. We examine the US economy and show how many industries depend on immigrant labor. While immigrants' contributions are much more than economic—and our biblical call to welcome remains regardless of whether or not immigrants make us marginally wealthier—the economic realities of immigration are a compelling part of the national conversation.

Chapter eight provides an overview of the political environment for immigrants and refugees within an unconventional presidential administration. While the Trump administration has implemented a number of dramatic changes in its first several months in office, members of Congress have also debated a wide range of policy proposals, from mass deportation to amnesty for all. Coming closer to becoming law—though there have been no major changes as of this writing—are compromise bills that include both stricter border enforcement as well as an earned legalization for at least some of the undocumented, requiring them to pay a fine and meet other criteria in order to receive their legal status. We draw on Jenny's experience in representing World Relief's position in Washington over the past decade as we walk through the most recent policy proposals.

In chapter nine, we examine how many of the churches and denominations in our country—particularly those of the evangelical tradition, with which we both identify—have engaged the immigration dilemma, documenting a significant shift in evangelical engagement with immigration issues over the past decade. We will also examine how immigration is changing the church itself in America today and what this means for how the church should respond to immigrants.

Finally, chapter ten provides some suggestions for moving forward. There are many responses: by serving and getting to know our immigrant neighbors through volunteering, by advocating for more just governmental policies, by educating our churches and communities, and by addressing the larger structural issues that lead to poverty, war, and environmental disasters in other countries and thus to the waves of immigration we face today.

We hope you will be convinced—not necessarily of which policy to support but at least, as a follower of Christ, that we each are called to love and serve our foreign-born neighbors. Appendixes at the end of the book provide resources for getting started in this process.

We expect that readers will look at this immigration dilemma from a wide range of perspectives. We may have already offended some of you just in the first chapter, as immigration is a highly charged topic. Our sincere prayer is that you will continue to journey with us to explore these difficult questions, and that each of us, personally and corporately as the church, would seek God's heart on this issue. To begin, we need to understand who the immigrants at the center of this controversy *are*, which is the topic of chapter two.

TWO

"ALIENS" AMONG YOU

Who Are Undocumented Immigrants?

We have no idea who these people are,
where these people are.

DONALD J. TRUMP, IN A CAMPAIGN SPEECH
ON IMMIGRATION, PHOENIX, AUGUST 31, 2016

THE MILLIONS OF UNDOCUMENTED IMMIGRANTS living in the United States—approximately eleven million of them, according to researchers—are at the center of the immigration debate.[1] For many Americans the issue is compounded by a great confusion about who these undocumented immigrants are: Why do they come here? Where do they come from? What do they do once they are here? And what effect do they have on our communities?

The reality is that many American citizens have limited meaningful interaction with immigrants (any individual from one country who now resides permanently in another) and even less interaction with undocumented immigrants. Today, immigrants live in just about every corner of the United States. While, historically, most immigrants once lived in large cities like New York, Chicago, Los Angeles, and Miami, increasingly immigrants are also showing up in small towns in places like Iowa, North Carolina, Wisconsin, and Idaho. While many immigrants are themselves Christians, there are many in the church who could count on one hand the number of immigrants they would consider friends.

SIFTING THROUGH THE RHETORIC

For those who do not know many immigrants personally, much of what is known comes from secondary sources—particularly anecdotal stories passed around the water cooler at work or the coffee pot at church, forwarded in an email, shared on Facebook or Twitter, or heard on television or radio. Much of what we hear is inaccurate.

For example, an email that has been circulating for several years, citing the *Los Angeles Times* as its source, claims that "95 percent of warrants for murder in Los Angeles are for illegal aliens," "75 percent of people on the Most Wanted List in Los Angeles are illegal aliens," and "over [two-thirds] of all births in Los Angeles County are to illegal alien Mexicans on [Medicaid] whose births were paid for by taxpayers."[2] In reality, as Chuck Colson pointed out in a 2006 column calling on Christians to think more critically and compassionately about immigration, none of these "facts" are true, nor did they come from the *Los Angeles Times*.[3] That has not stopped the email from spreading: I (Matthew) recently received a version of it in my inbox more than a decade after the now-deceased Colson lamented Christian participation in spreading the slanderous message.

Most of us are savvy enough not to believe everything we read on the Internet, but we may be more likely to trust what we hear from news sources. Yet even here, we find that not everything reported about immigrants is accurate. For example, a 2015 *Fox News* report claimed that undocumented immigrants "account for far more crimes than their 3.5-percent share of the US population would suggest, [accounting for] 13.6 percent of all offenders sentenced for crimes committed in the U.S. [and] twelve percent of murder sentences."[4] The report was influential, confirming the suspicions of many viewers and online readers and even being cited by lawmakers who voted in favor of a House of Representatives bill that purported to crackdown on "criminal aliens."[5]

However, these statistics are incredibly misleading. The *Fox News* report draws its conclusions primarily from data within a 2014 US Sentencing Commission report on *federal* crimes, not, as the *Fox News* piece implies, all crimes committed in the United States. That distinction actually is incredibly important, because about 90 percent of criminals in the United States are *not* convicted of federal crimes but of violating state and local laws.[6] Undocumented immigrants make up a disproportionate share of *federal* prisoners because certain federal offenses (such as unlawful entry to the country) are specifically related to immigration, but undocumented immigrants are actually 44 percent *less* likely to be incarcerated in local, state, or federal facilities than native-born US citizens.[7]

The menacing finding that undocumented immigrants were responsible for 12 percent of all murder sentences was based on a grand total of *nine* convictions (out of a total of forty-five mentioned in the report on federal crime). But there were more than *fourteen thousand* murders committed in the United States in 2014, and those charged federally are not a representative sample of the whole. It's like surveying people at your family reunion and concluding that most Americans share your surname.

Sadly, this sort of misuse of statistics is persistent: it's very similar to a 2005 report on CNN by Lou Dobbs, making the same inflated claims of immigrant criminality based on federal (but not state or local) prison statistics.[8]

In addition to manipulating statistics, some opposed to immigration tend to rely on isolated, anecdotal situations to build stereotypes. Author James Russell, for example, begins his book (a critique of the role of American churches in guiding immigration policy) with the story of an undocumented immigrant in Oregon who raped a Catholic nun and then strangled her to death with her own rosary beads.[9] Similarly, many politicians have highlighted the 2015 death of Kate Steinle in San Francisco at the hands of an undocumented man who had already been deported on multiple occasions. Each of these instances are true and absolutely horrific; the perpetrators should be prosecuted to the full extent of the law and deported if they were ever to be allowed out of prison. However, it's inaccurate to presume that they are representative of *all* or even *most* undocumented immigrants, who researchers consistently find commit crimes at lower rates than US citizens. In fact, as Ed Stetzer notes, an undocumented immigrant from Latin America is more likely to be an evangelical pastor than they are to be a murderer.[10]

While most American Christians reject obviously prejudiced and hateful statements, it is easy, if we hear false statistics and stereotypes repeated frequently enough, to subconsciously suspect they are at least partially true. As followers of Christ who are committed to the truth, we need to carefully consider what we read, see and hear, fact-checking carefully and always asking who the source is and what their motivations are.

That is particularly important because many of the misconceptions about immigrants (of all legal statuses) are disseminated by organizations rooted in a philosophy of population control, whose central conviction is that there are too many people living in the United States. The same concerns that have led some to advocate dramatic immigration restrictions have also led some to seek to limit population growth by supporting abortion or even forced sterilization.[11] For example, John Tanton, who was involved in founding three of the most prominent groups advocating lower immigration levels and harsh policies toward the undocumented (NumbersUSA, the Federation for American Immigration Reform, and the Center for Immigration Studies), also began a Planned Parenthood chapter to help broaden access to abortion and speaks favorably of China's "one child" forced abortion policy, saying it is "unfortunate" that India has not slowed its population growth as China has.[12] Few Christians would affirm such extreme views, but many consume misinformation about immigrants from sources motivated by the same population-control ideologies without realizing it—and end up with a skewed view of who immigrants are.

WHO ARE IMMIGRANTS?

If immigrants are not necessarily who we hear they are on television or the Internet, we are still left wondering: *Who are these people?* Statistics about the undocumented population are always going to be estimates, as those without immigration status are sometimes wary to participate in surveys or census questionnaires. Still, we consider the demographic information from governmental agencies and from the Pew Research Center and the Migration Policy Institute, two nonpartisan research institutions, to be among the most reliable, unbiased data.

I (Matthew) have also included a number of stories from immigrants; most are my friends and acquaintances and for that reason are geographically concentrated near my home in Illinois. Indeed, anecdotal evidence can be twisted easily, but the stories I have selected generally represent the diversity of immigrant experiences I have encountered in the immigrant neighborhoods where I have lived and through my work as an immigration counselor with World Relief. All of the stories in this chapter and throughout the book are factual, personal stories, shared with the individuals' consent, but to guard their privacy we have changed names and identifying details in some cases.

IMMIGRANTS: DOCUMENTED AND UNDOCUMENTED

In any discussion about undocumented immigrants, it is important to remember that most foreign-born people in the United States have legal status. Of an estimated 44.7 million people born outside but living inside the United States, about twenty million are already naturalized US citizens, and roughly twelve million are Lawful Permanent Residents.[13] There are also about two million people who are lawfully present but who do not yet qualify for Lawful Permanent Resident status, such those on temporary work visas or refugees in their first year within the country. Thus, most foreign-born individuals—about three out of four—are present lawfully. The rest of the immigrants currently in the United States—an estimated eleven million people—have no legal status, meaning either that they entered the country without inspection or overstayed a visa.[14] We focus most of this chapter on stories and statistics related to undocumented immigrants not because they are the most "typical" immigrants but because they arguably have been the most misunderstood.

Pedro, Martha, and family: Economic realities. Pedro and Martha are both originally from Morelos, a small Mexican state just south of the capital city. They married young and have long struggled economically, as many do in Mexico; in the mid- to late-1990s, when migration levels from Mexico to the United States began to rise dramatically, roughly 30 percent of the Mexican population survived on less than $3.10 per day, though that percentage has fortunately declined significantly in recent years.[15] Early in their marriage, Martha recalls, they had nothing to eat besides simple corn tortillas and salt. They considered migrating several decades ago to find better work and a better future in the United States, but under US immigration law their financial situation made it unlikely that they would be granted even a visitor visa.

Pedro found work in a factory, making fabrics for export; it was hard work at a relatively low wage, but the family was able to support themselves. The couple had four children over the years. It was a challenging life, but they were surviving. Then the factory where Pedro worked went bankrupt and closed, and Pedro lost his job. Pedro found other jobs but could not make enough income to support the family. Afraid to ask her husband for money that she knew they did not have, but unwilling to see her children drop out of school, Martha began to take out loans for their children's school expenses. Eventually, she had to tell her husband that they were severely indebted, with interest payments for the school loans using up the better part of the income Pedro was bringing in.

Desperate, the couple decided their only option was for Pedro to head north; their seventeen-year-old son, Harold, decided to accompany him. Martha would stay behind along with the three other children. Pedro had relatives living in the Chicago suburbs—two sisters and some cousins—who offered a temporary place to stay and to help them find work. They would send money back to pay off the debt and support the rest of the family.

The family took out one more loan, enough to cover the $3,800 Pedro would have to pay a *coyote*, or smuggler, to bring him and his son illegally into the United States. Pedro and Harold set out. Their group consisted of two smugglers, one male and one female, and eighteen migrants. As they crossed the Mexico-Arizona border in the desert, the group was spotted by US Border Patrol agents, and everyone ran in different directions. Harold remembered his father's instruction: "Whatever happens, we stay together."

They ended up together, but they were separated from part of their group, including the more experienced smuggler. They now had no way to arrive in Phoenix, as had been the plan, so they jumped on a slow-moving freight train, holding on for twelve hours and trying desperately to stay awake.

When they finally arrived in Phoenix, several days later than planned, Pedro was able to call Martha by telephone and assure her that, though tired and traumatized by the journey, they were okay. Only then did Martha complete the payment to the smuggler.

Pedro and Harold were taken by van from Phoenix to Chicago, where they were reunited with Pedro's sisters and cousins. They helped them to secure false Social Security cards, since, having entered illegally, they were not eligible to obtain authentic work documents. Very soon after arrival, both Pedro and Harold became busboys in a family restaurant, each working about fifty hours a week. It was hard work, but they were grateful for employment. They lived very frugally, sharing a small space with family members, and were able to send money home to Martha and the children.

With each paycheck, a sizable portion of Pedro and Harold's income is deducted for payroll taxes, but Pedro knows he will likely never receive any benefit for all the money he is paying into Social Security or Medicare, since he has been using a false Social Security card. At one point, a new manager took over at the restaurant where Pedro worked, began paying him in cash instead of through the payroll system, and lowered his hourly wage to less than $3 per hour plus irregular tips. Eventually, he quit and found work in a different restaurant, where he is once again paid on the books, at just over Illinois' minimum wage, and has payroll taxes deducted.

Within a few years of their arrival, Pedro and Harold saved enough money to hire smugglers to bring the rest of the family north: the oldest son, Homero, arrived first, then Martha, each undertaking the same dangerous journey. When I met the family in 2007, when their household consisted of four adults living in a one-bedroom apartment in the same cockroach-infested building as mine, Martha described their seemingly modest life in the United States with exuberance: "I feel like I'm in glory here," she told me then, noting the luxury of a small fiber-optic Christmas tree that they would never have afforded back in Mexico while serving me another helping of her expertly cooked food. "Back there, we didn't even have enough to eat."

A few moments later, though, Martha was in tears as she spoke of her two youngest children still in Mexico, left as a ten- and eleven-year-old, respectively, with Martha's sister. It did not surprise me when, a few months later, the two youngest children eventually arrived as well, smuggled in just like the others. The four adults working far more than full-time hours (albeit at barely the minimum wage) had saved their money.

Eventually, Pedro and Martha's family moved away from my neighborhood, and I lost touch with them. Recently, though, I reconnected with Pedro and Martha, now living in a three-bedroom house, a decade after we first met. They're both still working—Pedro, along with Harold, at a restaurant; Martha at a Mexican grocery store—and both paying their taxes. There have been high points over the past decade: they're now grandparents several times over, and their housing, while far from luxurious, is much more spacious. They go frequently (maybe too frequently, Martha acknowledged, joking that I'd gained some weight just as she had) to get ice cream, enjoying small luxuries they would not have had in their hometown.

Overall, though, their disposition as we spoke was somber. While Harold, now a father of three, is still with them and doing well, their other three children are not. Their daughter married—a happy occasion—but then returned to Mexico with her husband when her father-in-law was thought to be dying. Without legal status, and with heightened border security, her mother does not want her to risk trying to come back illegally. Martha and Pedro now have a grandchild they have never met in person.

Their youngest son, Juan, was among more than three million immigrants formally removed from the United States under the Obama administration, a figure higher than in any other administration in US history.[16] Martha and Pedro insist that their son is innocent of the crime that brought him into police custody—he was arrested driving a car he borrowed from a neighbor, which unbeknownst to him had a small amount of drugs inside the glove compartment—but after being transferred from one prison-like detention facility to another, Juan was deported to Mexico.

Homero was arrested for driving under the influence of alcohol, an offense that landed him in immigration court in addition to facing criminal penalties. Rather than being formally deported like his brother, Homero accepted a "voluntary departure," signing a promise that he would leave the country (at his own expense) by a certain date, which he did. Homero was one of the 2.2 million individuals returned to their country of origin "voluntarily," rather than being formally deported, during the Obama years.[17]

Ten years ago, Pedro and Martha spoke glowingly of life in the United States, as if they had just landed in the Promised Land. Now, like about 60 percent of all undocumented immigrants, they have resided in the United States for more than a decade.[18] But while some feel deeply integrated at this point and could not imagine returning to their home country, Pedro and Martha are more circumspect. They seem dejected; lately they have been contemplating returning to Mexico. They are tired of living apart from most of their family, and they read the results of the recent presidential election as a clear sign: "*Este país ya no nos quiere*," Martha says. *This country doesn't want us anymore.* While they have very little cash on hand, they have purchased a property back in Mexico, which they've been sending money to relatives back in Morelos to slowly build up. Sooner or later, they say, they will likely return. Their American dream may be coming to its end.

Francisco and Alison: A mixed-status marriage. Like Pedro and Martha, Francisco grew up in Morelos, south of Mexico City, into a tight-knit family that struggled economically throughout his childhood. He recalls one particular morning as a small child when he woke up to find his mother crying, devastated that she had nothing to feed her children. That day, along his three-mile walk to school, Francisco found the equivalent of a

UNDOCUMENTED IMMIGRANTS, TAXES, AND PUBLIC BENEFITS

A common frustration with illegal immigration stems from the presumption that undocumented immigrants fail to pay taxes while receiving governmental services. In reality, the reverse is often true: almost all undocumented immigrants pay taxes in one form or another, even though they are ineligible for many of the services that tax dollars support.

Just like anyone else residing in the United States, undocumented immigrants pay state and local sales and excise taxes when they go shopping, fill up their tank with gas, or purchase a vehicle: nationwide, undocumented immigrants pay approximately $7 billion annually in sales and excise taxes, including more than $1 billion in Texas and nearly $2 billion in California.[19] Undocumented immigrants also pay property taxes, approximately $3.6 billion each year across all states,[20] whether directly (about 30 percent own their own homes) or indirectly by paying rent to a landlord who pays property taxes.[21]

Beyond that, though, while many undocumented workers are paid in cash "under the table," and thus generally do not have payroll taxes deducted from their paychecks, the Social Security Administration estimates that nearly half are paid "on the books," with payroll taxes deducted from each paycheck.[22] That basically implies that they presented something that looks like a Social Security card to their employer when they were hired: some may have been issued a valid Social Security number previously (such as those who had temporary work authorization under a student or temporary work visa), while others used a fake document with either an invented or stolen number. Using a false Social Security number is unlawful, but it also facilitates these undocumented workers' contribution of approximately $12 billion per year in Social Security contributions that they will likely never be eligible to draw upon, effectively subsidizing the system for older Americans who benefit from Social Security.[23] "Earnings by unauthorized immigrants result in a net positive effect on Social Security financial status generally," concludes the chief actuary of the Social Security Administration.[24]

In fact, many undocumented immigrants actually file tax returns each year. False Social Security numbers are not valid for filing taxes, but the Internal Revenue Service offers special Individual Taxpayer Identification Numbers (ITINs) to those who do not qualify for valid Social Security numbers. In recent years, about 4.6 million federal tax returns have been filed with an ITIN, most (though not all) of which likely come from undocumented immigrants.[25] Though some may be wary to submit their name and address to the federal government, many undocumented workers seem to have trusted the commitment the IRS has publicly made to not communicate with immigration enforcement authorities. "We want your money whether you are here legally or not and whether you earned it legally or not," IRS commissioner Mark Everson told the *New York Times* in 2007.[26]

While many criticize undocumented immigrants because of certain societal costs related to illegal immigration, immigrants often pay more in taxes than they take in services, while also contributing overall to the US economy. That is particularly true because, while they benefit from governmental services such as roads, parks, police, and fire department services, and the national security maintained by the US military, undocumented immigrants do not qualify for most public benefits. Without evidence of valid legal status, undocumented immigrants cannot benefit directly from any means-tested federal public benefits, including our country's welfare system (the Temporary Aid for Needy Families program), food stamps, public housing, Supplementary Security Income for the disabled, the Earned Income Tax Credit, Medicaid health insurance for low-income people, or purchasing subsidized health insurance through the Affordable Care Act. Although public benefit eligibility varies somewhat from one state to another, the only benefits an undocumented immigrant might be eligible for in most states are emergency and prenatal healthcare, immunizations, and treatment for communicable diseases, certain nutritional programs aimed primarily at children, and noncash emergency disaster relief (such as in the wake of Hurricane Katrina).[27] Five states and the District of Columbia also extend health insurance to low-income children regardless of their legal status, and, because of the Supreme Court's 1982 decision in *Plyler v. Doe*, all children are allowed to attend public schools.[28]

In fact, even immigrants with legal status are generally ineligible for most means-tested public benefits for the first five years they are in the country (those admitted as refugees are the largest exception). And even when they are eligible, immigrants tend to utilize public benefits at lower rates than US citizens of the same income level.[29]

While the perception persists that people migrate to milk America's social safety net, the reality is that almost all immigrants come to the United States to work. Immigrants overall are significantly more likely than native-born US citizens to be employed, a difference that is particularly pronounced among undocumented men, whose labor participation rate is above 90 percent, far higher than either work-authorized immigrants or native-born US citizens.[30]

$20 bill: *We're going to eat today!* he remembers thinking. Their family, all Christians, saw God's provision more than once.

Francisco quit school before graduating high school in order to go to work with a landscaping business and then in a factory. In 1999, when he was twenty, his father, who had worked long hours in construction, could not find work for several months. With his mother facing serious health challenges, Francisco decided the only way he could help his family was to migrate.

Aiming to reach his aunt and cousin in Chicago, Francisco set out, accompanied by another uncle who had also decided to make the illicit crossing. They took a bus to the Mexican state of Sonora, across the border from Arizona. The *coyote* they had hired instructed them to stay there and wait for his instructions; they ultimately waited about two weeks before they attempted to cross. On their first attempt to cross, they were left in the middle of the desert at night, unsure of where to go. Francisco was robbed—the thieves took even his shoes and his shirt—and then they were caught by the Border Patrol and returned across the border.[31]

On their second attempt, Francisco made it across undetected, though his uncle broke his ankle running through the darkness at night. The smuggler directed them—and the roughly forty other people who had crossed illegally, including children as young as two years old—to a garage, where they were left for three days without food or water. Francisco remembers a feeling of despair, wanting to return home, but mindful that his family was relying on him.

Eventually, Francisco and the others were ushered into the back of a semi-truck, where they stood in silence, cognizant of Border Patrol checkpoints, for several hours. Dirty, hungry, and anxious, they eventually reached Phoenix, and from there boarded a series of buses to Chicago. Francisco was finally able to communicate with his family back in Morelos, who, after more than two weeks without communication, had begun to fear the worst. Indeed, those fears were not baseless: more than six thousand people have died in their attempt to illegally cross the US-Mexico border since 2000; that averages to at least one documented death per day.[32]

Francisco, gratefully, survived the journey. As a Christian, his conscience bothered him when he illegally obtained the false documents necessary to work, but his mind was on his family in Mexico: *I've got to do this in order to help them*, he told himself. He eventually found work, working about seventy hours per week among three restaurants. Sometimes, on the weekend when restaurants tend to be most busy, he would begin work before dawn and not end until after midnight, occasionally sleeping in his car when his time between shifts was too short to commute back to the apartment he shared with five extended family members.

Their lack of legal status makes many undocumented workers wary to report abuses, and thus they are vulnerable to unfair labor practices: one survey of low-income workers in Chicago, Los Angeles, and New York City found that 37 percent of undocumented workers had been paid less than the minimum wage and 76 percent had been expected by their employer to perform work "off-the-clock," for which they were not paid at all.[33] Francisco, however, had a positive experience with his employers. One particular boss noticed that he looked stressed one day and asked Francisco what was wrong. He explained the situation facing his family in Mexico, which at that point had escalated such that his mother was near death. His boss wrote Francisco a personal check for $1,500 and told him to ask for additional help as needed. As Francisco learned English in an English as a Second Language class, his boss also gave him the opportunity to move to a better-paying job in the "front of the house," interacting with customers.

While the vast majority of his waking hours were spent working, Francisco found a home in a Spanish-speaking congregation. As is the case for many immigrants, especially those who have left behind their immediate families, church became like a family to Francisco. He began playing music in the worship band, something he had done back at his home church in Mexico, and became involved as a leader in the church's youth group, which grew from about 25 students to 150 in just over a year under his leadership. At one point, the pastor also invited Francisco to preach, and in that experience he began to feel a call he could not shake—as much as he told himself it was impossible, given his lack of legal status or formal education—to serve as a pastor. Though he had never been able to finish high school, he enrolled in theology classes.

Early in 2007, Francisco was introduced by a mutual friend to Alison, a US citizen who worked as a special education teacher; by the end of the year, they were engaged.

Francisco was up front about his legal status issues, but Alison presumed as they dated and moved toward marriage that, if he married a US citizen, this could be resolved easily. In hindsight, Alison says she was naive about immigration issues, having grown up in an ethnically homogeneous community where she had no real personal interaction with immigrants. If anything, she was confused by why Francisco wouldn't have just come legally in the first place: "As Americans," she says, "We have this skewed perspective. Since we can go anywhere, [we presume] anyone can go anywhere; since we can just fill out the paperwork, [we suppose] anyone can just fill out the paperwork" and be given legal status.

One of Alison's first clues that the US immigration system was more complicated and sometimes harsh than she had presumed came as they were preparing for their wedding. Francisco's parents were denied tourist visas to be allowed to attend. Francisco had thought it was a waste of money for them even to apply, because he knew that people as poor as his parents would be suspected as potential visa overstayers and almost certainly denied. But Alison insisted. She was devastated when, after paying for the privilege to apply for visitor visas, they were given "a very expensive no."

The wedding proceeded without Francisco's parents, and the newlyweds visited an immigration attorney shortly after they were married, Alison confident and Francisco at least hopeful that they would be able to "fix" Francisco's legal status. It was not so simple. The lawyer warned them, first, that having been married for just a few months, there was a risk that the federal immigration service would suspect them of committing marriage fraud, when a US citizen legally marries a noncitizen with the sole intention of helping the immigrant to obtain legal status. If they waited a year, the lawyer suggested, they would have more time to build up the evidence that their marriage was legitimate: jointly filed tax returns and other financial documents, photographs, maybe even a baby.

The attorney also warned that, because Francisco had entered the country unlawfully, he would be required to return to Mexico to obtain his immigrant visa—which would trigger another challenge. Because of a law signed by President Clinton in 1996, any immigrant who is in the country illegally for one year or more who then *leaves* the country triggers a ten-year bar on lawful reentry. There is an exception if a consular officer decides to grant a waiver, based on evidence of the "extreme hardship" that the US-citizen spouse would face, but there was no guarantee that a waiver would be granted, even though it sure seemed to Francisco and Alison that it would be "extremely hard" to either be separated for a decade or for Alison to move with Francisco to Mexico. In fact, many such waiver requests were denied—but you could only receive that decision *outside* the US. Francisco and Alison debated whether they should take that risk. Plus, there was the cost: "minimum $5,000," the lawyer had said, which was more than they could come up with immediately.

Francisco and Alison lived as what's called a "mixed-status family," a family where at least one family member has permanent legal status and at least one does not. Overall, about 1.5 million undocumented immigrants are married to a US citizen or Lawful Permanent Resident.[34] About one-third of all undocumented immigrants have at least one US-citizen child, accounting for 4.5 million US-citizen children.[35]

Living in a mixed-status marriage has occasionally generated friction between Francisco and Alison, fueled by the fear that the couple could be separated if Francisco were to be deported. The couple became increasingly guarded, sharing their situation with only a small circle of friends and close family members, avoiding social situations, even with Alison's extended family, where anyone might ask questions. Alison became increasingly protective—perhaps overly protective, she now says—even once insisting that Francisco hide in the closet when there was an unexpected knock at the door (it turned out be a neighbor, dropping off some misdirected mail).

The birth of their twin sons brought immense joy to the couple, but also new fears. The prospect of Francisco being deported became even more cataclysmic. Raising twins was difficult with two parents, and Alison could not fathom doing so on her own. But the possibility of relocating the entire family to Mexico also became even more fraught, particularly when the twins were diagnosed with health issues for which treatment options are limited in Mexico.

Fortunately, around the time that the twins were born in 2013, a few policy changes dramatically affected the family for the better. The Illinois legislature passed legislation making the state among just a few states—as of this writing, twelve plus the District of Columbia—to allow undocumented immigrants to obtain a version of a driver's license.[36] After years of avoiding driving, obtaining this permission was life-changing for Francisco.

The same year, the US Department of Homeland Security implemented a new policy, allowing individuals who would require a waiver to apply for permanent legal status to prequalify from within the United States, such that Francisco and Alison could know *before* departing for Mexico that their waiver had been approved and Francisco would be allowed to return with permanent legal status (or if the waiver was denied, to not trigger the ten-year bar to legal status by leaving in the first place). They continued working with their attorney to try to move their case forward, now without the same level of risk.

By 2015, the couple gave up on one attorney, who had made a number of mistakes on their case and been less than forthcoming, and found a new legal counselor at World Relief's immigrant legal-services program in suburban Chicago.[37] In March 2017, with their waiver application provisionally approved, they traveled to Ciudad Juarez, Mexico, where the final application was approved. Eighteen years after he first arrived in the United States and almost a decade after he and Alison were married, Francisco reentered the United States with Lawful Permanent Resident status.

In the two years prior to finally receiving his legal status, with strong encouragement from Alison as well as from the pastor of their former church, Francisco also became a pastor, planting a Spanish-speaking church in a neighboring county where the Latino community is relatively new and there are few local churches to serve them. With training and oversight from an evangelical denomination that embraced Francisco and Alison, the church has grown to about sixty people attending each week, 80 percent of which are new believers.

Given Francisco's lack of work authorization, the denomination could not extend to him the salary that other church planters receive, so he has pastored the church as a volunteer and the couple has lived on Alison's salary as a teacher. Even now that he has legal status and could legally receive a salary from the church, the fledgling congregation's finances are not enough to cover a salary, but Francisco is grateful for the opportunity to live out the calling he has sensed for many years.

Reflecting back on their journey, Alison struggles with what she perceives as hostility toward immigrants among many within the larger American church. "It's hard for me to know that there are people within our faith family that would still turn him away, or would still think badly of him," she says, tears forming in her eyes. Still, as Francisco volunteers, they have also seen many ways that local churches have stood with them, embodying Christlike love for him and others who are vulnerable and relating to them with mutual love and respect as fellow brothers and sisters in Christ. He notes in particular the various ways that the nearly all-white evangelical church that has shared their space with their new church plant has been a blessing.

Francisco, too, has been a blessing to his adopted country. "As far as someone who can do good in this country," his wife testifies, "he pours himself out every day." She lists the selfless ways he serves his congregation, from late night visits to the hospital to consistently seeking out those who are struggling, both proclaiming and living the gospel.

Fernando: Waves of migration. While Mexican immigrants like Francisco have long accounted for the majority of undocumented immigrants in the United States, that may no longer be true: fully 50 percent of undocumented immigrants are now from countries *other* than Mexico.[38] In fact, during the past several years, the net flow of Mexican nationals between the United States and Mexico has actually been *toward Mexico*, with more leaving the United States than arriving, some as a result of deportations, others leaving voluntarily to be reunited to family.[39]

Concurrently, however, the number of undocumented immigrants from other countries, particularly countries in Central America and Asia, has risen slightly. Central Americans now account for approximately 15 percent of all undocumented immigrants, with most coming from Guatemala, El Salvador, or Honduras.[40] The increase in migration from these three countries has coincided with a dramatic increase in violence, most of it tied to gang activity: all three countries have homicide rates among the highest in the world.[41]

Central Americans, though, have also been coming to the United States for decades. Fernando was among the hundreds of thousands who sought refuge in the United States during the civil war in El Salvador, reaching the United States in 1987 after a dangerous, illegal journey by boat up the coast of Mexico.[42] Eventually, he and many other Salvadorans who had fled the war were granted "Temporary Protected Status," allowing him to stay and work lawfully in the country. But after a peace agreement was finally reached, Fernando chose to return home to El Salvador.

There, he married and eventually became the father of three children. In the mid-1990s through early 2000s, though the war was over, the country still struggled to recover economically, and a second wave of migration toward the United States began, fueled this time primarily by poverty. When Fernando's car was damaged in a rollover accident, it precipitated a spiral of financial challenges that left him deep in debt. He concluded there was no hope of recovering financially and supporting his young family if he remained in El Salvador. He went home and asked his wife, Ana, pregnant with their third child, to help pack him a suitcase, which she presumed was for a trip of a few weeks within the country looking for work. Eight days later, he called her from Houston, Texas, having successfully crossed the border illegally a second time.

Fernando stayed for twelve years in the United States, making roof trusses in Houston, then accepting an invitation from his employer to move to Kentucky and train others in the craft. That company was eventually subjected to a raid by immigration authorities, and most of the undocumented employees were deported; Fernando avoided being deported, but, with most of its workers gone, the company closed. He found a new job in landscaping, then in carpentry, all the while staying in close contact with his wife and children via telephone and providing as much financial support as he could.

On one of his twice-weekly calls home to his daughter, though, she broke into tears: she appreciated how hard her father worked to send back money to support the family, but what she most wanted was her father. After twelve years in the U.S., Fernando made the decision to return home. While about two-thirds of Latino immigrants say they intend to stay permanently in the United States, many others intend to return to their country of origin.[43]

Fernando returned reluctantly, worried that his family would be unable to survive without the income he could earn working in the United States, but he has done well since his return. With a loan from his brother (still in the US) and help from a local church, Fernando now owns 1,200 chickens and two cows. His home community now has access to potable water, made possible in part because the local church, equipped by a Christian ministry called Enlace, has helped Fernando advocate with the municipal government.

Fernando and Ana are happy to be reunited, and they are proud of their daughter, now studying veterinary science in college. Tragically, though, their family is once again divided: their sixteen- and seventeen-year-old sons were among many in El Salvador threatened by vicious gangs in the past few years. In 2016, Fernando's sons were threatened when they rebuffed invitations to join local gangs, and the family decided that their best hope for survival was to flee to the United States; they were among more than 17,500 Salvadoran children who reached the United States unaccompanied by any parent or guardian, a twelvefold increase since 2011.[44]

Unlike those who illegally cross the border and try to evade the Border Patrol (which has become much more difficult in recent years, with fewer attempting to cross and more Border Patrol agents), unaccompanied children generally are *looking* for the Border Patrol, and almost all are apprehended. Under US law, unaccompanied children (unlike adults or those arriving with families) are transferred from the custody of the Border Patrol to the Department of Health and Human Services, which is charged with protecting the children until a court can determine if they will be allowed to stay (such as if they are granted asylum) or returned to their country of origin. In most cases, the Department of Health and Human Services puts these children into the care of nonprofit organizations until a family member can be identified. Fernando's sons are now safely with relatives, but awaiting further decisions from a court that will determine if they are to be returned to El Salvador or allowed to stay lawfully in the United States.[45]

Liz: Unlocked potential. Much of the political rhetoric surrounding illegal immigration focuses on the US-Mexico border. However, more than 40 percent of all immigrants who are unlawfully present in the country never crossed a border illegally: they came in lawfully on a valid visa, usually through an airport, and then did not return when their visa expired.[46] In fact, "visa overstayers" have accounted for most *new* undocumented immigrants over the past decade.[47]

In some of those cases the individual did not even intend to overstay. Our friend Liz is a good example. Liz was born in China. When she was a child,

REFUGEE STORIES

When the first edition of *Welcoming the Stranger* was released in 2009, undocumented immigrants were very clearly the subcategory of immigrants who were most controversial and subject to widespread misconception, which is why we've highlighted several of their stories in this chapter. Now, however, another subgroup of immigrants, refugees, has become similarly misunderstood.[48]

Refugees in the United States are, by definition, not undocumented immigrants: any individual admitted as a refugee first undergoes a thorough vetting process conducted by various agencies of the US government overseas; then, if selected, they come to the United States at the invitation of the US State Department. They have legal status from the day they arrive in the United States; they can apply for their green cards one year after arrival and, in most cases, for naturalization four years after that.

Though all refugees meet a precise legal definition as individuals who have fled their countries because of a well-founded fear of persecution, the refugees admitted to the United States over the past decade are incredibly diverse in terms of nationality, religion, and educational background. Just as the media stereotype of an undocumented immigrant as a Mexican who illegally crossed the border does not capture the full story, the media focus on Muslim refugees from Syria is also incomplete. In fact, of the roughly 680,000 refugees admitted in the past decade, 45 percent have been Christians of one tradition or another, many of them individuals who faced persecution particularly because of their faith in Christ, while about one-third have been Muslims.[49] The top countries of origin for refugees who came to the United States in the past decade have been Burma (also known as Myanmar), Iraq (including many individuals whose persecution is tied to their Christian faith, as well many others who served alongside the US military and as a result faced threats from terrorist groups), Bhutan, Somalia, and the Democratic Republic of Congo.[50]

Our colleague Durmomo Gary is one of the many refugees resettled to the United States in recent years. Durmomo was born in southern Sudan. Durmomo's work as a Bible translator drew the attention of the government of Sudan based in Khartoum, and he was forced to flee to Egypt in 2002. After several years living in Cairo and completing a lengthy vetting process, Durmomo and his family were selected by the US State Department to be resettled. He landed at O'Hare International Airport in Chicago on October 31, 2006. While initially troubled by the Halloween celebration going on around him, Durmomo and his family have adjusted well to life in a new country. Durmomo pastored a Sudanese church in Wheaton, Illinois, for several years and also took a job with World Relief, helping other refugees adjust to life in a new country. He's also completed his seminary degree at the Moody Theological Seminary and become a US citizen.

Adam Babiker's story parallels Durmomo's in several ways: he too fled Sudan for Egypt and then ultimately was resettled in the United States in 2006. In Adam's case, the persecution he faced was based not on his faith (Adam is a Muslim, as are most in the government-backed militias), but because of ethnic and political tensions that culminated in a horrific genocide in the region of Darfur. Just three years after being resettled in the United States, Adam joined the US military; he served for four years, including a tour of duty in Iraq. "America stood with me the time I really needed it," Adam says, "and that's why I joined the United States Army." Adam now works in the Houston area, helping other Darfuris as well as refugees from other countries, including many who worked with the US military in Iraq and Afghanistan.[51]

her mother was granted a student visa and came to pursue her master's degree in the United States; because she did not have the financial means to support her in the United States, Liz stayed behind with her grandparents. But when her mom graduated and was offered a job, along with a temporary work-based visa, Liz moved from China to Chicago, with temporary legal status as a dependent on her mom's employer-sponsored visa. She arrived with excitement as a ten year old, knowing no English and very little about the United States, beyond that it was home to Disney World.

The adjustment to life in a new country, in a classroom where everything around her was in a new language, was difficult. But Liz gradually learned the language. With time, she excelled academically, graduating among the top of her high school class. Her teachers and friends were understandably confused when she expressed ambivalence about applying for college.

In reality, Liz was desperate to attend college, but she was repeatedly told she would be unable to do so without a valid Social Security number and valid legal status. She found out in high school, around the time that most of her peers were applying for driver's licenses or for a summer job, that she had neither. A couple years after she arrived, her mother had changed jobs, which required her to file for a new temporary worker visa. The attorney helping them with this process, however, made an error: he forgot to attach Liz's application to her mom's. Without realizing, Liz became undocumented as a twelve year old. By the time the error was realized, they were told it was too late to fix it, even after consulting with various elected officials.

Liz struggled with her identity as she came to terms with the reality that, legally, she did not belong in the place she considered her home. She found support, though, in her church. Her family back in China were atheists, but Liz's mom had been welcomed by Christians from the days that she was in graduate school in Iowa. Those friends connected her to a local church when she moved to Chicago, and though it took years, eventually both Liz and her mom became believers.

Liz was initially wary to disclose her legal status challenges to others within her church, which occasionally presented awkward situations. She would have loved to participate in an overseas mission trip, for example, but could not, because she would not be allowed to reenter the country. But she could not explain that without revealing her status, which for her involved a sense of shame.

When she ultimately found the courage to share the truth of her legal situation with her youth pastor, he became an advocate, helping to make sure she had rides to go beyond where her bike could take her, praying with and for her, and even meeting with legislators, urging them to pass legislation that would allow Liz and other young people to earn permanent legal status. "It meant so much to me that my pastor would speak up for me, when I felt like I could not," Liz recalls.

Eventually, Liz found out that, unlike some of the other colleges she had initially consulted, the local community college would allow her to take classes even without legal status. From there, she says that God opened up doors she never dreamed possible: she applied for and was offered a private scholarship that allowed her to finish her bachelor's degree at Northwestern University. She's now completing her master of business administration degree at the University of Chicago's prestigious Booth School.

She also now (as of this writing) has employment authorization—at least for the moment. The Deferred Action for Childhood Arrivals (DACA) program announced by President Obama in 2012 has allowed approximately 800,000 undocumented individuals who, like Liz, came or were brought to the United States as children, and meet certain other requirements, to be granted a "deferral" of deportation and receive work authorization.[52] After working in the private sector for a while, Liz joined our staff at World Relief, helping to mobilize local churches to advocate for immigration policies consistent with biblical values through the Evangelical Immigration Table.

For Liz, though, the future is uncertain. In September 2017, President Trump terminated the DACA program, which means Liz will be unable to renew her work permission when it expires in fall 2018. Barring intervention from Congress (which President Trump has said he would welcome, but which has not occurred as of this writing) or the courts, Liz will likely lose her job and could even be at risk of deportation. Still, having seen him provide in so many ways already, she trusts that God will provide: "I know that my ultimate security lies in the hands of a just and compassionate God," she says.

CONCLUSION

The individuals whose stories I have included in this chapter—Pedro and Martha, Francisco and Alison, Fernando, and Liz—are representative of the many undocumented immigrants (and their families) I (Matthew) have interacted with over the past several years in my work with World Relief and living in neighborhoods with many immigrants. As I have gotten to know them, I have found them to be good friends, neighbors, and, often, brothers and sisters in Christ. They are not perfect, but they are also certainly not the criminals that the media often portrays them to be. Like me, they are concerned about their families, their faith, and the day-to-day realities of paying rent and affording groceries.

I worked for a number of years as a legal counselor, tasked with informing the immigrants who came to me for advice about what the law says. In rare cases, the law provides them an option to obtain legal status, but more often I have had to break to them the bad news that under current law they have no real options. This realization made me wonder: how is it that my ancestors, who I am told came much for the same reasons as those described here, were able to immigrate to the United States? In chapter three, we will look at how American immigration (and immigration policy) has changed over time.

THREE

NATION OF IMMIGRANTS

A Historical Perspective on Immigration to the United States

> Do not oppress a foreigner; you yourselves
> know how it feels to be foreigners,
> because you were foreigners in Egypt.
>
> **EXODUS 23:9**

THE BIBLICAL MANDATE to take special concern for foreigners, which we will look at in more depth in chapter five, is frequently paired with God's injunction to the people of Israel to remember their own history. They knew how it felt to be strangers living in a foreign land—Egypt—and God said that their own immigrant experience should inform how they were to treat sojourners in their land.

The problem, God knew, was that we human beings are apt to forget our own history. Often when we move out of difficult places, we tend to forget the grace that brought us through. To help keep their immigrant history in front of them, God imposed on the Israelites something of a liturgy, to be repeated to the priest when bringing forward an offering:

When you have entered the land the LORD your God is giving you as an inheritance and have taken possession of it and settled in it . . . you shall declare before the LORD your

God: "My father was a wandering Aramean, and he went down into Egypt with a few people and lived there and became a great nation, powerful and numerous. But the Egyptians mistreated us and made us suffer, subjecting us to harsh labor. Then we cried out to the LORD, the God of our ancestors, and the LORD heard our voice and saw our misery, toil and oppression. So the LORD brought us out of Egypt with a mighty hand and an outstretched arm, with great terror and with signs and wonders. He brought us to this place and gave us this land, a land flowing with milk and honey; and now I bring the firstfruits of the soil that you, LORD, have given me." Place the basket before the LORD your God and bow down before him. Then you and the Levites and the foreigners residing among you shall rejoice in all the good things the LORD your God has given to you and your household. (Deut 26:1, 5-11)

The Israelites were commanded to rehearse their history, lest they forget it and then treat immigrants who would come into their land as badly as Pharaoh had treated them as foreigners in Egypt.

American Christians are in a unique position in that, as spiritual descendants of the Israelites, we too are commanded to remember and learn from the Israelites' history as immigrants in Egypt. At the same time, we have the unique distinction of being a nation of immigrants, where more than 99 percent of the population—everyone except for those few whose ancestry is entirely Native American—has an immigrant history. It's important to remember that the first immigrants did not come to a land undiscovered but to a land already inhabited by Native Americans, who were forcibly displaced, disenfranchised, and sometimes killed for their land. It took the systematic and targeted displacement of Native Americans and their subsequent dehumanization for the first European immigrant pilgrims to inhabit a land that was deemed "free" for the taking.

As did the Israelites, we need to remember our history—where God has brought us and our ancestors from—to remember God's grace, especially as we think about how God would have us interact with immigrants reaching our country today.

AMERICA AS A LAND OF IMMIGRANTS

Immigration holds an important place in our national mythology and lore. Our ancestors, generations of grandparents have told their grandchildren, came to this county with nothing, worked extraordinarily hard, and realized the American Dream. Historian Nancy Foner describes the common sentiment about immigrants of a century or two ago, which has been perpetuated and sometimes glorified by films, television, and literature: "They worked hard; they strove to become assimilated; they pulled themselves up by their own Herculean efforts; . . . they had strong family values and colorful roots. They were, in short, what made America great."[1]

Curiously, though our collective image of the immigration of a century or two ago has become more romanticized with time, many Americans do not have the same warm feelings toward contemporary immigrants. Historian Roger Daniels suggests that most Americans hold a dualistic opinion about immigration: "On the one hand reveling in the nation's immigrant past and on the other rejecting much of its immigrant present."[2] They make a firm distinction between the immigrants of Ellis Island and earlier eras—who, they are quick to note, immigrated the legal way—and those who are coming today, some of them illegally, and most of them not from Europe but from Latin America and Asia.

Immigrants today, whatever their manner of entry, come primarily for the same reasons that immigrants have always come to our country. Though immigration policies have changed quite drastically over the last two centuries, immigrants themselves are still pushed out of their countries of origin by poverty, war, and persecution, and are still drawn to the United States by promises of jobs and economic advancement, freedom, and family reunification. These push-and-pull factors explain most, if not all, of immigration to the United States from the time of the first settlers to today.

Likewise, the rhetoric around immigration and immigrants themselves has not changed much. Immigrants have always been simultaneously praised and resented, welcomed and scapegoated, from the earliest days of our country's existence to the present. Consider the following quote:

Why should [immigrants] establish their Language and Manners to the Exclusion of ours? Why should Pennsylvania, founded by the English, become a Colony of Aliens who will shortly be so numerous as to [change] us instead of our Anglifying them, and will never adopt our Language or Customs, any more than they can acquire our complexion?[3]

These words could feasibly come today from some media personalities who have made their dissatisfaction with contemporary immigration a central theme of their broadcasts and social media platforms, but the words were actually Benjamin Franklin's, writing in 1751 about the mass arrival of German immigrants into Pennsylvania. Anti-immigrant attitudes, and concerns that immigrants will not assimilate, are nothing new (though few Americans of German origin speak their ancestral tongue today and few could distinguish their skin tone from that of Americans with British blood).

Much of the lore of immigration is built around the Statue of Liberty, standing majestically on Liberty Island in New York Harbor, where millions of immigrants entered the United States for the first time. The words of a sonnet by Emma Lazarus, penned in 1883 and later inscribed on the base of the Statue of Liberty, have immortalized the idea of America as a refuge of freedom and opportunity:

Give me your tired, your poor,

Your huddled masses yearning to breathe free, The wretched refuse of your teeming shore.

Send these, the homeless, tempest-tost to me, I lift my lamp beside the golden door![4]

The poem suggests an era when immigrants, even the poor and outcast of their home countries, were welcomed into the United States—but just a year prior to the poem's publication, in 1882, the US Congress had passed the first significant federal law restricting immigration, the Chinese Exclusion Act, which legally forbade Chinese immigrants from entering the United States for more than sixty years. That same year the federal government also passed, for the first time, laws banning the immigration of any "lunatic, idiot, or any person unable to take care of himself or herself without becoming a public charge"—excluding precisely many of the tired, poor, huddled masses that Lazarus would write about the following year.[5]

Throughout American history, pro- and anti-immigrant voices have coexisted, and public policy has generally responded to whichever voice commanded the majority of public opinion at the time. The various perspectives on the immigration debate cannot adequately be described as conservative or liberal, or as Republican or Democrat: the debate has, throughout history just as it does now, divided otherwise homogeneous ideological blocs.[6]

To understand the contemporary debate over immigration, we must first understand at least a little bit of the historical context. What follows is a brief, and certainly not conclusive, review of the various waves of immigration to the United States.[7]

IMMIGRATION IN THE EARLY DAYS OF THE UNITED STATES

As Benjamin Franklin's concerns about German assimilation suggest, immigration to the United States has had its opponents since even before the United States became an independent country. Most of the founding fathers, though, looked favorably on continued immigration, believing there was plenty of space to fill in the nascent nation. George Washington's words, addressed to Irish immigrants in 1783, are representative:

> The bosom of America is open to receive not only the opulent and respectable stranger, but the oppressed and persecuted of all nations and religions, whom we shall welcome to participate in all of our rights and privileges, if by decency and propriety of conduct they appear to merit the employment.[8]

Following these ideals, Congress imposed no significant restrictions on immigration until after the Civil War, though there were some changes in law during this time that affected the foreign born. For example, a 1790 law limited naturalization—the process of becoming a US citizen—to free, white people. A few years later, the Alien and Sedition Acts of 1798, pushed through by John Adams and his Federalist Party out of wariness of French immigrants, gave the government the right to deport immigrants it believed to be a danger to the United States or who came from countries at war with the United States.[9] Though there were many groups that faced unjust treatment—Native Americans were not included as citizens, African Americans were enslaved, and women were not allowed to vote—new immigration remained open to all.

Among the earliest to arrive in what would become the United States, of course, were men and women from Africa, who were enslaved and taken against their will to the New World. An estimated 645,000 Africans were involuntarily displaced and forced to work as slaves in what is now the United States, with millions more being sent to other parts of the Western Hemisphere.[10] It is important to remember this tragic element of our country's immigrant history, particularly since involuntary migration—now termed human trafficking—continues to be a problem today.

The first great European wave: 1820–1860. Throughout American history, immigration levels have ebbed and flowed, depending both on what was happening in the United States and in other parts of the world. As is still often the case, events in the particular country of origin often precipitated large waves of immigration: in the 1840s, for example, a massive famine caused by the failure of the potato crop in Ireland provided the push that many Irish needed to leave their homeland and come to the United States, where farmland was abundant.[11] German immigration spiked around the same time, as people fled a government that had stomped out an attempted revolution in 1848, seeking the liberty and democracy offered by the United States.[12] These Irish and German immigrants, in particular, created a wave of immigration unlike anything the United States had seen up to this point. Over five million immigrants arrived between 1820 and 1860, about twenty times more than the number of immigrants who had arrived in the previous forty-four years since the nation's independence.[13] By 1860, 13.2 percent of the population of the United States was foreign born, a percentage that would roughly stay the same through the 1920s.[14] Beyond the sheer numbers, most of the German and Irish immigrants of this era were also distinct from the previous generations of immigrants in that they were primarily Roman Catholic, not Protestant.

This surge in non-Protestant immigration fueled a sharp rise in anti-immigrant sentiment among earlier generations of immigrants, mostly Protestant Christians of various denominations. Many Protestant laypeople genuinely believed, following the rhetoric of some church leaders, that Roman Catholicism represented "an invading enemy, audaciously conspiring, under the mask of *holy religion*, against the liberties of our country."[15] This anti-Catholic rhetoric led to a rash of arson against Catholic churches and convents, beginning in the 1830s, that lasted several decades, while continued and increasing Irish and German immigration meant that the number of Catholics—and thus the alleged threat—kept on growing.[16]

This anti-Catholic and anti-immigrant hysteria had political manifestations as well. A political movement known officially as the American Party—though more popularly known as the "Know Nothing" party—relied on anti-Catholic and anti-immigrant rhetoric and policy proposals to grow to 1.25 million members and to have elected seven governors, eight US senators, and 104 representatives by 1856, though federal immigration policy was not substantially altered by their presence.[17] The movement fell apart only when its membership sharply divided over the issue of slavery in the years leading up to the Civil War.

During this period when many immigrants from Europe arrived in the United States, the country also instituted the forced migration of thousands of indigenous Americans. In 1830, Congress passed the Indian Removal Act, which gave President Andrew Jackson the authority to force Native Americans to leave the United States and settle in unsettled lands west of the Mississippi River.[18] While the Indian Removal Act was strongly supported in the South as several states were in jurisdictional disputes with the Cherokee, many Christian missionaries, such as Jeremiah Evarts, opposed it.[19] After a bitter debate, the Act passed, and from late 1838 to early 1839, approximately four thousand Cherokee died on the forced march to the west, which became known as the "Trail of Tears."[20]

The Treaty of Guadalupe Hidalgo: 1848. Even while immigration was booming from Western Europe, the demographic characteristics of the

United States were also changing because of US military activity along the southern border. On February 2, 1848, approximately 100,000 foreign-born individuals became US citizens in a single day—not because they crossed the border but because the border itself migrated south and crossed them.[21] On that day, the United States and Mexico signed the Treaty of Guadalupe Hidalgo, putting an end to the Mexican-American War that had raged since 1846. The terms of the treaty ceded more than half of what had been Mexican territory—including modern day California, Nevada, Utah, and parts of Colorado, Arizona, Wyoming, and New Mexico—to the United States. Those Mexican citizens living in the territory were granted the right to automatically become US citizens by simply taking an oath of allegiance, without undergoing any naturalization process.[22]

The Mexican-American War began when the Mexican government, unhappy with the annexation of Texas, broke off diplomatic relations with its northern neighbor. US President James K. Polk responded by offering to buy California and New Mexico from Mexico for $25 million; when Mexico refused the offer, the United States declared war—and in the end, forced Mexico into a treaty that gave the United States not just California and New Mexico but several other future states for just $15 million.[23] The war, and the treaty that ended it, were the consequence of an idea known as "Manifest Destiny," which claimed that the United States had the God-given responsibility to expand its territory—spreading democracy in the process.

The treaty, though, and the war that preceded it, were not uncontroversial. Ulysses S. Grant considered the war to be "one of the most unjust ever waged by a stronger against a weaker nation."[24] Abraham Lincoln, in one of his earliest speeches on the floor of the US Congress, asserted his belief that the war constituted an unprovoked attack against Mexico and warned that President Polk, who insisted that the US's military incursions had been just and warranted, would feel "the blood of this war, like the blood of Abel . . . crying to Heaven against him."[25]

Whether just or unjust, the treaty that ended the Mexican-American War shifted the border south and made many Mexicans into Americans practically with the stroke of a pen. With the prominence of Mexicans in today's immigration debates, it is important to remember that not all people of Mexican descent are recent immigrants: some are living in the same locations that their ancestors have lived for centuries. In fact, despite the common presumption that most Hispanics[26] living in the United States are immigrants, in 2016, about 78 percent of Hispanics were US citizens, most of them by birth.[27]

Chinese immigration and exclusion: 1848-1890. Mexico signed away the rights to California with the Treaty of Guadalupe Hidalgo unaware that, just nine days before the document was signed, gold had been found there. It did not take long, though, before news of the potentially lucrative discovery spread throughout the world.[28]

Hundreds of thousands eagerly set out to strike it rich in California—including many of the European immigrants arriving around this time in New York and the Mexicans and Native Americans who were already on the land. As news spread beyond the United States, other immigrants came as well, in some cases having been actively recruited. Among these new immigrants were many Chinese men, lured by promising advertisements such as this:

> Americans are rich people. They want the Chinaman to come and will make him welcome. There will be big pay, large houses, and food and clothing of the finest description. . . . Money is in great plenty and to spare in America. Such as wishes to have wages and labor guaranteed can obtain the security by application at this office.[29]

The Chinese, mostly men and mostly from the region of Canton, poured into California for several decades, lured first by the promises of gold and later by the employment created by construction of the Union Central Pacific Railroad.[30] Many had no intention to stay permanently, seeking to make money in the United States and then to return to their families in China. By 1870, the census counted sixty thousand Chinese living in the United States, most of them in California.[31]

As has proven to be a theme throughout American history with immigrants from across the world, though, the Chinese were welcomed when their labor was needed, but once work became scarce, the welcome wore thin.

Particularly on completion of the railroad in 1869, public sentiment on the West Coast turned against the Chinese, who were viewed as racially inferior and as taking jobs from US citizens.[32] In many cases, as historian Jean Pfaelzer has documented, Chinese immigrants were forcibly driven from their homes and were in other cases victims of lynching and other violence.[33] Californian legislators began to pass a series of ordinances and laws designed to drive out the Chinese: for example, the state legislature passed bills making it illegal for the Chinese to obtain a business license, fish, or marry a white person.[34] Local ordinances aimed specifically at the Chinese immigrant population and their particular customs were also passed in various places, such as an ordinance in Santa Cruz that declared, "No person shall carry baskets or bags attached to poles carried upon back or shoulders on public sidewalks."[35]

As West Coast legislators carried the anti-Chinese hysteria with them to Washington, the US Congress authorized a joint congressional committee to investigate Chinese immigration in 1876. The final congressional report stated, among other inflammatory statements, that there "was not sufficient brain capacity in the Chinese race to furnish motive power for self-government" and that "there is no Aryan or European race which is not far superior to the Chinese," and on these bases recommended a full halt to immigration from China.[36]

While there was no immediate action on these recommendations, by 1882 a bill passed the Congress and was eventually signed by President Chester A. Arthur that prohibited the entry of any new Chinese laborers—a bill that would become known as the Chinese Exclusion Act.[37] The Chinese Exclusion Act marked the first significant federal legislation limiting immigration, such that historian Roger Daniels considers the signing of the bill to be "the moment when the golden doorway of admission to the United States began to narrow."[38] New immigration by people from China would be closed until the bill was repealed in 1943, at which time the Chinese—though not most other Asians—were finally allowed to naturalize.[39]

That the law prohibited entry of the Chinese, though, is not to say that no new Chinese immigrants entered the United States after 1882. Many came as "paper sons"—presenting birth certificates to suggest that they were the children of American-born citizens of Chinese descent, and thus citizens themselves according to the laws that governed the derivation of citizenship from a father to a child.[40] This phenomenon, as immigration attorney and policy advocate Fred Tsao points out, demonstrates a reality that is important to the current immigration debate: that "if you set up restrictions, . . . particularly restrictions on established patterns of immigration, you'll find [that] people will find ways to get around them."[41]

The second great European wave: 1880–1920. As the earlier wave of European immigrants—primarily the Irish and the Germans—began to ebb, a new wave began, with immigrants now arriving from southern and eastern Europe, particularly Italians, Poles, and people of Jewish descent fleeing Russia. These immigrants, whose arrival bookended the turn of the twentieth century, are often remembered as the Ellis Island immigrants, because, beginning in 1892, they were processed into the United States through Ellis Island in New York Harbor. Between 1881 and 1920, an estimated 23.4 million immigrants entered the United States—many times more than had entered in all of the country's history prior to that time—and the percentage of the population that was foreign born was steadily between 13 and 15 percent, setting a historical high mark that has not been reached since that time.[42]

The Italians were primarily peasant farmers from southern Italy. The population of Italy had been growing substantially during this time period, requiring farms to be divided into smaller and smaller plots. Peasant farmers "were left barely clinging to their fields and hence vulnerable to any agricultural setback."[43] The economic situation for Italian farmers was further complicated by the globalization of the era, as grain from the American Great Plains began to enter the European markets at cheaper prices, while the growth of the citrus industry in Florida and California meant less demand internationally for Italian oranges.[44]

Unable to support themselves and their families as farmers as they once had, many Italian peasants set sail in cramped steamships for America. They established themselves primarily in New York and quickly sent money and letters back home to Italy, which "spread the news of opportunities and inspired prospective emigrants."[45] By the turn of the century, many regions of Italy were experiencing "America fever," with immigrants leaving every day for the promises of a better life in the United States; one mayor of a southern Italian town during this era greeted visitors "in the name of the five thousand inhabitants of this town, three thousand of whom are in America and the other two thousand preparing to go."[46]

While the Italians came primarily for economic reasons, Russian Jews came to New York fleeing political and religious discrimination. In 1882, following the assassination of Czar Alexander II, the passage of the May Laws made life nearly impossible for people of Jewish descent and faith. They were barred from living anywhere except in the large cities of a particular region of the country, and strict quotas limited their access to education. Government-approved anti-Semitic violence became increasingly common. Facing such repression, and the economic challenges that accompanied it, Jews began leaving for America, which had the reputation as "a free country for the Jews."[47]

Most of these immigrants entered the United States through New York harbor during this time, but immigrants also entered through other ports in Boston, Philadelphia, Baltimore, and Miami.[48] First- and second-class passengers who arrived at New York harbor did not undergo further inspection on arrival at Ellis Island and were free to enter the United States, but third-class passengers who were assumed to be more susceptible to medical issues and more likely to become a "public charge" were inspected on arrival, which typically took a few hours. The journey on passage to Ellis Island was not easy, with the passenger mortality rate at 10 percent per voyage at one point. Many ships were overcrowded, unventilated, and unsanitary. The United States Immigration Commission found in 1911 that "the unattended vomit of the seasick, the odors of not too clean bodies, the reek of food and the awful stench of the nearby toilet rooms make the atmosphere of steerage such that it is a marvel human flesh can endure it."[49]

Still, immigrants came. In 1907 alone, 1.25 million immigrants were processed at Ellis Island, which was the highest number of immigrant arrivals in a single year until the late 1980s.[50] Ninety-eight percent of all immigrants who came through Ellis Island were processed and allowed to proceed to the United States, while the small number of people who were excluded were not allowed to enter primarily for public health reasons or because they were thought likely to become a public charge. Today an estimated one-third of all Americans can trace their ancestry to immigrants who entered the United States through Ellis Island.[51]

Predictably, these new waves of immigrants spurred a new nativist backlash. The Immigration Restriction League, founded by recent Harvard graduates in 1894, became one of the most effective voices opposed to the new immigration, relying heavily on supposedly scientific theories that argued that the new immigrants were biologically inferior to, and thus less capable of assimilation than, the races that had populated America in the previous centuries.[52] Many Americans accepted this rhetoric, as well as continued rhetoric based on religious grounds, and they began to actively lobby their political leaders for increased restrictions on immigration.

In democratic fashion, political leaders responded to the nativist concerns of the voting electorate, gradually adding piecemeal restrictions on who could enter the United States and initiating a federal bureaucracy to control and monitor immigration. In 1911, under pressure from the Immigration Restriction League and other nativist groups, a commission of the US government published a report, named after the commission's chair, Senator William Dillingham. The Dillingham Commission report suggested that racial distinctions made the "new" immigrants biologically inferior to the old, and thus less likely to become good Americans.[53] For example, the Commission found that "certain kinds of criminality are inherent in the Italian race" and that "the high rate of illiteracy among new immigrants was due to inherent racial tendencies."[54] The Commission thus recommended "restriction as demanded by economic, moral and social considerations."[55]

After several years of debate, Congress responded to these recommendations by passing a literacy requirement for immigrants in 1917 and also excluding additional Asian immigrants to the United States.[56] Though World War I slowed immigration levels from Europe substantially, public opinion toward immigrants continued to be harsh, and demand for further restrictions led to temporary restrictions on immigration that were passed in 1921 and 1922, leading up to permanent restrictions passed in 1924 that would redefine immigration to the United States of America.

The quota system: 1924–1965. The Immigration Act of 1924 marked a turning point in US immigration history. The new law tightly restricted immigration, setting strict quotas for immigrants based on their nationality. The new law allowed the admittance into the United States of no more than 2 percent of the foreign population from a given country that existed in the United States in 1890. The 1890 census data was used, rather than the recently completed 1920 census, precisely because the older census predated the most recent wave of immigration, meaning the earlier baseline date would more tightly limit the immigration of new Italian and Jewish immigrants. The effect was to cap new immigration at about 180,000 people, the vast majority of whom would come from northern European countries such as England, France, and Germany.[57] The "new immigrants" from southern and eastern Europe, as well as Asians, were effectively shut out.

Race and eugenics played a major role in US immigration policies at the turn of the twentieth century. Eugenics is the practice of seeking to genetically improve the human population; its practice in the United States is thought to have inspired eugenics programs in Nazi Germany.[58] In the early 1920s, Immigration Restriction League President Prescott Hall asked his former Harvard roommate, Charles Davenport, who was with the Eugenics Record Office, for assistance to influence Congressional debate on immigration.[59] Davenport and Harry Laughlin with the Eugenics Record Office provided Congressional testimony that the "American" gene pool was being polluted by a rising tide of intellectually and morally defective immigrants—primarily from Eastern and Southern Europe.[60] Laughlin traveled through Europe to gather data to convince Congress to pass the bill. When President Calvin Coolidge signed the Immigration Restriction Act of 1924, he commented that "America must remain American."[61]

Notably, the quota system did not apply to immigrants from the Western Hemisphere, so Mexican and Canadian immigrants were still allowed to immigrate outside of numerical restrictions. This exception came about at the insistence of legislators from the western and southwestern states, who argued that their regions depended on Mexican agricultural labor.[62]

The act also introduced, for the first time on a permanent basis, the requirement of a visa to enter the United States of America.[63] Whereas previous generations of immigrants could simply board a steamship and show up in the New World without securing permission from the United States government beforehand, immigrants have henceforth needed the permission of the US State Department in their home country before they would be allowed to legally enter the United States.

The importance of this new rule should not be understated. While it sounds reasonable to expect that today's immigrants come legally, the way that many Americans' ancestors did, the rules have changed entirely.[64] For those of us whose ancestors came prior to the 1920s, without the requirement of a visa, to proudly note that our ancestors came *legally* to the United States is quite like a basketball coach bragging that his team scored 120 points in a game while a baseball coach's team scored only six—the boast is illogical, because the rules are completely different.

The bracero program: 1942–1964. While immigration from most countries dwindled after the drastic change in policy in 1924, immigrants from Mexico continued to come north in increasing numbers in response to an increasing need for labor. The agricultural industry, in particular, depended on migrant laborers.

THE CHURCH AND IMMIGRATION HISTORY

Just like the American public at large, American churches have espoused differing and ever-changing opinions on immigration. Protestant Christians were among those most opposed to the waves of Irish and German immigrants who arrived in the mid-nineteenth century, because they saw their Roman Catholic faith as a threat.[65]

In contrast, Protestant church leaders were, with some exceptions, among the foremost defenders of the Chinese immigrants on the West Coast during the late nineteenth century, with Presbyterian, Methodist, and Baptist clergy beginning churches among the new immigrants. They also displayed "stubborn courage in their advocacy of the Chinese," opposing local and national policies designed to exclude the Chinese, even when this meant battling public opinion.[66]

As the second great wave of European immigration commenced in the 1880s, with Italian Catholics and Russian Jews, in particular, pouring into New York City, most Protestants, while still skeptical of Catholicism, advocated welcoming the newcomers and attempting to convert them, with very few considering the political solution of restrictions on immigration.[67] That perspective gradually changed, though, and by the 1890s most prominent Protestants were advocating some level of immigration restriction.[68]

Interestingly, the general sentiment among Protestant believers reversed course again, quite dramatically, in the first decade of the twentieth century. Historian Lawrence B. Davis suggests that the evolution in attitude was the result of increased personal acquaintance with the vilified new immigrants: "One might speak disparagingly of foreigners in the abstract," Davis writes, paraphrasing a Baptist pastor of the era, "but would regard them as brothers upon personal confrontation."[69] The change came about as Christian men and, in particular, women, heeded the call of evangelical leaders such as Howard Grose, who in a series of popular books extolled the arrival of the "incoming millions" as "an opportunity" to "carry the gospel to [foreigners] in our own land" and provided a number of practical suggestions for caring for one's immigrant neighbors, such as helping them to learn English.[70]

The change in perspective toward immigrants affected Protestant attitudes toward immigration policy, as well. Though many had been fervently calling for immigration restrictions around the turn of the century, by the 1920s, many Protestant denominations vocally renounced the restrictions based on national origin that, nevertheless, became law in 1924.[71]

Forty years later, though, when Congress was reconsidering the national origins quota system of immigration restriction, evangelicals, speaking through the National Association of Evangelicals,[72] opposed the opening of immigration policy proposed by John F. Kennedy.[73] Ironically, as evangelical historian Douglas Sweeney notes, the passage of the 1965 immigration reform has been a boon for evangelicalism, as Asian and Hispanic immigrants "have quietly contributed several million new adherents to the evangelical movement."[74]

Today, as throughout American history, American churches are divided over the question of immigration. We will look more closely at how churches are responding to the immigration issue, and to immigrants themselves, in chapter nine.

Beginning in 1942, when World War II led to shortages in the labor market, the United States and Mexican governments agreed to implement a specific guest-worker program known as the *bracero* program, which lasted in various forms until 1964, with as many as 400,000 Mexican agricultural laborers entering in some years.[75] Bracero workers were supposed to be temporary nonimmigrants, but many stayed in the United States illegally rather than returning to Mexico at the end of the season. When migrants arrived to the United States, they were put into holding pens and waited for a job opportunity with numbers hanging around their necks. They were then stripped naked and sprayed with a delousing agent before entering the United States.[76] The President's Commission on Migratory Labor in 1951 also documented abysmal living conditions of migrant workers who were found living in orchards and irrigation ditches, working in unsafe conditions, in "virtual peonage."[77] The program was criticized both by organized labor, who felt that the Mexican laborers were stealing jobs from American citizens, and by those who were concerned that the Mexican workers themselves were being exploited. Braceros, who worked under contract, complained of "violations of wage agreements, substandard living quarters, exorbitant charges for food and clothing, and racist discrimination."[78]

The lobbying efforts of the agricultural interests, though, proved strong, and the program was consistently renewed until 1964. When the bracero program was finally disbanded, it was, at least in part, due to the concerns raised by Cesar Chavez, a union organizer who was concerned that the bracero program undermined the rights of workers—both the braceros themselves and those in the United States who could not compete with their cheap, contracted labor. Chavez, who cofounded the United Farm Workers union, would become a revered leader in the Mexican American community.

The 1965 reforms. As the bracero program officially ended, a new era was dawning in immigration law. The quota system that began in 1924 had been, with slight modifications, the immigration law of the land for approximately forty years, though not without criticism. President Harry Truman called the 1924 law and subsequent variations of the law based on the same national-origins premise "a slur on the patriotism, the capacity, and the decency of a large part of our citizenry," but the will of the Congress prevailed over Truman's criticisms, and the law remained generally in place.[79]

It was not until President John F. Kennedy's administration, in the 1960s, that the quota system would be effectively challenged. As the civil rights era was bringing questions of racial and ethnic discrimination to the forefront of the public discussion, the blatantly racial nature of the existing law was called into question.[80] Kennedy argued, in a book on the topic of immigration, that the United States should have an immigration policy that was generous, fair, and flexible, allowing the nation to "turn to the world, and to our own past, with clean hands and a clear conscience."[81] To Kennedy, this meant a system based on a series of preferences, based primarily on family relationships and job skills.

When Kennedy was assassinated in 1963, President Lyndon Johnson, who had supported the status quo as a senator, voiced his support for his predecessor's reform plan.[82] After much debate and some significant modifications—including the insertion of a numerical limit on immigrants from the Western Hemisphere, which had never before existed—the bill was finally approved by the Congress and then signed by President Johnson. In a speech given after signing the bill, in the shadow of the Statue of Liberty in New York Harbor, President Johnson stated, "The days of unlimited immigration are past. But those who do come will come because of what they are, and not because of the land from which they sprung."[83]

Though there have been significant modifications—some of which have been generous toward new immigrants and some of which have added further restrictions, usually in response to the public sentiment of the era—our current immigration system, which is described in chapter four, is still modeled after the 1965 law. As Johnson noted, the bill certainly did not bring us back to the era of unrestricted immigration that existed through our country's first century of existence. The 1965 law did, though, dramatically change who was entering: though it may not have been the intention of the bill's supporters, the 1965 bill opened up immigration for people from Asia, Africa, and other parts of the world beyond just Europe. At the same time, it subjected many Mexicans and other Latin Americans, who had historically crossed the border without numerical limit, to new legal bars to their entry.

The 1965 law permanently changed the nature of immigration to America, resolving some problems with the previous immigration system while creating new problems, many of which we, as a nation, are wrestling with today.

THE REFUGEE ACT OF 1980

During World War II, millions were forcibly displaced from their homes; in its wake, various nations came together to create a global system to protect and assist refugees. The United Nations created the 1951 Refugee Convention and the subsequent 1967 Protocol, which outlined the framework to define a refugee and afford them legal protections and rights for the global community.

In the United States, the 1970s and 1980s marked an era of forced migration in which thousands of Indochinese and Soviet Jews were coming to the United States. Senator Edward Kennedy started a conversation in the Senate about streamlining the United States response to the global refugee crisis. The Refugee Act of 1980 was the first comprehensive legal system that codified the definition of a refugee based on the UN Convention and Protocol on the Status of Refugees while also establishing a uniform and permanent system for the admission of refugees of the United States. The Act, signed into law by President Jimmy Carter on March 17, 1980, was passed unanimously by the Senate and the by the House by a significant majority.

The Refugee Act authorized the president, in consultation with Congress, to determine the annual refugee admissions ceiling (the maximum number that the country could receive for a given year, though in many instances the actual number has fallen well short of the ceiling), and established the Office of Refugee Resettlement, which provided assistance to refugees after their arrival to the United States. The Refugee Act has provided the basic framework for the United States refugee admissions program, which continues today, although the presidentially determined ceiling of refugee admissions has declined dramatically in recent years: the ceiling was set at 231,700 for FY1980, at 142,000 for FY1993, and at 110,000 for FY2017, but was set at a historical low 45,000 for FY2018.[84]

Immigration from the 1970s to today. The 1970s started a new era of large-scale immigration to the United States of both those entering lawfully and unlawfully. Because previous immigration from Latin America was not subject to strict numerical limitations, the phenomenon of illegal immigration increased dramatically this time, with immigrants from Mexico making up the largest share of both authorized and unauthorized immigrants in the United States.[85] By the mid-1980s, an estimated three to five million immigrants were in the United States illegally, sparking a national debate over how to reform our immigration laws.[86]

When President Reagan ran for office in 1980, immigration was a hot topic in both the Republican primary and the general election. In a GOP primary debate, candidates Reagan and George H. W. Bush were asked about their position regarding the education of children of unauthorized immigrants.[87] Bush answered by saying that a response "would be so sensitive and understanding about labor needs and human needs that that problem wouldn't come up.... I would reluctantly say that they [children of the undocumented] would get whatever the society is giving to their neighbors."[88] Reagan also responded by saying, "Rather than talking about putting up a fence, why don't we ... make it possible for them to come here legally."[89]

When Reagan defeated Jimmy Carter in the general election, he used his first State of the Union address to ask Congress to pass a comprehensive immigration reform bill.[90] President Reagan, considered the father of modern conservatism, knew from his experience as the governor of California that immigrants were critical to the economy. "Our nation is a nation of immigrants," he said in 1981.

More than any other country, our strength comes from our own immigrant heritage. We have a special relationship with our closest neighbors, Canada and Mexico. Our immigration policy should reflect this relationship. We must also recognize that both the United States and Mexico have historically benefited from Mexicans obtaining employment in the United States. A number of our States have special labor needs, and we should take these into account.

Illegal immigrants in considerable numbers have become productive members of our society and are a basic part of our work force. Those who have established equities in the United States should be recognized and accorded legal status. At the same time, in so doing, we must not encourage illegal immigration.[91]

In running for reelection in 1984, Reagan said, "I believe in the idea of amnesty for those who have put down roots and who have lived here even though some time back they may have entered illegally."[92] President Reagan worked with both Republicans and Democrats in Congress to pass the bipartisan Immigration Reform and Control Act of 1986.

The Immigration Reform and Control Act of 1986 had three significant components: employer sanctions, which required employers to verify their employees' immigration status; increased enforcement of immigration laws and border security personnel; and a legalization program that allowed individuals who entered the United States before January 1, 1982, and were continually present in the United States without a criminal record, to be able to acquire legal status.

As was common to every immigration debate, various interest groups weighed in on the bill. Before this bill was enacted, while it was unlawful to enter the country without inspection, it was never a crime to employ someone who had done so. The US Chamber of Commerce opposed the sanctions against employers, while agricultural groups asked for more visas for migrant laborers, and civil rights groups asked for labor protections. But as the bill worked its way through Congress, opposition from employers lessened as an amendment released employers from checking the authenticity of workers' documents. There were also provisions included for agricultural guest workers and protections for immigrant workers' rights.

When President Reagan signed the bill, he said immigration shouldn't be seen as "a problem between the United States and its neighbors," adding, "Our objective is only to establish a reasonable, fair, orderly and secure system of immigration into this country and not to discriminate in any way against particular nations or people."[93]

Approximately 2.7 million previously undocumented immigrants were legalized by the bill, popularly termed "the amnesty."[94] For those who received legal status, the bill was a game-changer; these immigrants made significant wage gains in the years after legalization and many became naturalized US citizens.[95] However, because the employer sanctions implemented through this bill were inconsistently enforced and because the legislation did not increase legal immigration at all, the bill certainly did *not* halt illegal immigration.

The unauthorized immigrant population in the United States rose significantly during the 1990s and the early 2000s, peaking at 12 million in 2007.[96] In 1996, in his State of the Union address, President Bill Clinton said, "We are a nation of immigrants, but we are also a nation of laws. It is wrong and ultimately self-defeating for a nation of immigrants to permit the kind of abuse of our immigration laws we have seen in recent years. And we must do more to stop it."[97] Later that year, he would sign the Illegal Immigration Reform and Immigrant Responsibility Act, which created harsher penalties for immigration offenses, including bars to reentry for immigrants who had been unlawfully in the country, departed, and tried to reenter lawfully, new restrictions on Lawful Permanent Residents federal public benefits, and an increase in border security spending.

President George W. Bush campaigned on the idea of immigration reform, famously proclaiming that "Family values do not stop at the Rio Grande."[98] By the time his administration focused on a big push for an immigration reform bill in 2007, though, he had spent much of his political capital, and a bipartisan comprehensive immigration reform bill the president supported failed in the Senate in 2007. This year marked the highest point of unauthorized immigrants in the United States, after which there was a steady decline as the country hit a recession. Immigration reform wasn't brought up again until President Obama took office.

During President Obama's second term, a "Gang of Eight" US Senators worked together for months to craft legislation that would comprehensively reform our immigration system. The Border Security, Economic Opportunity, and Immigration Modernization Act of 2013 passed the Senate by a vote of 68-32 with all Democrats, two Independents and fourteen Republicans voting in favor of the bill. The bill would have substantially increased border security, created a process by which most undocumented immigrants could pay fines and earn permanent legal status and eventual citizenship, eliminated certain visa categories, and changed the visa system to a merit-based points system. However, the House of Representatives never took up the Senate-passed bill, and the legislation died in the 113th Congress.

CONCLUSION

Jason de Leon is an anthropologist at the University of Michigan leading the "Undocumented Migration Project" in which he collects artifacts left by immigrants crossing the border in the Sonoran Desert. He believes the journey that immigrants take today will be remembered one day as the Ellis Island of this era. He's intent on preserving backpacks, broken shoes, bloody socks, and other materials that demonstrate that the journey was not easy because

> the worry is that it's going to get whitewashed, you know, in 50 years. I mean, people reminisce about Ellis Island as if it was, you know, a vacation spot. Ellis Island was a horrible place if you were Italian, if you were Eastern European. The human rights abuses that were happening when folks were migrating here have largely been forgotten with some historical distance.[99]

Immigration has always been and will remain a defining issue for the United States of America. Whether we trace our roots to the original peoples of the land, to the early western European colonists, to the Africans who were forced to migrate prior to the abolition of the slave trade, to the southern and eastern Europeans who journeyed through Ellis Island, to the more recent waves of immigrants from Latin America and Asia, or to some combination of the above, each of us has an individual immigrant history.

Understanding the history of immigration to the United States will help us have perspective on how to view and act toward newer immigrants entering the United States. The distinctive immigrant-rich history of the

United States demonstrates that the lines drawn around favored and disfavored immigrant groups are constantly shifting; groups deemed unassimilable when first arriving to the United States are now often considered fully American. Our history also reminds us that the immigrants of today are driven by the same motivations that drew the earlier colonists to come to the United States: the journey is never easy, and by sheer resilience, courage, and fortitude, many immigrants have established themselves as contributing, successful members of society for themselves and their families.

Like the Israelites, whose ancestors were immigrants in Egypt, we each have a story that can—and, Scripture suggests, should—inform the manner in which we treat immigrants entering our country today.

As we have seen, though immigrants themselves still come to the United States for many of the same reasons that immigrants have come since the colonial period, immigration laws and policies have changed drastically. In chapter four, we will examine how immigration law works today, which goes a long way toward explaining why there are so many undocumented people living and working in violation of the law.

FOUR

IMMIGRATING THE LEGAL WAY

Our Immigration System Today

American citizenship is priceless and it ought to be done the legal way, just like my ancestors did.

US REPRESENTATIVE JAMES SENSENBRENNER, ON CBS NEWS'S *FACE THE NATION*

ONE OF THE GREATEST POINTS OF CONFUSION for many native-born US citizens, such as those whose ancestors came through Ellis Island, is why *illegal* immigration has become so common. It is reasonable to expect that immigrants wishing to start a new life in the United States go about the proper legal channels to reside here. Much of the frustration revolves around why eleven million people decided to enter the country illegally (or to overstay a temporary visa).

Misconceptions persist about how our immigration system works today. Many believe people stay undocumented to avoid paying taxes, preferring to be paid in cash under the table. It simply is not right, they argue, for people to receive government services, like education and emergency healthcare, when they refuse to pay their taxes like everyone else.

Others think the undocumented are simply unwilling to fill out the proper forms to obtain a green card and a Social Security number. Once, at a training session on citizenship and immigration law for social workers, a well-meaning social worker, whose clients were mostly immigrants, expressed his bewilderment at the apparent unwillingness of many of his Mexican clients to get a Social Security card. His Polish clients, he said, go to the Social Security office as soon as they arrive, but many Mexicans never go. He was under the impression they never acquired a valid Social Security card because of sloth. He was genuinely surprised to learn that they were almost certainly ineligible to apply for a Social Security card since they had not been legally admitted to live and work in the United States, while his Polish clients were apparently lawful residents, with valid green cards or work authorization.

Still others are vaguely aware of the legal processes necessary to obtain a green card—knowing this involves filling out various forms available from the government, which are then adjudicated by the United States Citizenship and Immigration Service (formerly the Immigration and Naturalization Service)—and recognize that, as with any bureaucracy, this process will likely take some time. Some suppose that immigrants who come illegally have chosen to forgo this legal process because they are simply too impatient to wait their turn in line.

If the issue were really (as anti-immigration activists often suggest) that people who are undocumented refuse to go through the legal channels and wait their turn, or are lazy, it would be entirely reasonable to think them outrageous for demanding to be subsequently rewarded for having entered (or overstayed) illegally. If this were really the situation, Christians, who are directed by Scripture to be welcoming and hospitable to the stranger but who do not want to be taken advantage of, might therefore prefer to reserve their hospitality exclusively for legal immigrants.

The reality, though, is that immigration today is not so simple, and most undocumented immigrants are undocumented not because they choose to remain in that state but because there is no process for them to enter legally or obtain legal status. As we saw in chapter three, the immigration policies in our country have changed drastically since the era of Ellis Island, when 98 percent of immigrants who arrived were admitted into the United States, usually after just a few hours of processing and without need of a visa.[1] In those days, while the journey to the United States was often a harrowing voyage by ship and required great bravery and risk, it was easy to immigrate "the legal way." In fact, it would have been difficult to find an illegal way to immigrate.

Now, though we might encourage undocumented immigrants to wait their turn in line, there is often no line they can stand in. They can repeatedly line up at the US consulate, pay a substantial fee, and apply for a visa, but for the majority, especially those without substantial education or financial resources, they will leave the consulate disappointed, finding there is not even a line in which to wait.

IMMIGRATION STATUSES

If we are to understand the current immigration problem, we need to start by understanding how the US immigration system works today, which is the root of why we have so many undocumented immigrants living among us.

In general, there are three basic statuses that a foreigner residing in the United States can have: legal nonimmigrant, Lawful Permanent Resident, or US citizen.[2] Most foreigners who do not have one of these statuses are undocumented, meaning they have no legal status and could be legally deported solely on that basis.

Nonimmigrants. Foreigners on a nonimmigrant visa are admitted into the United States on a temporary basis, usually either as tourists, business travelers, temporary workers, or students. These nonimmigrants have come to stay for a limited period, and their home is still in the country they came from. Depending on the specific details of their visas, they may or may not be allowed to work during their time in the United States. If they are not authorized to work but do so anyway, they could risk deportation.

Visitor visas are typically granted at the US consulate in a foreign country. The visa is sealed into the foreign passport, and in most cases the visitor will then be allowed to enter the United States. To be granted a visa, the US government must determine that the potential visitor meets all of the admissibility requirements set forth in the Immigration and Nationality Act, which is the federal law that governs immigration. These requirements include prohibitions against people with certain infectious diseases, people who have committed certain crimes, and people who are expected to be a "public charge" (costing the country money), among other requirements.[3] Even with a visa, visitors can be refused entrance when they arrive if they meet one or more of the grounds of inadmissibility.

Nonimmigrant visas generally have a specific expiration date. If a person stays in the United States beyond that time and has not arranged to change their status, they become undocumented. In fact, about 42 percent of the estimated eleven million people who are undocumented came on a valid visitor visa but overstayed, including the majority of those who arrived in the past decade.[4] These visa *overstayers* come from every country in the world. For obvious geographic reasons, undocumented immigrants from locations other than Mexico, Canada, and Central America are more likely to have entered on a visitor visa and overstayed than to have crossed a border illegally.

It is precisely because so many temporary visitors overstay their visas, often with that intention in mind even before they leave their home countries, that it can be very difficult to obtain a visitor visa. The US government is wary about granting a visa to anyone it deems likely to overstay. So it is nearly impossible for many of the world's poor to obtain a visitor visa, because the potential for economic advancement is so strong by staying in the United States that consular officials consider them too high a risk. Conversely, most western Europeans, who live in and have steady employment in countries where the economic standards are roughly equivalent to those in the United States, can enter the United States without difficulty as nonimmigrant visitors. In fact, for certain countries, the visa requirement is waived.

In some cases, visitors who were admitted to the United States on a temporary basis can apply to adjust their status to that of a Lawful Permanent Resident, even if they have already overstayed. For example, a student who falls in love with and marries a US citizen while studying at a university in the United States would in most cases be eligible to adjust status and obtain a green card without ever leaving the country. In other cases, the only option is for individuals to leave the United States and process their petition for Lawful Permanent Resident status through the US consulate in their home country, which often causes further complications.

Lawful Permanent Residents. Lawful Permanent Residents possess a *green card* that identifies them as having been legally admitted to live permanently in the United States. They have the right to live and work, and their status never expires, although their green cards need to be renewed every ten years.

To be granted a green card, a potential immigrant must meet all of the same requirements of admissibility as a visitor or anyone else who wants to enter the United States as a noncitizen, in addition to other requirements. Once admitted, a green card holder still could be deported, for example, if the immigrant commits certain crimes, claims to be a US citizen or votes illegally, stays outside the United States for too long, or is suspected of threatening the national security of the United States.[5]

Lawful Permanent Residents have the right to petition for certain family members—spouses or unmarried children of any age—to immigrate to the United States as Lawful Permanent Residents, although they will need to wait—sometimes for a long time—for a visa to become available.

Lawful Permanent Residents can apply to become US citizens after having resided in the United States lawfully for four years and nine months, if they meet all other requirements for naturalization, including passing a test in English (with limited exceptions) of US history, civics, and government that a study has found at least one-third of native-born US citizens would fail.[6] Applicants must also generally pay a fee, currently $725. Lawful Permanent Residents married to a US citizen may apply earlier, after two years and nine months.

US citizens. US citizens include naturalized citizens, who must first have been Lawful Permanent Residents, pass a test, demonstrate that they are of good moral character (as vaguely defined by immigration law), swear an oath of allegiance to the United States, and meet certain other requirements. In recent years, about 700,000 Lawful Permanent Residents per year have naturalized.[7]

Other US citizens, of course, receive that title simply by being born in the United States (whatever the immigration status of their parents), based on the Fourteenth Amendment of the Constitution. Still others acquire US citizenship at birth abroad, if one or both parents are US citizens, while others derive citizenship if a parent naturalizes before their eighteenth birthday.

US citizens, by whichever of these means they acquire that title, have several rights that Lawful Permanent Residents do not. These rights include the rights to vote, to run for public office, to travel with a US passport, to apply for certain jobs, and to petition for certain family members (children of any age, married or unmarried, as well as spouses, parents, and siblings) to immigrate as Lawful Permanent Residents. US citizens are also free from the risk of deportation.

The undocumented. Most of those who are present in the United States and do not fit into any of the previous three categories are undocumented.[8] We discussed in chapter two exactly who these people are, what motivates them to come, and how they live. While some undocumented migrants have no intention of living permanently in the United States, many others yearn for the legal status offered by a green card—and with that the freedom from fear of deportation, the confidence to demand fair labor conditions, and particularly the ability to travel back to their home country and be reunited, even temporarily, with family. Many of these immigrants yearn to eventually to be citizens, but the current system, in most cases, makes that difficult if not impossible.

Since the first edition of this book was published, the US Department of Homeland Security opened and then closed an opportunity for a subcategory of undocumented immigrants: to be granted "deferred action."[9] Given that Congress has never appropriated more than a fraction of the money that would be necessary to deport everyone who is undocumented (not to mention those *with* legal status who become deportable because of criminal activity), every administration prioritizes immigration enforcement activities to focus on those with criminal convictions or who pose a threat to public safety. When a particular individual is considered *lowest* priority for deportation, the government in some cases formally "defers action" on their case, offering them a formal (albeit withdrawable) acknowledgement that they do not intend to deport them and allowing them to apply for temporary employment authorization.

While deferred action is not a new concept in immigration law—every administration since Dwight Eisenhower has employed some version of it[10]—it had never been made available to as large a number of individuals as it was in 2012, when President Obama offered Deferred Action status to undocumented individuals who had entered the United States before their sixteenth birthday (generally brought by one or both parents), who had been in the United States for at least five years as of that time, had not committed serious crimes, and met other criteria.[11]

This Deferred Action for Childhood Arrivals (DACA) program allowed individuals to renew their status each two years, giving beneficiaries access to work authorization, which in turn allowed them to obtain a valid Social Security number and then a driver's license, though it did not qualify them for federal financial aid or means-tested public benefits, nor did it allow an individual to apply for a green card or citizenship. In September 2017, the Trump administration announced the termination of the DACA program, such that—barring congressional or court intervention—all those granted permission to work and protection from deportation under DACA would be unable to renew those privileges. If the courts allow the termination of DACA to proceed and Congress has not taken action, an estimated thirty thousand individuals per month could lose their jobs and be at risk of deportation (like any other undocumented immigrant).[12]

PATHS TO LEGAL STATUS IN THE UNITED STATES

Elena is a typical example of the millions of undocumented people in the United States who yearn to be on the path to citizenship but at this point are not. She came to the United States for the first time in 1990. Like many others, she came because there were insufficient work opportunities in her home country. Elena graduated from high school in Guerrero, Mexico, in the mid-1980s. After working for a few years for little pay as an accountant and spending too much of her income just on transportation to reach the difficult-to-find job, she decided to try to go north to the United States. She had relatives in the Chicago area who assured her that she could make a better life there for herself, and even more so for the family that Elena hoped to have one day. Many immigrants are willing to work a difficult job for their entire lifetimes in exchange for the hope offered for advancement for their children—who within one generation can, with lots of hard work and education, be successful.

Elena thought about trying to obtain a visa, but with little money she knew that she would be denied a tourist visa, as she would be suspected (rightly) of being a potential overstayer. She would have liked to have immigrated legally as a Lawful Permanent Resident, but there were no accessible legal options for her to immigrate. So, instead, she paid about $600 to a *coyote*, trekked three days across the desert without food and drink, and eventually arrived to the welcome of her relatives in the suburbs of Chicago. With their help, she secured a false document to work and began flipping burgers at a fast-food restaurant within a month of arrival. She has since married and had two children—US citizens by birth—but she still does not have a green card.

Within the four general processes by which a person can obtain a green card under current immigration law, Elena has no options. Those four options are employment, family, the diversity lottery, or a fear of persecution in the home country.

Employment-based immigration. Employers may petition for immigrants to come as permanent resident workers or temporary workers, filling positions within their companies, with the intention of meeting the labor demands of the US economy. Within the permanent resident worker program, preference is given to immigrants with unique skills and high levels of education who meet a particular labor shortage within the United States. This path always requires an employer sponsor. The US Department of Labor must also certify that the employment of the immigrant will not adversely affect the wages and working conditions of US citizens. The employer thus obtains a labor certification from the government allowing them to hire the immigrant, who after thorough criminal background checks, would be admissible to the United States. This process usually requires the services of an immigration attorney, as extensive paperwork has to be filed by the hiring company.

Employment-based visas are also granted to investors who invest large amounts of money (at least $500,000, at present) in the United States and employ US citizens or Lawful Permanent Residents. This provision has been criticized as selling green cards to the wealthy, though the rationale is that these investors generate employment within the United States.[13]

A minimum of 140,000 immigrants is allowed to enter the United States each year based on employment.[14] The majority of these visas are reserved for individuals who have "extraordinary" or "exceptional ability," for "outstanding professors and researchers," and for others "holding advanced degrees."[15] For example, some medical professionals—especially doctors and nurses—may be able to obtain a green card through employment-based channels. Special employment-based visas are also available for religious workers and a few other specific categories of workers.

The current employment-based immigration system has little to offer, though, to the low-income, relatively low-education migrant like Elena, who came to the United States expecting, at least initially, to do what most Americans would consider menial labor. In fact, just five thousand employer-sponsored immigrant visas annually can be granted to those who are *not* considered highly skilled.[16]

Although Elena has now worked at fast-food restaurants for more than twenty-five years, and has seen her hourly wage rise as she has demonstrated her assiduousness, her employer would not be likely to expend the money necessary to pursue an employment-based visa, nor would it be likely to be granted, since Elena's high school education in Mexico does not meet the requirements for highly educated skilled workers for which most employment visas are designated. Indeed, few of those currently undocumented have any chance to receive a visa on the basis of employment, even if they could afford to initiate the application process.

Family-based immigration. Most immigrants who come to reside permanently in the United States immigrate on the basis of family relationships, with the intention of reuniting families. Each year a minimum of 226,000 immigrants are granted Lawful Permanent Residence based on a relationship to a US citizen or a Lawful Permanent Resident.[17]

Lawful Permanent Residents have the right to petition for a spouse or for a son or daughter of any age, so long as the son or daughter is unmarried. Citizens can petition for spouses, sons or daughters (whether married or not), siblings, and parents (but not until the petitioning child is at least twenty-one years old). In many cases, if a person is granted a visa on the basis of a family relationship, their spouse and children under age twenty-one are granted green cards as well.

However, although a person may have a qualifying relationship with a US citizen or Lawful Permanent Resident, that person still must wait for a visa to be available. Visas are available immediately, without limit, for certain relatives of US citizens (spouses, unmarried children under age twenty-one, and parents). They must simply file the proper form, pay the required fee, and wait the time that the government agencies involved require to process and adjudicate the request, often about one year. Nevertheless, the immigrant relative must still qualify with all other eligibility rules to be granted Lawful Permanent Residence.

WAITING YOUR TURN IN LINE:
The Current Family-Based Immigration Preference System

The following are examples of wait times for a visa to be available, based on family relationship, immigration status of the petitioner, and (in some cases) country of origin of the beneficiary:*

Spouse of a US citizen (from any country): No wait time, beyond the six months to two years usually required to process all required paperwork

Spouse of a Lawful Permanent Resident from Canada: Two years

Minor child (unmarried) of a Lawful Permanent Resident from China: Two years

Brother or sister of a US citizen from India: Fourteen years

Unmarried adult child of a US citizen from Mexico: Twenty-one years

Brother or sister of a Lawful Permanent Resident: No option to immigrate

Unmarried adult child of a Lawful Permanent Resident from Iran: Seven years

Unmarried adult child of a Lawful Permanent Resident from Mexico: Twenty-one years

The situation is much more challenging for other family-based petitions. Visa availability is based on the particular relationship to the US citizen or Lawful Permanent Resident, and then further affected by country quotas, as no single country is allowed more than 7 percent of the family-based visas for any given year.[18] The visa categories are divided on a preference system in which each preference is based on the status of the person petitioning in the United States (a US citizen or US Lawful Permanent Resident) and the relationship of the US sponsor to the intending immigrant.

The *first preference* is for unmarried adult children of US citizens; currently, the wait time for these people, from most countries, is approximately seven

Married adult child of a Lawful Permanent Resident: No option to immigrate

Parent of a US citizen: No wait time, beyond the six months to two years required to process all required paperwork

Parent of a Lawful Permanent Resident: No option to immigrate

Brother or sister of a US citizen from the Philippines: Twenty-three years

Unmarried adult child of a US citizen from Italy: Seven years

Married adult child of a US citizen from Ghana: Twelve years

Married adult child of a US citizen from the Philippines: Twenty-three years

Having a visa available is just the first step: would-be immigrants could still be prohibited from immigrating for criminal problems, health problems, previous unlawful presence in the United States, and for many other reasons. They also could face problems if they change their status during the years that the petition is pending, such as if an adult child of a Lawful Permanent Resident decides to marry.

---

*These wait times are taken from the most recent US Department of State Visa Bulletin, and wait times are rounded to the nearest year. The Visa Bulletin is updated monthly, and wait times may vary slightly from one month to another.

years.[19] For immigrants from the Philippines, though, the wait time is about eleven years, and for those from Mexico, more than twenty-one years.

The *second preference* includes spouses and children of Lawful Permanent Residents. For a Lawful Permanent Resident applying for their spouse or children under age twenty-one, the wait time for most countries is currently about two years.[20] If a child turns twenty-one before the visa is available, they move to the lower-preference category of unmarried adult children of Lawful Permanent Residents (twenty-one or over), who generally have wait times of about seven years.[21] Mexicans and Filipinos again prove the exception: Mexican adult, unmarried children of a Lawful Permanent Resident are currently waiting about twenty-one years for a visa, while Filipinos are waiting about eleven years under this category. If they marry before the visa becomes available, they become ineligible to immigrate, as Lawful Permanent Residents do not have the right to petition for married children. (If the immigrant has a live-in girlfriend or boyfriend and has children but does not legally marry, he or she can maintain a spot in line—which has the not-so-family-friendly effect of discouraging marriage.)

The wait times for the *third preference*, which is for married sons and daughters of US citizens, are particularly long. The wait time is around twelve years for those with family in most parts of the world, while for Mexicans it is currently about twenty-one years, and for Filipinos it is twenty-three years.[22]

Finally, the *fourth preference* category is for brothers and sisters of US citizens. For immigrants in most countries of the world, the wait time for a sibling to come is about thirteen years, with slightly longer waits for those from India and much longer waits—twenty and twenty-three years, respectively—for those from Mexico and the Philippines.[23]

Given these long wait times during which would-be immigrants are separated from their families, it is not entirely surprising that some, particularly from Mexico or Central America (who are geographically proximate to their relatives, if they can make it across the border), choose to wait their turn for a visa while already living in the United States, albeit without the benefit of legal status. In some cases, they may be able to adjust their status from undocumented to Lawful Permanent Resident once the wait time is up. Yet in most cases they must return to their country of origin to claim their visa, often to find that their unlawful presence in the Unites States has made them ineligible to immigrate for up to a decade.

A further barrier to family reunification is financial. The United States Citizenship and Immigration Services (USCIS), the division of the US Department of Homeland Security that is responsible for approving family-based immigration petitions, is funded almost entirely by the fees paid by immigrants themselves, rather than by taxpayer monies.[24] USCIS has increased fees charged to immigrants several times over the past several years. Since 1998, for example, the fee for Adjustment of Status (filing for a green card for someone already physically present in the United States, usually on a nonimmigrant visa) jumped from $130 to $1,140.[25] When the additional required fees for a family member petition (currently $535) and biometrics processing ($85) are added on, plus the costs of an attorney to help to prepare the application (which can cost thousands of dollars in some cases) and a medical exam that is usually not covered by insurance, the financial costs can be prohibitive.

An understanding of the actual waits and costs implied when we suggest that immigrants wait their turn and immigrate the legal way is helpful. It is equally important to acknowledge, though, that many (probably most) of the people who immigrate illegally to the United States did not even have the option to get in line, because they have no qualifying family member who is a US citizen or Lawful Permanent Resident. Elena is a good example. She chose to come to Illinois because she had family living there—a US-citizen uncle and Lawful Permanent Resident cousins—but they did not have any right to petition for their niece or cousin, respectively. So Elena had no one to apply on her behalf for a family-based visa, and instead she came, as many others have, by crossing the border illegally.

Elena's son, who was born in the United States and is thus a US citizen, turned twenty-one a few years ago, so he is technically eligible to petition for his mother. Under current law, though, this would not really benefit Elena, because she would have to return to Mexico to apply for the visa—no adjustment of status within the United States would be possible in her case, at least under current law—and the moment she crosses the border, leaving the United States, she would trigger a ten-year bar to legal reentry because of a tough law passed by Congress in 1996. In her circumstance, there is no waiver or exception available, so unless she wants to be separated from her children for ten years, she does not have a particularly good option.[26]

Diversity immigration. Since most immigration to the United States is based on family relationships, the countries that already have the most immigrants living in the United States are also the countries that send the most new immigrants each year. For countries that have historically sent few immigrants to the United States, there are few naturalized US citizens or Lawful Permanent Residents who can apply for family members to come, and immigration from these countries is limited. To address this imbalance, Congress instituted a new means of obtaining a green card in the early 1990s, known as a diversity visa. These visas, which are distributed by a random lottery of qualifying entrants, can be applied for, free of charge, by anyone from an underrepresented country who has completed high school or has at least two years of work experience in a skilled profession. Those selected by lottery must demonstrate that they meet all other requirements for admission into the United States.

In recent years, fifty thousand visas have been issued annually through the diversity lottery. Indeed, it really is a lottery, as the odds of being selected in recent years have generally been between one in 250 and one in 400, depending on the number of entrants.[27] For countries that already have the most immigrants in the United States, however—including Mexico, the Philippines, India, China, Canada, Haiti, El Salvador, England, Nigeria, South Korea, and Vietnam, among others—the diversity lottery is not currently an option.[28] Elena, from Mexico, would thus have had no possibility of a diversity lottery visa, either.

Refugees and asylees. Another way in which a person might obtain a green card is by entering the United States as a refugee or, on entering the United States, claiming and ultimately being granted asylum. Both refugees and asylees, according to the definition accepted by the United Nations and the

United States, flee their home country based on "a well-founded fear of being persecuted for reasons of race, religion, nationality, membership in a particular social group, or political opinion."[29]

The United Nations High Commissioner for Refugees estimates there are currently 22.5 million refugees in the world, of which only a small fraction of 1 percent are resettled each year in the United States.[30] Asylees are individuals who arrive in the United States as nonimmigrants but, once here, request asylum based on fear of returning to their home country. Both refugees admitted into the United States and those asylees approved by the US government are eventually granted green cards in most cases, allowing them to live permanently in the United States and, ultimately, to apply for citizenship. Refugees and asylees generally go through harrowing, tragic life circumstances to become a recognized refugee or asylee in the United States, but from there it is usually not a complicated process to receive a green card.

The total number of refugees admitted annually varies each year, based on a maximum "ceiling" set by the president and also impacted by the funds appropriated by Congress for processing, vetting, and resettling refugees. In 1980, President Carter set the refugee ceiling at 231,700, and nearly that many refugees arrived, primarily from Vietnam. Throughout the early 1990s, the ceiling was set by Presidents George H.W. Bush and Bill Clinton above 100,000 per year, with many refugees arriving from the former Soviet Union in addition to Southeast Asia. Throughout the George W. Bush and Barack Obama administrations, the ceiling was between 70,000 and 85,000 each year (though some years the actual number of arrivals did not reach the maximum set by the president), with most refugees coming from Africa (particularly Somalia, Sudan and later South Sudan, Rwanda, Burundi, Sierra Leone, Liberia, and the Democratic Republic of Congo), Asia (particularly Burma and Bhutan), and the Middle East (primarily Iraq and Iran).[31] Most recently, President Trump has set this ceiling at 45,000, the lowest level on record, and as of this writing the US seems unlikely to reach even half that target in fiscal year 2018 as a result of slowed overseas processing.

Another group who have received significant media attention in the United States in recent years are unaccompanied children; most have fled the Central American countries of El Salvador, Honduras, or Guatemala and arrived at the US-Mexico border. Under current law, these children are transferred from the Department of Homeland Security to the custody of the Department of Health and Human Services, which seeks to provide or arrange temporary care (usually with a family member already in the United States) until the child can go before an immigration judge. Many of these individuals—who are frequently fleeing threats of violence in El Salvador or Honduras, which compete for the ignominious title of the highest homicide rate of all countries in the world[32]—are ultimately granted asylum by proving they meet the legal definition of refugee. Many others are eventually deported. Some never show up for court and have entered the ranks of the undocumented.

The definition of refugee does not include those who flee their home country because of environmental or natural disasters—such as a famine, tsunami, or earthquake—or those who flee dire economic circumstances, which would include many who have come to the United States illegally, particularly from Mexico and Central America. Elena came to the United States because she could not find work to sustain herself in Mexico, but fleeing economic hardship is not a valid reason to be classified as a refugee or to be granted asylum under the US system.

CONCLUSION

Almost all Lawful Permanent Residents and naturalized US citizens living in the United States today received their status through one of these four manners: for family unity, employment, by winning the diversity visa lottery, or seeking protection from persecution.[33] For those like Elena who are un-documented, though, none of these legal paths may be an option. For her, there was no hope of an employment-based visa, no qualifying relationship to apply for a family-based visa, no diversity lottery, and no persecution that would merit a plea for asylum or refugee status.

That was true for Elena when we wrote the first edition of this book, and it's still true a decade later. In many ways, her family has excelled in the United States: her son, born a few years after she arrived in the United States, graduated from a competitive Christian liberal arts college a few years ago; he is now pursuing a master's in social work while working full-time as a teacher at an after-school program for low-income students operated by his church. Elena's daughter just graduated from high school and is deciding between several colleges that offered her admission. Elena's hopes for her children are bright—but, without changes to law, she is unlikely to gain legal status. Her undocumented status has limited her options for economic advancement, and, with the constant threat of deportation, she lives with the fear that she could be separated from her children.

Millions of others are in similar situations to Elena; they elected to come illegally or to overstay a temporary visa years or even decades ago because there was no legal path to permanent status as an immigrant. For many others all over the world, particularly from countries where the economic situation is dire, coming to the United States seems to be the only hope—just as it has been for immigrants throughout our country's history. However, there is simply no legal way to immigrate for the majority of those who would like to do so, even though those who can arrive anyway do not seem to have difficulty finding willing employers.

I (Matthew) lived for a while in Nicaragua, the economically poorest country in Latin America. Many there see the United States—whose streets are rumored to be paved in gold, whose federal minimum wage of $7.25 per hour sounds to many like a fortune to be made, and whose extravagance is displayed to the Nicaraguan people on the ubiquitous television—as the great hope for a better life for their families.

While in Nicaragua, I heard story after story of people who had tried in vain to secure a visa to go to the United States. When there was no avenue to apply for an immigrant visa, many would apply for a visitor visa, sometimes with the intention of overstaying. In almost every case, they were denied the visa, but they still had to pay a $100 fee—more than a month's income for many Nicaraguans—just for the privilege of the appointment at the US consulate.[34] For many Nicaraguans facing extreme poverty, unsure of where the next meal for them and their children will come from, spending their last $100 (or, more likely, borrowing $100 from a better-off relative) is like buying a lottery ticket, hoping they might beat the odds and win the chance to live and work in the United States.

That immigrants should wait their turn and immigrate the legal way sounds entirely reasonable, but the realities of our present immigration system complicate this truism. The immigration system, many would agree, is broken. Just how we fix this broken system, though, is a question of heated controversy—in Washington, DC, and even in our churches. As Christians, our response to these challenging issues should be informed by Scripture, which guides us toward how God would have us think about immigration policy and about immigrants themselves. We turn to Scripture in chapter five.

FIVE

THINKING BIBLICALLY ABOUT IMMIGRATION

Welcoming the stranger (the "immigrant," we could say today) is the most often repeated commandment in the Hebrew Scriptures, with the exception of the imperative to worship only the one God. And the love of neighbor (especially the more vulnerable neighbor) is doubtlessly the New Testament's constant command. . . . Whatever the cause of immigration today, there can be no doubt as to where the Church must stand when it comes to defending the immigrant.

THEOLOGIAN ORLANDO O. ESPÍN

FOR CHRISTIANS WHO TAKE the authority of Scripture seriously, all of life should be viewed through the lens of what God tells us about himself and his world in the Bible. While the Bible does not provide a specific prescription for a US immigration policy—or for any other particular policy decision—it certainly offers principles that guide us as we consider the immigration dilemma and seek to influence policy in a way that reflects God's love, compassion, and justice.

In fact, immigration is a common theme in the Scriptures. There are several words in the original Hebrew of the Old Testament rendered into English as *alien, stranger, sojourner, foreigner,* or *immigrant*, depending on the translation. The most common word, and that which best describes the immigrants we encounter—not just tourists traveling through but strangers who establish themselves, at least for a time, in a foreign land—is the Hebrew word transliterated into English as *ger*. Based on textual, historical, and archaeological evidence, scholars believe that *ger* (in the context of the Hebrew Scriptures) refers to "a person not native to the local area" and thus often without family or land; the same term is used to refer both to the Israelites when living (whether as welcomed guests or resented laborers) in Egypt as well as to non-Israelites living among the Israelites.[1] The noun *ger* alone appears ninety-two times in the Old Testament. Throughout the text, we find stories of *ger* (sojourners or immigrants), as well as guidance and commands from God to his people about how to treat the immigrants living among us.

IMMIGRANTS AND IMMIGRATION IN SCRIPTURE

When we read the Bible as a sacred narrative of God's interaction with humanity, we find that immigrants play many of the most important roles in the story. Throughout Scripture God has used the movement of people to accomplish his greater purposes. Like immigrants today, the protagonists of the Old Testament left their homelands and migrated to other lands for a variety of reasons.

Abram, later Abraham, is introduced in Genesis 11 as an immigrant from Ur to Haran. Abram's journeys did not stop there: this Ur-born immigrant later journeyed on to Canaan, with a stay in Egypt as well. Abram's decision to leave Haran and bring his family to Canaan parallels the stories of many historical and contemporary immigrants who leave the lands they know and cross borders in pursuit of a promise—in this case a divine promise that God would bless him, make of him a great nation, and bless all nations through him (Gen 12:1-5). Indeed, Abram's courage in making the journey and his faith in God's promise mark one of the pivotal moments in the Old Testament narrative.

Like many migrants in our world today, though, Abram also faced some complex ethical decisions in the course of migration: when a border stood behind him and the sustenance he and his family needed in the midst of a famine, Abram urged his wife, Sarai, to tell Egyptian officials that she was his sister, rather than his wife, under the presumption that he would then be treated better by the Egyptians (Gen 12:10-20). In US immigration law, that would be considered a "material misrepresentation of the facts," but rightly or wrongly—and the text leaves that somewhat ambiguous—Abram did what he thought he had to do to protect himself and provide for his family.

Abraham also serves as a model of hospitality toward foreigners. When three strangers—unbeknownst to Abraham, messengers from God—passed by Abraham's home, he was so eager to offer them food and drink that he ran out to greet them (Gen 18:1-6). As an immigrant himself, he understood the experience of being a stranger in a foreign land, and he was eager to make others feel welcome. Likewise, today's immigrants to the United States are often embraced by earlier immigrants, who have already learned English and sufficiently understood US culture to help the new arrivals orient themselves.

A few generations later, Abraham's great-grandson Joseph becomes a different sort of immigrant—one who leaves his homeland not by choice or in pursuit of a better life, but as one sold into slavery and forced across a border. Joseph's brothers, tired of their younger brother's haughtiness, sell him to slave traders and invent a story to explain his absence to their father. Historically, of course, millions of people have been forced into involuntary migration; Americans are particularly aware of the slave ships that brought Africans to the New World against their will. Most would be surprised to know, though, that there are likely more victims of human trafficking—people forced by violence, coercion, or deception into either sexual exploitation or labor—today than there were at the height of the transatlantic slave trade.[2] Like Joseph, some of today's victims of human trafficking are betrayed by their families, who profit from their relatives' suffering.

Eventually, through a series of divinely directed events, Joseph's status was raised from slave to the second-most-powerful person in Egypt, and God used him in powerful ways to save both his own family *and* his host country, Egypt. Joseph's experience, as theologian Justo González notes, reminds us that immigrants can make important contributions, economically and otherwise, to the country that receives them.[3] In the United States, for example, immigrants or their children were responsible for founding 40 percent of Fortune 500 companies, including brands such as Apple, AT&T, Boeing, Disney, General Electric, Google, and McDonald's.[4]

In God's plan, Joseph was ultimately reconciled to his family, who then took up residence in Egypt and lived there as foreigners for several generations. As the Israelites multiplied in Egypt, though, their growing numbers began to concern the native-born Egyptians, who began to oppress them, forcing them into slave labor. Likewise, many immigrants arrive eager to work in the United States, only to be viewed with suspicion, mistreated, paid less than they were promised, or subjected to unsafe working conditions.

The book of Exodus explains how God used an unconfident man named Moses to lead his people out of Israel, fleeing a tyrannical government that had decreed death for all Israelite male infants. The Israelites, under Moses' leadership, became refugees, fleeing persecution in Egypt and escaping, with God's help, to a new land where, like many refugees today, they found new challenges. God ultimately used Moses to bring his people out of Egypt, so they could live in a "good and spacious land, a land flowing with milk and honey" (Ex 3:8).

Not all of the migrants in Scripture were *from* Israel: as the Israelites became established, there was also immigration *into* Israel. A woman named Ruth, from the land of Moab, married a foreigner in her home country and then, after her husband's death, decided to follow her mother-in-law, Naomi, to the foreign land of Judah. Ruth was like many immigrants today, who leave their homeland for the sake of family unity. God used Ruth's migration to Israel, and her subsequent marriage to Boaz, to form part of the lineage of Jesus, the Messiah.

Ruth's great-grandson David was thus born as a descendant of an immigrant. In God's perfect plan, that did not stop him from becoming Israel's greatest king. Likewise, many of the great heroes of American history have been immigrants or second- or third-generation immigrants. Before becoming king, David also crossed borders himself, fleeing the wrath of King Saul and seeking asylum from King Achish of Gath, in the territory of the Philistines; David established himself there in Gath, along with his family (1 Sam 21:10; 27:3).

Just as immigrants and refugees are important actors in the Hebrew Scriptures, they feature prominently in the New Testament too. The most notable refugee was Jesus himself, who fled, the Gospel of Matthew tells us, with his parents to go to Egypt, legitimately fearing King Herod would kill them if they remained in Judea (Mt 2:14). In another sense, of course, Jesus was a divine immigrant, leaving the glories of heaven to live among us and save us on earth (Phil 2:6-8).

Persecution was also the impetus for the great scattering of the earliest Christians in Jerusalem, as described in Acts. When Stephen was martyred for his strong defense of the gospel, "a great persecution broke out against the church in Jerusalem, and all except the apostles were scattered" (Acts 8:1). God used this dispersion of Christ-followers to spread the gospel throughout Judea and well beyond. For example, Philip went south toward Gaza and encountered an Ethiopian pilgrim who accepted the good news and presumably brought it back to Africa (Acts 8:26-30).

Furthermore, Scripture suggests that all of us who follow Christ, whatever our nationality, have become aliens in this world, as our allegiances are to lie not primarily with any nation-state but with the kingdom of God. Paul reminds the believers at Philippi that their citizenship is in heaven (Phil 3:20), while Peter (1 Pet 2:11) and the author of Hebrews describe believers as foreigners and strangers on earth (Heb 11:13).

God used migration throughout Scripture to accomplish his purposes and bring his people to a greater understanding of his will for creation. God, who used migration so vividly throughout the Bible, works today to move his people from one place to another.

THE BIBLICAL MANDATE TO CARE FOR IMMIGRANTS

Since so many of the characters of the biblical story were migrants of one sort or another, it is not surprising that God gives us a great deal of guidance about interacting with immigrants. God reminds the Israelites early on of their own history as strangers in a foreign land, commanding them that, given their own experience, they should welcome the immigrant among them. In Leviticus 19:33-34, God commands the Israelites, "When a foreigner resides among you in your land, do not mistreat them. The foreigner residing among you must be treated as your native-born. Love them as yourself, for you were foreigners in Egypt. I am the LORD your God." In fact, Israel's very identity was tied to how they treated the foreign born, as it reflected Israel's trust in God to provide and their willingness to follow his commandments.

God commands his people to extend the same legal protections to immigrants as were available to the Israelites themselves, including rights to a sabbath rest (Ex 20:10), fair labor treatment (Deut 24:14), and prompt payment for work (Deut 24:15). The words of Exodus 12:49, repeated throughout the Pentateuch multiple times, make clear: "The same law applies both to the native-born and to the foreigner residing among you."

At the same time, immigrants are recognized as being particularly vulnerable, and God therefore commands the Israelites to take special concern for them. The term usually translated as *foreigner* or *sojourner* appears repeatedly in conjunction with two other categories of people of special concern to God: the fatherless and the widow. For example, Deuteronomy 10:18 says that God "defends the cause of the fatherless and the widow, and loves the foreigner residing among you, giving them food and clothing." Psalm 146:9 echoes this concern:

> The Lord watches over the foreigner
> and sustains the fatherless and the widow,
> but he frustrates the ways of the wicked."

The same linkage extends throughout the Old Testament, such as in Ezekiel, where the evil rulers of Israel are condemned for having "oppressed the foreigner and mistreated the fatherless and the widow," and in Zechariah, where God commands, "Do not oppress the widow or the fatherless, the foreigner or the poor" (Ezek 22:7; Zech 7:10).

Given God's particular concern, the Israelites are commanded in Deuteronomy 24 to make special provisions for immigrants, as well as for orphans and widows:

> When you are harvesting in your field and you overlook a sheaf, do not go back to get it. Leave it for the foreigner, the fatherless and the widow, so that the LORD your God may bless you in all the work of your hands. When you beat the olives from your trees, do not go over

the branches a second time. Leave what remains for the foreigner, the fatherless and the widow. When you harvest the grapes in your vineyard, do not go over the vines again. Leave what remains for the foreigner, the fatherless and the widow. (Deut 24:19-21)

Likewise, the Israelites are commanded in Deuteronomy 14 to participate in a special triennial tithe, when they set aside a portion of their harvest so immigrants, along with the Levites, the orphans, and the widows, may have a feast (Deut 14:28-29).

Many of these biblical imperatives also warn that those who disregard God's instructions—who do not specially care for the immigrant and others who are vulnerable—will face God's judgment. The prophet Malachi lumps those who deny justice to foreigners with sorcerers and adulterers: "I will be quick to testify against sorcerers, adulterers and perjurers, against those who defraud laborers of their wages, who oppress the widows and the fatherless, and deprive the foreigners among you of justice, but do not fear me" (Mal 3:5).

The Hebrew Scriptures, particularly the books of the Law, are full of instructions on how to treat immigrants. Old Testament scholar Daniel Carroll Rodas notes that such frequent and specific injunctions in the Mosaic law toward care for the sojourner are unique in that the law codes of other nations in the ancient Near East "are almost totally silent" about how to treat immigrants.[5] While these instructions (along with the rest of the law) were directed to the people of Israel as rules to structure their society, and few American Christians believe that we should adapt the entire law as given to Moses (with its sacrificial system and dietary guidelines) directly to US policies, the many commandments to care for the immigrant demonstrate that God has a special concern for immigrants, a concern that, as God's people, we are commanded to share. Our concern for the foreign born in our own society will have personal manifestations, but should also inform our positions as we consider immigration policy.

While the New Testament speaks less frequently about immigrants, the same ethic of concern for the alien and stranger is consistent. The author of Hebrews advises us to care for and welcome strangers with hospitality, because in doing so, we may be entertaining angels "without knowing it" (Heb 13:2). Likewise, Jesus told his disciples that whenever they welcomed and invited in a lowly stranger, they welcomed him (and, alternately, whenever they shut the stranger out, they shut him out as well—and would be judged harshly) (Mt 25:31-46).[6]

Caring for immigrants is a central theme in Scripture. We have reviewed just a sampling of the many passages woven throughout the text that tell us we are to take special concern for immigrants. God does not suggest that we welcome immigrants; he commands it—not once or twice, but over and over again.

NO LONGER FOREIGNERS AND STRANGERS BUT FELLOW CITIZENS

Scripture teaches that each of us who comes from outside the bloodline of Israel has something in common with immigrants today. Paul tells the Gentiles of the church at Ephesus that because of their nationality they were previously "separate from Christ, excluded from citizenship in Israel and foreigners to the covenants of the promise, without hope and without God in the world" (Eph 2:12). The promises of God in the Old Testament, which we celebrate in our worship songs, were *not* initially directed at us (the Gentiles) but to the Jewish people God had specially chosen. Simply for reason of the location of their birth—which, of course, they had not chosen, any more than someone today chooses to be born in Mexico, Poland, or Vietnam rather than in the United States, Canada, or western Europe—most of the world was without hope and without access to the God of Israel, the one true God. Like most Asian immigrants in the United States until 1952 and like any undocumented immigrant today, we who are Gentiles were once barred from citizenship.

Thanks be to God, though, this was not his final plan; by his grace, we have now been naturalized into God's kingdom and adopted into his family through the blood of Jesus Christ (Eph 2:13). What is more, Christ has personally

> destroyed the barrier, the dividing wall of hostility, by setting aside in his flesh the law with its commands and regulations. His purpose was to create in himself one new humanity out of the two, thus making

peace, and in one body to reconcile both of them to God through the cross, by which he put to death their hostility. (Eph 2:14-16)

The parallel to our current immigration situation, of course, is inexact—to be naturalized into the United States is almost unmentionably insignificant in contrast to becoming a citizen of God's kingdom—but many immigrants today know keenly what it means to have a law standing between them and really belonging as citizens. Even as many immigrants gratefully find their citizenship in heaven (through Christ, not through keeping the law of the Old Testament), they yearn for a change to laws in the United States that do not allow them to admit their infraction of undocumented presence and proceed to become fully integrated members of our society. We, who now "are no longer foreigners and strangers, but fellow citizens with God's people and also members of his household" (Eph 2:19), might remember the grace we have received on a cosmic scale and, corporately, seek appropriate ways to extend to those who seek it the much smaller grace of being allowed to pursue citizenship in the United States. While we need not necessarily advocate open borders—there is an appropriate role for the government in monitoring and controlling those who enter our country—we ought to have a strong bias toward generosity in light of the enormous blessings we have received.

Furthermore, we do well to note that by bringing Jews and Gentiles together as one person—though not, the apostle Paul makes clear, by requiring Gentiles to become as the Jews in every way—God creates a single body, his church (Acts 15:10; 1 Cor 12:27). Each part of Christ's body—Jew and Gentile, Asian, African, Hispanic, Native American, Caucasian, and every other group of people—must be reconciled to one another and to God to effectively be the unified body God has called us to be, doing his work in the world.

THINKING BIBLICALLY ABOUT ILLEGAL IMMIGRATION

We believe it is evident from the many references to immigrants and immigration, aliens, sojourners, and strangers in both the Old and New Testaments that God has clearly commanded his people to welcome and care for foreigners. We can appropriately extrapolate that Christians seeking to influence a national immigration policy should push for laws that are welcoming to and specially concerned with immigrants, just as God decreed for the nation of Israel.

The present immigration situation in the United States, however, presents a special challenge, as Scripture's many references to immigrants never mention or consider their legal status—a concept that may not have applied during the biblical era, just as it did not apply during the early history of the United States, when there were practically no limits on immigration and when all immigrants were, as far the governing authority was concerned, legal.

Indeed, many Christians would readily recognize that they should care for immigrants in a general sense, but they are troubled by the legal status issue and are not sure that they want to or should assist individuals whose presence in the United States is unlawful.

The current state of immigration helps to explain (if not necessarily justify) why so many people are in the United States without documents: the present laws make it impossible for most people to immigrate legally, while the economic or political situations in their home countries make it exceedingly difficult to stay put there.

Nevertheless, many Christians are uncomfortable with the idea of, and some even openly hostile toward, undocumented immigrants. Micah 6:8 commands us "to do justice, love mercy, and walk humbly with your God,"[7] but some Christians feel a tension between doing justice—which they might define as following and enforcing the law—and loving mercy—which might mean giving a break to those who have violated a law, especially without malicious intent in doing so.

James Edwards, for example, recognizes sympathetically the situation that many migrants are in, but he argues, "Even desperate circumstances don't make a lawless act moral."[8] He notes Proverbs 6:30-31, which says that, although most people would not blame a starving man for stealing some food, the thief is still responsible for the consequences of his crime. Many others have pointed to Romans 13, which states emphatically that everyone should "be subject to the governing authorities" since "there is no authority except that which God has established" (Rom 13:1). The text continues to say that those who disobey the civil authorities should expect judgment from those same authorities, who "do not bear the sword for no reason" (Rom 13:4).

We seem to be faced with a dilemma, then: Scripture tells us to welcome and care for immigrants, without reference to legal status, but it also commands us to obey and respect the laws created by the governing authorities. Given this apparent paradox, it is understandable that Christians who take Scripture seriously have diverging opinions on this topic.

The issue needs closer scrutiny, though. The words of Micah 6:8, translated above as a command to "do justice," are translated as "act justly" or "do justly" in alternate translations of the text (the New International Version and New King James Version, respectively). To many North American ears, to "do justice" implies law enforcement, whereas to "act justly" implies doing what is right and fair. We believe the latter understanding is closer to the justice that God calls us to.

In many situations throughout history, the laws of the civil authorities have not been just according to the principles that God gives to his people. Nor were civil authorities in the Bible always just: the Egyptian government of Pharaoh commanded Hebrew midwives to murder newborn boys (Ex 1:15-21), Babylonian King Nebuchadnezzar required people to bow before a statue of his image (Daniel 3), and the authorities forbade the earliest apostles from proclaiming the name of Jesus (Acts 5:27-28). In response to these unjust laws, God's people insisted that, "We must obey God rather than human beings" (Acts 5:29), defying the unjust injunctions—while remaining nonviolently subject to the authorities and submitting to the punishment they imposed, whether prison or a fiery furnace.

The question for us if we are to seek God's justice, then, is not only what the law is and is it being followed, but is the law itself just? Ultimately the laws must answer to God's higher law, which requires us to treat all human life with sanctity. All persons bear God's image and thus should be treated with dignity. Valuing persons includes doing what we can to preserve them, to care for them, and to create fair systems that lead to healthy societies.[9]

For most Christians, this is intuitive; for example, the majority of evangelical Christians across ethnicities believe that our federal government's allowance of abortion under almost all circumstances, through the Supreme Court's 1973 decision in *Roe v. Wade*, is unjust.[10] While recognizing that we are called to be subject to the state—few call for anarchy or violent revolution over this policy—many Christians feel strongly that to seek justice as God commands us means to seek to make abortion illegal within the law, through protest, lobbying, and voting. In a democratic government, the governing authorities to which we are called to submit actually invite us to be a part of changing laws we disagree with.

When unjust laws remain in place, there may be times when civil disobedience is permissible or even required if we are to practice "divine obedience."[11] The African American Christians who led the civil rights movement violated unjust laws in order to expose their injustice and end legalized segregation. Brave Christians such as Corrie ten Boom harbored Jewish people during the Holocaust. Today, many churches send missionaries to countries where it is illegal to preach the gospel.

Fortunately, at least in most cases and as of this writing, most US citizens need not cross this bridge: we can love, serve, and welcome immigrants, regardless of their legal status, and still be fully in compliance with the law. With the exception of employing someone who is undocumented and not authorized to work (which is quite clearly unlawful) none of the ways that a church as an institution or an individual Christian would interact with undocumented immigrants—welcoming them into a local church, offering English classes, running a food pantry or clothing closet, teaching them in Sunday school, or allowing them to teach Sunday school (so long as it is not a paid position)—is against the law. There is no legal requirement or expectation that a citizen report someone they suspect might not be lawfully present in the country.[12]

It is important to note, though, that the law could change so that even *ministry* to undocumented immigrants could be made a crime. For example, a 2005 bill that passed the US House of Representatives (but did not pass the Senate and is thus *not* current law) would have made a felon of anyone who knowingly "assists" a person to unlawfully "reside or remain in the United States," language broad enough that many church leaders feared that they could be legally liable for providing English classes or food assistance.[13]

Efforts to criminalize care for or even interaction with undocumented immigrants—whether at the state or federal level, legislative or administrative—present a significant threat to religious liberty, with the potential to legally bar citizens from obeying the biblical commands to love their immigrant neighbors. As pastor Rick Warren says, "A good Samaritan doesn't stop and ask the injured person, 'Are you legal or illegal?'"[14]—and the state should not expect him to do so.

At least under current law, though, there are few legal restrictions on ministry to immigrants, regardless of legal status, so there really is no tension between the biblical commands to be subject to governing authorities and the many Scriptural instructions to welcome and love immigrants. However, the ethical challenges for believers who are themselves undocumented—and there are many of them, as the US church is flourishing in immigrant communities even as it experiences a decline among white, native-born citizens—are more complex.

In fact, many immigrant believers who are present unlawfully are deeply anguished by their legal status. The vast majority are *desperate* to be right with the law and would be willing to do just about anything to earn legal status— but as we explained in chapter four, that's not possible in most cases.

I (Matthew) have a former neighbor who is typical of many undocumented Christians. He came illegally to the United States several decades ago in search of economic opportunity for him and his family. Once in the United States, he heard the gospel and committed his life to following Jesus. As his faith grew, nourished by his Baptist congregation, he became a lay leader in his church and began taking theology classes to gain a deeper understanding of his newfound faith. He is well-acquainted with Romans 13 and Paul's instructions to the Roman believers to subject themselves to the governing authorities, and he is deeply troubled. He wants to be right with the law, and he has sought to become so, consulting with attorneys and legal experts, but they all have given him the same message: the only way for him to fully comply with the law is to self-deport to Mexico. For someone in his circumstance, there is no possibility of "getting legal"—no matter how much money he is willing to spend. He can leave, but he cannot "come back the legal way," as some Christian brothers and sisters would advise him with all the best of intentions: someone in his circumstance would not qualify to return legally for at least a decade, and possibly ever.

Given that harsh reality, but deeply committed to faithful obedience to Scripture, he has considered returning to Mexico. Indeed, some in similar circumstances have done so, following their convictions and trusting that God would provide. But it is certainly not a simple decision. For one thing, he has teenage children who were born in the US, who have never been educated in any language other than English. If their father were to depart, they would likely want to stay in the United States, live with cousins or friends, and finish their education—but their dad believes he has a God-given responsibility to be present with them. These decisions are also complicated for marriages, particularly when one spouse feels the conviction to return, but the other does not. Most notably, my neighbor is also mindful of the biblical mandate that he provide for his family—"Anyone who does not provide for their relatives, and especially for their own household, has denied the faith and is worse than an unbeliever" (1 Tim 5:8)—and he sees no way that he could do so if he were to return to the situation of poverty that he fled decades ago, especially now that he has a large family to support.

We have each been asked by brothers and sisters in similar situation what to do in this circumstance. It's not the simple, cut-and-dry issue some might imagine, not just "what part of illegal don't you understand?" but also "what part of 'provide for your family' don't you understand?" We're wary to prescribe a one-size-fits-all instruction to situations that vary so dramatically, including situations in which returning to a country of origin could literally mean facing persecution or death.

Here's what we are sure of: we can exercise the responsibility inherent within a democratic system of government to advocate for changes to law, such that individuals in this circumstance could make things right, paying a fine or completing whatever restitution might be necessary for having overstayed a visa or entered the country within inspection, but stay with their families, where so many are also contributing to our local churches and to our national economy.

Ultimately, the Scriptures guide Christians to respect the rule of law, but our current immigration legal system actually makes a mockery of the law.

Our economy has created many jobs, particularly in sectors of our economy that do not require extensive formal education such as agriculture, hotels, and restaurants, but our immigration visa quotas, many of which were set in 1965, do not provide enough visas to meet the demand of our labor market. Rather than change the visa system, administrations of both parties effectively looked the other way for decades as desperate people overstayed visas or crossed the border unlawfully. Because the consequences of *fully* enforcing the law—deporting all those who are unlawfully present—would be cataclysmic both on an economic and a humanitarian level, few political leaders seriously support mass deportation of all undocumented immigrants, but they have also not found the consensus to create the mechanism to remedy their status.

Christians who advocate for immigration reform are not elevating compassion over the rule of law, but seeking solutions that would *restore* the rule of law, while also keeping families unified and affirming the inherent human dignity of all people. The comprehensive immigration reform proposals debated in Congress is recent years would make it *harder* to immigrate illegally (with increased spending on border security and systems to deter visa overstayers) while making it *easier* to immigrate legally (by increasing the number of visas available in particular categories), thus ensuring a more orderly legal system. It would also create a process by which those currently in the country illegally could admit their offense, pay a fine (which distinguishes this policy from "amnesty," which would be free grace without penalty), and earn permanent legal status and eventual citizenship over the course of a number of years if they can meet a series of requirements. We believe that proposals along these lines—which we will explore in more detail in chapter eight—would, as pastor and author John Piper says, both "give honor to the law and show mercy to the immigrants, whose situations are so varied and so many."[15]

THE GREAT COMMISSION AND THE GREAT COMMANDMENT

By loving and welcoming our immigrant neighbors, regardless of their legal status, the church has the opportunity to both carry out the Great Commandment and fulfill the Great Commission.

Perhaps the simplest reason that we, as Christians, should care for immigrants is that they are our neighbors—both figuratively and, increasingly, for many Americans, literally. When a legal scholar asked Jesus what the most important command of Scripture was, Jesus indicated that two elements of the Great Commandment sum up all of the Law and the Prophets: to love the Lord with all of our heart, soul, and mind, and to love our neighbor as ourselves (Mt 22:35-40).

Our natural tendency when we read this commandment is to apply the narrowest possible definition of a "neighbor," seeking to justify ourselves. In this, we are like the legal scholar, who pressed Jesus for a more precise, probably limited, legal definition. Were the definition of a neighbor limited narrowly, we could shirk the responsibility to love immigrants by arguing that they are of a different culture, ethnicity, and language, and by avoiding living where immigrants might move in next door. Of course, Jesus proceeded to tell the inquisitive lawyer the parable of the good Samaritan, where we find that our neighbor might be a person of an entirely different (and maybe even disliked) culture, far away from his homeland, with serious needs (Lk 10:25-37).

However we approach immigration policy, we must first approach immigrants themselves as neighbors—with love. The love we are called to is a conscientious decision based on commitment and trust, not simply a warm feeling or emotion.

In our experience, and in the historical experience of previous generations of American Christians, this sort of love becomes much easier when you actually meet and get to know the immigrants in your community and begin to realize that, for all your differences, you also have a great deal in common—probably a taste for good food, a concern for your families, and often a common Christian faith.[16]

To love our neighbors does not necessarily resolve any number of legitimate questions about how to construct a national immigration policy, but it ought to be our guiding principle both in personal interactions and as we think about structural issues that affect our immigrant neighbors.

Welcoming the stranger also opens up new opportunities to obey Jesus' Great Commission, to "go and make disciples of all nations, baptizing them in the name of the Father and of the Son and of the Holy Spirit" (Mt 28:19). With people from all nations arriving at our doorstep—most of a Christian background, but many others who are not yet believers—American Christians have the opportunity to share the good news with neighbors from around the world without even leaving their neighborhoods. Acts 17:26-27 reminds us that immigration is not accidental but a part of God's divine plan to bring people to know him: "From one man he made all the nations . . . that they should inhabit the whole earth; and he marked out their appointed times in history and the boundaries of their lands. God did this so that they would seek him and perhaps reach out for him and find him, though he is not far from any one of us."

Migration patterns are not just changing the social, demographic, and economic realities of the United States, but migration is also shaping the face of Christianity in the United States and around the world. There is a spiritual dimension to the movement of people, and God often uses the brokenness and suffering tied to migration to bring people into a closer understanding of his goodness and grace. As we welcome, love, and advocate with our immigrant neighbors, we have the opportunity to point to a relationship with Jesus for those who do not yet know him.

As people from various countries embrace Jesus, and as others who already have a vibrant Christian faith reach our shores, the church in the United States is becoming increasingly diverse. Revelation 7:9 paints a picture of heaven as a "great multitude that no one could count, from every nation, tribe, people and language, standing before the throne and before the Lamb." This heavenly picture of all cultures worshiping God should remind us that we are temporary residents of earth, and that diversity is a mere reflection of God's heavenly plan.

SIX

CONCERNS ABOUT IMMIGRATION

> Every year we issue a million green cards to foreign nationals from all the countries of the world, but we do so without regard to whether that applicant has demonstrated the skill that can add to the US economy, whether they can pay their own way or be reliant on welfare, or whether they'll displace or take a job from an American worker.
>
> STEPHEN MILLER, SENIOR ADVISOR TO PRESIDENT DONALD TRUMP, IN A WHITE HOUSE PRESS BRIEFING, AUGUST 2017

WHILE SCRIPTURE GIVES MANY explicit commands to care for immigrants, there are also principles within Scripture, as well as extrabiblical concerns, that lead some Christians to be cautious. In our own interactions with other believers about immigration (whether as an invited speaker at a church or just around the table at a family gathering), we have heard many arguments *against* a more generous immigration policy. Among others, we have heard that accepting more immigrants might detract from care for the poor already in our country; that welcoming immigrants may be inconsistent with protecting our national security; that allowing some immigrants in will create an unstoppable chain of immigrants; that supporting generous immigration policies could compromise other public policy goals; that immigrants are responsible for crime, both at the border and throughout the country; and that immigrants negatively change the culture of the United States. We'll seek to tackle each of these concerns in this chapter, informed both by Scripture and relevant data.

IMMIGRATION AND CARING FOR THE POOR *ALREADY* AMONG YOU

Some Christians are concerned that allowing more immigrants to enter legally may have a negative impact on those US citizens who are already living in poverty. Throughout the Bible, there is a consistent and indisputable mandate on God's people to take special concern for the poor and oppressed.[1] While immigrants come from all economic and education levels, just as they come from all countries, many immigrants enter the United States at the bottom levels of the economic ladder and accept low-wage jobs. By allowing immigrants to join the poor already here, competing for many of the same jobs, some Christians feel we are neglecting a primary responsibility to those poor born in our country.

For example, Christian scholar Carol Swain argues that allowing more low-skill and low-education immigrant workers into the United States depresses wages for historically disadvantaged groups of US citizens— particularly African Americans, Native Americans, and Latinos who have been living in the United States for many generations.[2]

Indeed, basic economics would seem to suggest that if fewer workers are available for a given job, the wages will rise, whereas if there is a plethora of labor, the wages will go down. For a low-income single woman, finishing her GED while raising two children, it is understandable that she might suppose that she'd make an extra dollar or two per hour at her fast food restaurant if her undocumented coworkers were still in Mexico.[3]

Swain argues that our first priority should be to care—and ensure employment—for the poor among us, not those outside of our borders. James Edwards, now a fellow with the Center for Immigration Studies, agrees, arguing, "Scripture indicates certain priorities of our obligations."[4] He notes 1 Timothy 5:8, where Paul advises Timothy that we have a responsibility to care for our own family members, and that the person who fails to do so is "worse than an unbeliever."

The context of the passage, though, is referring to the care of widows—and the greater point is not that we should look out just for our own but that we should look out for our own and then, as the church, look out for others as well. Whether or not this passage can fairly be applied to suggest that our first responsibility is to those who share our citizenship (as opposed to those who are our relatives, as in the text) is not the point; Paul's point is that the church should care for all widows in need. We should likewise be concerned about all those in need of work, whether born in the United States or born elsewhere. Our responsibility does not stop at our national boundary.

It may be fair to criticize other nations for not providing a livable wage for their citizens in some cases, just as Paul criticizes those who were not caring for widows within their own families.[5] However, Paul never suggests that if a widow's family is not caring for her that she should be left hungry; quite the contrary, he insists that the church should care for those widows "who are really in need"—who have no families or whose families have abrogated their responsibility to them (1 Tim 5:3). In the same way, to the extent that we can do so, we should not close work opportunities to those who desperately want a job to support their families.

Indeed, while the secular government may have a particular responsibility to its own citizens, Christ-followers are called to love indiscriminately. Some of the first disputes within the early church arose when Hebraic disciples of Jesus were elevating the care of their own widows ahead of those who spoke Greek. The apostles, guided by the Holy Spirit, appointed seven leaders (notably, all with Greek names, suggesting they were from among the marginalized Greek-speaking contingent) to ensure that all received care (Acts 6:1-7).

Jesus nearly got himself into serious trouble by highlighting God's love for those beyond his particular nation. In Luke 4 the crowds at the synagogue in his hometown of Nazareth are enthralled with his teaching (Lk 4:22). A few verses later, though, the same crowd is physically removing Jesus from the synagogue and tries to throw him off a cliff (Lk 4:28-29). What had he said that so dramatically upset the crowd? He said that God could have sent the prophet Elijah to care for the widows of Israel, but he was sent only to a foreigner; that Elisha could have been sent to any of Israel's many lepers, but he was sent only to Naaman the Syrian. This implied they were not the exclusive center of God's love and attention. "Nazareth First" might have won Jesus a local election, but it would not have been faithful to the universality of God's love.[6]

The other flaw with this argument is that the presumption that immigrants harm the economic prospects of native-born individuals of similar education levels does not actually hold up. The question of how the presence of less-educated immigrants impacts the wages of US citizens with a high school education or less is hotly debated among economists, but almost all (81 percent of economists surveyed by the *Wall Street Journal*) believe that there is either no impact or only a slight impact on the wages of US citizens.[7] A study by the conservative American Enterprise Institute concludes that "Overall, when looking at the effect of all immigrants on employment among US natives, there is no evidence that immigrants take jobs from US-born workers."[8]

Among those who believe there is an economic impact on less-educated US citizen workers, many economists actually believe the net impact is positive, albeit slight.[9] That's because, as we will explore in more depth in chapter seven, immigrant workers often complement the work done by US citizens. For example, take a US citizen waiter whose job depends on an immigrant worker cooking in the kitchen, or a native-born truck driver whose job is to transport produce harvested by immigrant farmworkers—and because, while accepting employment, immigrants are also adding to the number of jobs by consuming within the US economy (paying rent or a mortgage; buying groceries, cars, cell phones, and everything that US citizens buy; paying taxes that fund governmental jobs; and making donations that fuel employment in the nonprofit sector). It's not as simple as competing for a slice of the pie: immigrants actually expand the overall size of the pie.

We ought then to redouble our efforts to care for the poor born in the United States, but we should not allow the persistence of poverty within the United States to close off our borders and our hearts to those abroad.

IMMIGRATION, TERRORISM, AND BORDER SECURITY

Particularly after the terrorist attacks of September 11, 2001, and more recently in Boston, San Bernardino, and Orlando, another significant concern with immigration is that we may be allowing terrorists to enter our country, putting us at risk for further attacks.

It is entirely right that we take appropriate caution to avoid further attacks. Certainly it is within the rights of every sovereign nation to keep out those who intend to do harm, and there is some biblical basis for this idea as well. The Israelite tribes of Gad and Reuben, for example, established fortified cities east of the Jordan River specifically to protect their families (Num 32:17), and Nehemiah's great wall-building project was certainly designed, at least in part, to protect Jerusalem.

Without contesting the idea that we should keep terrorists and criminals from entering the United States, however, we cannot presume that most immigrants are terrorists and criminals. The vast majority of immigrants are well-meaning people seeking a better life, and we certainly should not exclude everyone on the grounds of self-protection; indeed, in a globalized society we could not conceivably do so.

A wise response, then, would be to carefully monitor who comes into the country, both through airports and at border crossings. We can do so to an extent by criminal records checks, as we already do for anyone seeking a visa. While no screening process is perfect, since September 11, 2001, our federal government has significantly increased screening processes for those entering the country, and, fortunately, there have been relatively few people killed in terrorist attacks within the United States; of the attacks that have occurred, most of the perpetrators have been native-born US citizens, not immigrants.[10]

Much of the particular concern over terrorism has focused, rather inextricably, on refugees in particular. In reality, those who enter the United States as refugees are already the most thoroughly screened of any category of immigrant: each comes at the invitation of the US State Department and only after completing a vetting process that usually takes at least eighteen months (and often much longer) to complete, including in-person interviews with trained officers of the US Department of Homeland Security, multiple biographic and biometric background checks, and a medical exam. Since the Refugee Act of 1980 established the current refugee resettlement framework, there has not been a single lethal terrorist attack in the United States perpetrated by an individual who entered the United States through the US refugee resettlement program.

Others are concerned that immigrants who enter *without* inspection, illegally crossing the US border, could include potential terrorists. In reality, there has never been a documented case of a terror attack perpetrated by an individual who entered the United States by illegally crossing the US-Mexico border.[11] Still, it certainly is not impossible that a would-be terrorist could seek to reach the United States by entering the country unlawfully. Particularly in the past few years, though, as far fewer individuals are seeking to enter the country via the US-Mexico border and more border patrol agents and technology have been employed to apprehend them, the likelihood of being caught is high: as of 2017, the US Department of Homeland Security estimates that as many as 85 percent of those who seek to enter unlawfully are either apprehended or blocked from entering the country.[12]

There is also a legitimate concern that the millions of undocumented immigrants who have entered the country unlawfully in years past have not undergone the background check process that those who come in on a visa are required to undergo. While there is little reason to think this poses a particular threat, especially when most have already been present in the US for more than a decade without doing harm, it is a vulnerability.

The best way to minimize the risks of terrorism perpetrated by someone who entered the United States unlawfully is to comprehensively reform our immigration system: if the vast majority who are merely seeking work or reunification with family were able to pay a reasonable fee, undergo a vetting process abroad, and receive a visa corresponding with the number of available jobs, the few who might have nefarious intent (and would thus be unwilling to subject themselves to such a process) would be far less likely to be able to sneak in among those simply looking for work. Similarly, our government could much more readily identify any undocumented immigrant already in the country who might pose a security risk to others if the vast majority who do not were given the opportunity to come forward, pay a fine for having violated US immigration laws, and undergo a thorough background check as part of an earned legalization process.

While it is entirely appropriate for our government to take reasonable steps to protect American citizens from the threat of terrorism, we can squander scarce resources and unfairly malign entire groups of people with no connections to terrorism if we overestimate the extent of that threat. A thorough analysis by the Cato Institute of all terrorist attacks since 1975 found that the odds of an American being killed in a terrorist attack perpetrated by a foreigner—including the large-scale attack of September 11, 2011—are 1 in 3.6 million annually. The odds of being killed by a terrorist who came to the United States as a refugee or who is in the United States illegally are much smaller still: 1 in 3.6 *billion* and 1 in 10.9 *billion*, respectively, per year.[13] For perspective, the average American is about 400 times more likely to die from being bitten by a dog, and more than 400,000 times more likely to die in a car accident, than by a refugee-turned-terrorist.[14] You are about 800 times more likely to die from being struck by lightning and 17,000 times more likely to die from an accidental gunshot than by a terrorist attack perpetrated by an undocumented immigrant. The level of collective fear over the possibility of immigrant-fueled terrorism is dramatically inflated.

FAMILY IMMIGRATION—"ANCHOR BABIES" AND "CHAIN MIGRATION"

Two of the most common concerns about the current immigration situation relate to families and children. Many are concerned that immigrants illegally enter the United States simply to have children born in the United States who, as US citizens by birth, will be able to help their parents. Building on the same concern, some fear that our immigration law's focus on family reunification allows one individual who gains (or is born into) legal status to sponsor an uncontrollable number of new immigrants.

The principle of birthright citizenship was enshrined in the US Constitution in 1868 (shortly after the emancipation of the formerly enslaved) as the Fourteenth Amendment: "All persons born or naturalized in the United States, and subject to the jurisdiction thereof, are citizens of the United States and of the State wherein they reside." This principle granted full equality and rights to those who are born in the United States and prevented any future tier of "second-class citizenship."

The idea of birthright citizenship, however, has been scrutinized in recent years because many purport that children born in the United States to undocumented immigrant parents should not automatically acquire US citizenship and all its benefits. Some suspect that immigrants, who have no other way to gain legal status in the United States, cross the border so they can have children (sometimes derogatorily termed "anchor babies") who will then be able to secure US rights and benefits for the entire family. Some support repealing or reinterpreting the Fourteenth Amendment so as to eliminate birthright citizenship and deter future flows of illegal immigration.

In reality, the birthright citizenship guaranteed by the Fourteenth Amendment does not provide any direct benefit to the US-born citizen's parents. Most undocumented people bear children in the normal process of living their lives here in the United States—not because they think their child is going to help them gain legal status. Having a US citizen child does not entitle the parent to any extra benefits, allow them to gain legal status in the United States immediately, or prevent deportation. In fact, as many as 92,000 parents of US citizens have been deported annually in recent years.[15] While many such US citizen children stay in the United States with a remaining parent or another relative, and many others go with their deported parent to the parent's country of citizenship, thousands end up in the foster care system.[16]

A US citizen child *can* file for the parent when that child turns twenty-one years old, but few people would have a child only to *perhaps* gain legal status twenty-one years later. Furthermore, under current law, if the parents entered the United States illegally (as opposed to entering on a visa) and do not have any other US citizen or Lawful Permanent Resident relatives (such as their own parent or a spouse), their US-born child's petition would probably do them no good, as they would need to leave the United States to be eligible for the visa through their child, and they would be ineligible for any waiver of a ten-year bar to their reentry for having been unlawfully present in the country for so long.[17] Thus, the parent would not benefit directly or immediately from having a US citizen baby, even though the baby would have US citizenship and could receive government services and benefits like any other citizen.

The ultimate question may not be whether that US-born child should be able to benefit the parents, but whether the baby should gain the benefits of being born a US citizen.

Ending birthright citizenship could leave children without citizenship or nationality, rendering them stateless: some countries do not provide citizenship to children born abroad to a citizen parent. They would be without alternatives or means to return to the country of their parents. And even when the parents' country will recognize them as a citizen or grant them a visa, it is extremely disruptive for a child raised and educated in one language and culture to be suddenly transferred to another.

The number of individuals affected by such a proposed change are enormous: approximately 4.7 million children in the United States live with at least one parent who is present illegally.[18] Children born in the United States to an undocumented parent have not broken any law themselves, yet they would bear the brunt for the infraction of illegal presence by not being granted citizenship. The effect on vulnerable populations, like asylum seekers and victims of trafficking, would also be significant, as many asylum seekers and victims of trafficking often do not have documentation before they flee persecution or forced servitude.

Most immigrants do not come to the United States specifically to give birth to children here, but rather to improve their economic lot by working. In the normal course of their lives, of course, many do fall in love and have children. Eliminating birthright citizenship would thus neither discourage them from coming nor encourage those already here to leave, but would rather create a second tier of human beings within our country, with huge numbers of children in legal limbo.

Many critics of our current immigration policy are also concerned that our immigration system leads to "chain migration," purportedly allowing immigrants to sponsor an unlimited number of family members, who in turn sponsor further family members, increasing the number of immigrants exponentially.

In reality, only immigrants who have already gained legal permanent residency or US citizenship can sponsor relatives, and they often face years or even decades of waiting between when the application is filed and when the immigrant relative is allowed to enter the United States (see chap. 4). Only children, spouses, parents, and siblings qualify for such sponsorship; cousins, aunts, uncles, grandparents, in-laws, and other extended family members cannot be sponsored to come to the United States. In addition, in order to sponsor a family member, US citizens or Lawful Permanent Residents must prove they have adequate income (at least 125 percent of the poverty guidelines based on household size) and commit to financially support their family members, to ensure they will not rely on taxpayer funded social services.

Laws that continue to needlessly separate families are problematic from a Christian perspective. In fact, we believe that the current backlogged family-based immigration system needs to be repaired.

God instituted the family unit saying, "It is not good for the man to be alone" (Gen 2:18), and he uses it as the building block of an ordered and procreative society through which people can grow and experience his love. Throughout the Bible we see the family as an integral structure through which God carries out his purposes. When God promised Abraham to make a great nation, he did not promise to do so through political influence or economic power. Instead, he was able to establish a great nation through family, telling Abraham, "I will establish my covenant as an everlasting covenant between me and you and your descendants after you for the generations to come, to be your God and the God of your descendants after you" (Gen 17:7).

In the story of Ruth, her loyalty to her mother-in-law is integral to God carrying out his plan—not only to show Naomi his faithfulness to her in her old age but also to bring Boaz and Ruth together. Ruth then bore a son,

Obed, who was the father of Jesse, the father of David. Throughout the Bible, families were often multigenerational, composed of clans and tribes with extended relatives. Immigrant families, who often treat extended family members such as cousins, nieces, and nephews as immediate family members, give us a more biblical picture of family. By reuniting families in the United States, we open up more opportunities for God to work today as he has in the past and also create stronger, more stable communities.

As we consider who should come to the United States and who should not, family values and the societal benefit of intact families should be central to the debate. Rather than trying to minimize family-based immigration, we should try to quickly reunite families who have been waiting years for their applications to be processed and visas to become available. Any policy that undermines the ability of families to be together can only weaken our society. Immigration based on market needs will strengthen our economy, but immigration based on family will strengthen our social fabric and culture. Immigrant families are no different from native-born families in many respects. In fact, many immigrants, in our experience, have stronger family ties than native-born families, which adds to the vitality of the family unit here in the United States.

Extended family has also helped immigrants adjust to their new unfamiliar environment by providing resources and social capital to care for children and start family businesses. The desire of some to limit the scope of immigration should not have to come at the expense of reunifying those immigrants who are already here, legally, with their family members. According to the Family Research Council, "The family is the great generator, and the intact family the greatest generator, of human capital."[19]

IMMIGRANTS, VOTING, AND OTHER POLICY CONCERNS

Occasionally, we've both encountered brothers and sisters in Christ who express a concern about immigration that goes something like this: "We want to welcome immigrants, but if we let them become citizens, they'll be able to vote . . . and we're not sure we'll like the people they'll elect." Especially for Christians who are passionate about particular policy issues, some fret that allowing undocumented immigrants to eventually earn citizenship (or allowing more immigrants to lawfully enter the country and eventually naturalize) could effectively harm the electoral prospects of the candidates or party they think are most likely to represent their views on other issues— whether standing against abortion or pushing for lower taxes or defending religious liberty. An article in the *National Review*, a conservative magazine, for example, argues that

> More immigration would mean more Democrats. One need not be a partisan or a cynic to believe that the term "undocumented Democrat" is not merely a conservative epithet but in fact exactly the way . . . Democratic leaders look on illegal immigrants in the U.S. today.[20]

This concern is most common among political conservatives, since whereas most white evangelicals consistently have voted for Republican candidates in recent decades, most Latino and Asian voters have voted for Democrats.[21]

While we both have strong opinions on a range of political issues—for example, we're both unabashedly pro-life—our goal with this book is not to help either the Republican Party or the Democratic Party. World Relief is a strictly nonpartisan organization, and we believe that the question of how the church responds to immigrants is of much greater importance than merely a political calculus.

For those for whom this is a primary concern, though, it's worth noting that, on many of the social issues that most motivate evangelical voters, immigrants—particularly Latino immigrants who represent nearly 80 percent of those who are undocumented—would actually be political allies if they were eventually allowed to vote. Take views on abortion, for example: 51 percent of US Latinos believe that abortion should be illegal in all or most circumstances, compared to only 43 percent of Americans as a whole.[22] But Latino *immigrants* are actually significantly more likely to express pro-life views on the question of abortion than US-born Latinos.[23]

"Most Latinos are pro-life," write Liberty Counsel's Mat Staver and the National Hispanic Christian Leadership Conference's Samuel Rodriguez for *FoxNews.com*, "but the reality is that a candidate's views on immigration policy—and the rhetoric that they use to discuss immigrants—trump all other issues for many Latino voters."[24] They note that while Latino *voters* are, by definition, already citizens, they tend to personally know people who are undocumented or who are otherwise impacted by immigration policy.

As some conservatives have sought to prevent Latino immigrants from becoming citizens lest they become reliable Democratic voters, this has actually become something of a self-fulfilling prophecy. When Republican governor Pete Wilson led a harsh push to crackdown on immigration at the state level in California in 1994, conservative commentator William F. Buckley warned that it represented a "strain of xenophobia which will very quickly . . . evolve into anti-GOP resentments by the majority of Californians [and] could lead to such electoral catastrophes as pursued many GOP candidates who were slow in boarding the civil-rights crusade."[25] Buckley's warning proved right: up until 1994, California's large Hispanic vote was largely split in both gubernatorial and presidential between Democrats and Republicans; by 1996, more than 70 percent of Californian Hispanics supported Democrat Bill Clinton, and in 1998 nearly 80 percent supported the Democratic candidate for governor.[26] By 2016, the state had become so reliably Democratic that both the winner *and* the runner-up of their contest for US Senate were Democrats.

In contrast, in Texas, where Governor George W. Bush pushed back against anti-immigrant proposals like those Wilson pursued in California, the Republican governor won fully half of the Hispanic vote in 1998.[27] Bush, who subsequently advocated for comprehensive immigration reform, including an earned path to legal status for undocumented immigrants, in his presidential campaigns, won 44 percent of the Hispanic vote nationally in 2004, far higher than any Republican presidential candidate previously or since.[28]

Those whose primary concerns are electoral will be more successful if they employ rhetoric and embrace policies—including on immigration issues—that will make their party appeal to the growing Hispanic (as well as Asian) electorate, rather than seeking to block immigrants from becoming voters and alienating those immigrants' US-born relatives and friends in the process.

IMMIGRANTS, CRIME, AND SANCTUARY CITIES

Many Americans associate immigrants, and especially immigrants in the country illegally, with crime. We all want to live in safe communities, and it is appropriate to expect our government to protect us from those who would do harm.

While it may seem like a technicality, it's important to note that unlawful presence in the United States is *not* a crime—it is a violation of civil, not criminal, law.[29] While unlawful *entry* to the United States can be a violation of a criminal statute, since nearly half of undocumented immigrants entered the country legally and overstayed their visas, it is simply not accurate to state that "all 'illegal immigrants' are criminals."

Beyond legal semantics, many Americans are concerned that immigrants could commit violent crimes or property crimes. A 2017 Rasmussen Reports survey found that 44 percent of Americans believe that illegal immigration increased the level of serious crime in the United States.[30]

Popular impressions, though—often fueled by anecdotal media narratives—are not always accurate. Many studies have looked carefully at this question, and they consistently find no correlation between immigrants and crime; in fact, immigrants (with and without legal status) consistently have lower crime rates than native-born US citizens.

One way to measure the relationship between immigration and crime is by examining incarceration: in 2014, based on US census data, 1.53 percent of native-born US citizens between the ages of eighteen and fifty-four were incarcerated, but only 0.85 percent of undocumented immigrants and 0.47 percent of immigrants with legal status of the same age cohort.[31] This disparity in incarceration rates has been consistent in studies based on census data going back to at least 1990, with the incarceration rate of native-born US citizens always at least double and sometime as much as five times the rate of immigrants.[32]

If undocumented immigrants disproportionately *caused* crime, we would expect crime to rise along with illegal immigration both nationally and in particular communities. Instead, the opposite has been true: from 1990 to

2013, while the number of undocumented immigrants in the United States more than tripled, FBI data shows that violent crime fell by 48 percent and property crime fell by 41 percent.[33] A separate study looking at 103 particular communities throughout the United States found "that violent crime rates tended to decrease as metropolitan areas experienced gains in their concentration of immigrants."[34]

That immigrants commit relatively few crimes is not necessarily because they are more virtuous than native-born US citizens: immigrants likely commit fewer crimes because the consequences for them if they do so are often much steeper than for a US citizen committing the same crime. If, as US citizens, one of us were to steal a candy bar in the state of Indiana, we would have committed a misdemeanor offense; if convicted, we would likely get off with paying a fine. But if an immigrant with legal status were to commit precisely the same crime, they would also then face immigration-related consequences beyond the criminal penalties: they would likely be found to have committed a "crime involving moral turpitude" that could put them at risk of deportation.[35]

That immigrants are generally very careful not to commit crimes because the consequences could be so stark is a good thing. But when immigrants who lack legal status are also afraid to interact with police when they are the *victim* of or *witness* to a crime, which they likely will be if local law enforcement officers are (or are merely perceived to be) tasked with detaining anyone present unlawfully, it creates a serious public safety problem, particularly in neighborhoods where undocumented immigrants make up a large percentage of all residents. "We really feel that when we have immigrants or immigrant families who live in fear of deportation, they're going to be less likely to report crimes or even come forward as witnesses to crimes and work with us to assist in investigations," notes Chief of Police Chris Magnus of Tucson, Arizona.[36]

To build trust within immigrant communities, many local law enforcement agencies have enacted policies that prohibit police officers from asking anyone about their immigration legal status (in most cases, unless and until they are convicted of a significant crime). Such cities and towns sometimes profess to be (or are labeled by critics as) "sanctuary cities," though this term does not have a legal or universally accepted definition. Federal immigration officers can (and do) still enter a city or initiate deportation proceedings for individuals living within these cities and towns, but usually there are limitations on how much local law enforcement is involved in that process. "Immigration enforcement always has been and should be a federal responsibility," explains Montgomery County, Maryland, Police Chief Tom Manger.[37]

IMMIGRATION, IDENTITY, AND CULTURAL HOMOGENEITY

A final concern over immigration that we hear, even among some Christians, is that we need to keep immigrants out because they are "polluting our culture."[38] They do not, it is said, share our American values. Immigrants—people from other countries and cultures, by definition—are of course going to look, talk, and to a certain extent live differently from people of the majority culture of the United States, especially when they have just arrived. While many come already speaking some English, other immigrants take years or even decades to master the language, and others, especially those who arrive at older ages, never learn to communicate in English. Many Americans are frustrated by the increasing prevalence of Spanish and other non-English languages they hear in the streets of their communities, at the supermarket, on the radio, and even in their churches. Out of this frustration has grown a movement to declare English the official language of the United States.

Others argue that immigration is a problem because immigrants will change the cultural, ethnic, and religious makeup of the United States, which has since its founding been a nation with a majority of light skinned people descended from European countries and a Christian majority country, but which will, within the next several decades, no longer have any ethnic majority.[39] This projection is viewed explicitly as a threat by some of the most extremist elements of American society, including self-described white supremacists, white nationalists, and some members of the alt-right that have gained public prominence in the past few years. There is also a growing fear that letting in Muslim immigrants, in particular, could mean sharia law will become the law of the land in certain cities and states, which could then have national ramifications.

While these attitudes have recently received significant attention, they are not new. In many ways, they echo former presidential candidate Patrick Buchanan, who throughout his career advocated harsh restrictions on immigration because he believes that the cultures descended from the original European settlers of North America are superior to (and are now being contaminated by) "third world" cultures, whose people he considers unlikely to assimilate in the United States.[40] In a 1984 column, Buchanan stated bluntly that "the central objection to the present flood of illegals is they are not English-speaking white people from Western Europe, they are Spanish-speaking brown and black people from Mexico, Central America and the Caribbean."[41]

While most would probably distance themselves from explicitly racist language, many Americans—including some Christians—share his concern that large-scale immigration is destroying the homogeneity of our culture. It is notable, though, that not even Buchanan, a Roman Catholic who was connected to the Christian Coalition during his rise to fame in the early 1990s, bases his arguments in Scripture: such ideas are not found in the Bible.

Likewise, Steve Bannon, former chief strategist to President Trump and former chief executive of Breitbart, a media organization he once called "the platform for the alt-right,"[42] dismisses the immigrant-welcoming views of the Catholic Church (of which he is a member) as "not doctrine at all."[43] His statement drew a harsh rebuke from the US Conference of Catholic Bishops, which cited several biblical passages that inform the Christian embrace of immigrants and those of all cultures and ethnicities.[44]

Scripture is clear that, under Christ, we who are his followers, whatever our cultural background, are united as one body—the church—and that each part is dependent on every other (1 Cor 12:12-27). "There is neither Jew nor Gentile, neither slave nor free, nor is there male and female, for [Christ's followers] are all one in Christ Jesus" (Gal 3:28). While in the Old Testament God commanded the Israelites not to intermix with their neighboring cultures—so that they would not be led astray by their false religions (which is exactly what they proceeded to do)—in the New Testament, all barriers based on ethnicity or culture were broken down, as Peter learned in a dream when God commanded him to break Jewish purity rules by dining and sharing the gospel with a Gentile, Cornelius. After the experience, Peter concludes, "God does not show favoritism but accepts from every nation the one who fears him and does what is right" (Acts 10:34-35). We are called to the same standard. As beneficiaries of Christ's reconciliatory work, the church is called to a "ministry of reconciliation," bringing people of different backgrounds and cultures together around Jesus Christ, not dividing ourselves by race or country of origin (2 Cor 5:18).

If we are to think biblically about immigration, we need to disavow arguments based on claims of racial or cultural superiority. To the extent that all of us might harbor some of these feelings and ideas, we need to recognize that they may be rooted in our upbringing, our experiences, or the media we watch, read, and listen to, but these ideas do *not* come from the Bible. While it may be natural to prefer our own native language, foods, and customs, and even to be frustrated as the culture we know is changing all around us with the influence of immigrants living among us, we must recognize there is no scriptural justification to claim superiority or to exclude others on this basis.

While Scripture is clear that there is no place for claims of ethnic or cultural superiority within the church, some Christians are most concerned about the national culture changing as a result of those *outside* of the Christian faith, particularly Muslims.

It's worth noting that Muslims make up just 1 percent of the US population, which makes fears of Muslims "taking over" seem rather far-fetched.[45] By 2050, they will be only about 2 percent of the population, with about half of that growth from immigration.[46] The rest is expected to be due to births within Muslim families plus converts, less those who leave the faith.

As we have already noted, terrorism remains incredibly rare in the United States, and when it does occur—at least between 2008 and 2015—it has more often than not been carried out by non-Muslims.[47] The vast majority of Muslims worldwide condemn terrorism and terrorist groups, which Muslim scholars condemn as heretics.[48] Muslim scholar Manal Omar notes,

"The most prominent Muslim academics agree extremist groups believe in a fringe version of Islam well outside the scholarly consensus."[49] In fact, American Muslims are slightly less likely than American evangelicals to say it "is often or sometimes justified to target and kill civilians in order to further a political, social, or religious cause," though in either case it is a small percentage of either community.[50]

While many Muslims seek to abide by principles of sharia as a matter of personal piety—not so unlike how most Christians would (hopefully) say that biblical commands should guide their lives—most Muslims in the United States do not believe that sharia should be used as a legal source, just as most Christians affirm the biblical teaching that adultery, lying, or greed are sinful but few advocate for them to be made illegal.[51]

In any case, the US Constitution already explicitly forbids establishing a religious law—whether Muslim, Christian, or otherwise—from being established as the law of the land in the United States. Internet rumors that sharia law has *already* taken over certain cities or states are false.

While Christian principles informed the writing of the US Constitution and Declaration of Independence, and the majority of Americans are Christian, the United States is not a Christian nation. The US Constitution guarantees freedom of religion, allowing all to practice whatever faith they choose without government interference. Having religious freedom as the bedrock of US democracy means religious plurality will be a core part of the identity of the United States. As Christians, whether we're in the majority or not, this means not excluding or fearing Muslims and people of other faiths, but living out *our* faith, including its commands to welcome strangers, in such a way that they might be attracted to Jesus. Christians should not fear people of other faiths living in community with them. In fact, Scripture exhorts us to make ourselves "a slave to everyone, to win as many as possible" for Christ (1 Cor 9:19).

The bulk of the biblical record on the treatment of immigrants commands us to welcome and take a special concern for foreigners entering our land. Rather than saying that immigrants do not share our values, it is our responsibility to demonstrate in action what our values are to our new neighbors.

Immigrants can influence our culture in positive ways and teac
values of hard work, family, and resilience.

That's not to say it is not appropriate for the United States to expect those who seek to immigrate to embrace the core principles and values of our nation. However, it is antithetical to those very values—to the biblically based American founding belief "that all men [and women] are created equal, endowed by their Creator with certain unalienable Rights"—to presume that an individual cannot embrace those values simply because of their ethnicity, culture, or religion.

Today, as they have at various points in US history, local churches can play a vital role in helping immigrants integrate into American society. Integration does not mean that immigrants must forfeit their foods, language, religion, or culture, but that those elements become a part of the American whole (just as past generations of immigrants have enriched and expanded what it means to be an American) while embracing the core American values outlined in the US Constitution. This integration process is a two-way street: it requires both a receiving community willing to allow immigrants to "become American" and immigrants who want to do so. In chapter nine, we will explore the many ways that churches are facilitating this integration process.

Next, though, having spent much of this chapter addressing purported risks and liabilities of welcoming immigrants, we will turn to the value that immigrants add to the United States, both economically and otherwise.

SEVEN

THE VALUE OF IMMIGRANTS TO THE UNITED STATES

Immigration is one of the major reasons why the U.S. economy is so robust, diverse, dynamic and resilient. This is not to minimize the negative impacts immigration can have on particular workers, families or communities. But, in general, U.S. policy should be supportive of, rather than resistant to, immigration.

ECONOMIST JOHN STAPLEFORD

LOOKING UP AT A SQUARE BUILDING in the middle of dusty Tijuana, Mexico, I (Jenny) tentatively stepped through the squeaky wrought-iron gates. There I was welcomed by a warm, Brazilian Catholic priest who was running a shelter for migrants recently deported from the United States. I sat down to dinner at the shelter with a young man named Guillermo, who had been living in Northern California for over eight years. While driving back home after a long day of work, Guillermo was pulled over at a traffic signal for a broken headlight, summarily detained, and then deported back to Mexico without the chance to even say goodbye to his three-year-old US-born daughter in person one last time. Since he arrived in Mexico, Guillermo had been communicating by phone every few weeks with his daughter, who was being cared for by his wife and by his father back in California. "She always asks me where I am, but what can I say? How do I begin to tell her where I am or what happened to me? She won't understand. I can never go back. I don't know if I'll ever see her again," he said quietly, pushing his fork into a bowl of salad. When asked what he will do next, he said, "I will probably go back to my home [in Mexico], but I don't know if I will be able to find a job."

Thousands of immigrants like Guillermo find themselves seeking economic opportunity in the United States. In Guillermo's case, he had worked picking grapes in Northern California for three years, working eight hours a day in the hot California sun for $6 an hour. Though his wages were low compared to what most Americans earn, they were more than he could have earned for the same work in Mexico, allowing him to provide his family with a better life. At the same time, his employer profits from his hard labor, and the many Americans who buy inexpensive fruit at their local supermarket benefit from his work.

Not everyone thinks the presence, and labor, of immigrants like Guillermo is so beneficial, though. At a town hall meeting in rural Iowa, for example, a group of over one hundred concerned citizens gathered to talk about immigration and its impact on their community. Over the past decade or so, many jobs that were once done by native Iowans, particularly in agricultural and manufacturing industries, have been filled by Mexicans and Central Americans. Naturally, these new residents also had changed the town in many ways, bringing with them their language, their culture, and their children, who attended the town's public schools. Citizens were uneasy about the arrival of new immigrants who seemed to be taking away jobs and resources. A man stood up and declared, "We can't have people who are not going to pay taxes that we just don't know here." Another stood up and opined, "Our schools shouldn't be educating these kids who shouldn't be here anyway." In a community traditionally receptive to immigration, there was growing concern of the negative effect it was having on the community.

There are competing stories being told all over the United States—including within local churches—as to the costs and benefits of immigration for the country. While six-in-ten Americans say they believe that immigrants are a net strength to the United States "because of their hard work and talents," many others, including a slight majority of white evangelical Christians, believe that immigrants are an economic burden.[1]

What effects do people like Guillermo, who come to the United States to pick our produce for a low hourly wage, have on the overall economy? Does immigration hurt the American worker? Are foreign workers even needed? What about the costs of providing education, healthcare, and other public services to these people? Can our country afford to welcome so many immigrants? Could we afford not to have them here?

From a Christian perspective, these questions ought not to be primary: the scriptural witness is that we are to care for the immigrant stranger living among us, without any caveat that exempts us from this responsibility if it is not in our individual or national economic interest. Furthermore, immigrants contribute much to our society that is not easily quantified, and we err if we reduce the immigration dilemma to one of mere mathematics. God created and delights in cultural diversity, and immigrants have added richly to our communities through their different cultures. Nevertheless, economic considerations are among the most common concerns raised in the ongoing immigration debate in our country, and they need to be addressed. In this chapter we will look at the balance of costs and benefits that immigration implies both to the United States and to immigrant-sending countries, as well as consider the global dynamics fueling migration—not just in the United States but also around the world.

THE ECONOMIC IMPACT OF IMMIGRATION

Since the time of the Puritans, who emigrated from northern Europe seeking religious freedom in the West, immigration has defined the United States as a country and added to the richness and vitality of America today. Although the earliest European immigrants were "discovering" land that was already inhabited, the ebb and flow of those seeking freedoms, whether religious, economic, or social, have defined the identity of the United States. Most immigrants in the United States today are driven by the same dreams and hope for prosperity that attracted past generations of immigrants to a new land. As the

United States continues to grow, the central question that has driven the immigration debate is whether continued immigration is beneficial to the United States and if so, how many more immigrants can the United States sustain?

First and foremost, we need to understand that migration is a global phenomenon affecting every country in the world. While the United States has the largest number of immigrants in total, immigrants form a smaller share of the total population than in many other countries. Countries in the Middle East have the highest percentage of immigrants as a percentage of their population, with the United Arab Emirates, Qatar, and Kuwait having over 50 percent of their population made up of immigrants, as do Monaco in Europe and Singapore in Asia.[2] Australia and Canada also have a greater share of immigrants as a percentage of their population, at 28 percent and 20 percent respectively, than the United States.[3] The uniqueness and diversity of the United States, however, cannot be denied, and any debate on immigration should be couched within the premise that immigration has built this country into what it is today.

From the founding of our country until now, peaks in immigration have often happened during periods of fundamental economic change in the country, playing a key role in helping us through these economic transitions.[4] At the height of the great wave of immigration around the turn of the twentieth century, the United States was turning from an agricultural society into a manufacturing economy, and many immigrants fled poverty and came to the United States to work in newly formed industries. The same questions about whether immigration was beneficial to the United States were asked then, and immigration restrictions eventually followed as the general public increasingly felt that immigration was not in their economic interest. In hindsight, even though income was not always equally distributed in the short term, we now know that the long-term economic impact of immigration during that time period was generally positive.[5] For example, the wages of residents increased over that time, and local employment of residents also increased despite heavy immigration.

The twenty-first century is marked by an era of globalization where the world is becoming increasingly interconnected. The United States is transforming from a manufacturing society to an information-based society, and immigration can help the United States adapt. As economists anticipate a period of relatively steady US economic growth over the next several years, we will see an increase in need for workers in the labor force.[6] From 1980 to 2000, most labor force growth came from an increase in native-born workers between twenty-five and fifty-four years old, mostly women and baby boomers entering the labor market. In the next few decades, however, both because of an aging native-born population and low fertility rates, the number of elderly will increase more rapidly than the number of children or working-age adults.[7] Future immigrants and their descendants will account for the only growth in the working-age population of adults between ages eighteen to sixty-four.[8]

Immigrants' role in the labor market will become even more vital in coming decades as the baby-boom generation reaches retirement age and as life expectancy gradually increases as a result of medical advances, skewing the ratio of workers to retirees in our national economy.[9] By 2029, those sixty-five or older will make up more than 20 percent of the total US population; by 2056, they will outnumber children under eighteen.[10] These shifts would be accelerated if it were not for the role that immigrants already play, as the annual number of US births would have declined since 1970 if it weren't for the increase in births to immigrant women.[11] A greater number of retired dependents will thus need to be supported by a worker who can pay into the Social Security and healthcare systems.

Even if new native-born workers replace the retiring native-born workers in their jobs, there will not be enough native-born workers to fill new jobs created by a growing economy. The Bureau of Labor Statistics estimates that "replacement needs" (job openings created when workers leave their occupations, generally due to retirement or shifting to another job field) will generate 35.3 million job openings between 2014 and 2024. In addition, economic growth is expected to generate 9.8 million additional job openings. As demand for workers increases, though, the labor force is on track to grow by just 7.9 million, at an annual average growth rate of just 0.5 percent, in the same time period.[12] To fill in the gaps, older workers will either need to continue to work, or more immigrants will need to join the labor force.

The economic dependency ratio, or the number in the total population who are not in the labor force, is expected to increase from fifty-nine dependents per one hundred working-age people in 2005 to seventy-two dependents per one hundred workers in 2050. With lower immigration, the number of dependents would increase to seventy-five dependents per one hundred working-age people, while having higher immigration would decrease the number of dependents to sixty-nine dependents per one hundred working-age people.[13]

Not only is the US workforce aging, the native-born worker is also becoming more educated, but particular industries will continue to rely on workers who, while possessing unique skills, do not need to have a high level of formal education. In 1960, for example, half of all American men dropped out of high school, presumably to seek work in a labor field considered "unskilled," whereas nearly 83 percent of all adults ages twenty-five and over have completed high school now.[14] Two-thirds of the occupations projected to add the most new jobs typically require a high school diploma or less.[15] Given native-born US workers are becoming more educated and increasingly skilled, and most new jobs projected for 2022 are expected to be in occupations requiring only a high school diploma or equivalent, immigrants with a variety of skills can fill critical needs in fast-growing industries like healthcare and social assistance.[16] The construction industry is another example of a sector that is expected to have positive employment growth from 2014 to 2024. In an industry in which 14 percent of the workforce is composed of undocumented immigrants, the industry will need to continue to meet the demand to build more while finding workers to do the job. The National Association of Home Builders has found that labor shortages are one of the greatest impediments to housing recovery.[17]

Foreign-born workers of all legal statuses account for 23 percent of the US construction labor force and as high as 28 percent in construction trades like carpentry and brick masonry, areas that require less formal education but consistently have some of the highest labor shortages. In the country's most populous states, Texas and California, immigrants make up 41 percent and

40 percent of the construction work force, respectively. According to Hugh Morton, a board member of the National Association of Home Builders,

> Illegal immigrants have . . . supplemented American workers and provided the labor for an expanding housing market. . . . Builders who were struggling to find quality roofers, concrete finishers . . . etc., found the immigrant trade contractors a godsend.[18]

In 2014, immigrants accounted for 16 percent of all civilian employed workers. However, they represented much higher shares of workers in some of the fastest growing occupations in the United States, including roughly 32 percent of computer programmers, 30 percent of health-care support professionals, and 26 percent of physicians.[19] Undocumented immigrants specifically hold a high share of the total workforce in certain sectors, including 26 percent of farm labor and 17 percent of cleaning and maintenance workers.[20]

The restaurant industry, the country's second-largest private-sector employer, is projected to grow at a rate of 14.7 percent through 2017. In an industry dominated by younger workers, whose overall number is expected to decrease in coming years, immigrants can play a key role in fueling economic growth in this sector as well.

Some of the industries expected to grow significantly in the next decade are those in which human labor cannot be mechanized by greater technology or shipped overseas to another company, but require work to be done in the United States. Given the need for an ever-increasing labor market, almost all economists agree that immigration (whether legal or illegal) provides and will continue to provide a net benefit to the economy of the United States. In fact, according to a survey by the *Wall Street Journal*, forty-four out of forty-six economists surveyed thought that illegal immigration was beneficial to the economy.[21] Most economists agree that "on balance, immigration is good for the country. Immigrants provide scarce labor, which lowers prices in much the same way global trade does. And overall, the newcomers modestly raise Americans' per capita income."[22] As is often the case in economics, though, a phenomenon that carries an overall net benefit may incur costs and benefits disproportionate to particular subgroups.

ARE IMMIGRANTS A DRAIN ON PUBLIC RESOURCES?

One of the disproportionate effects of immigration is on governmental expenses, with federal, state, and local governments affected unequally by immigration. As we have already explained, most immigrants *are* paying taxes—taken out of their payroll checks for Social Security, Medicare, and income tax, as well as sales tax and property taxes—thus their presence involves an input of funds into the governmental coffers. It's estimated that half of undocumented immigrants pay payroll taxes, but because undocumented immigrants are not eligible for most federal benefits, undocumented immigrants have heavily subsidized Social Security without being able to benefit from it. In 2010 alone, undocumented immigrants paid $12 billion more in payroll taxes into the Social Security Trust Funds than what they qualified to receive in benefits.[23]

At the same time, of course, immigrants' presence results in expenses for the state: even though all undocumented immigrants and many other immigrants are ineligible for most public benefits, they will still be treated at a hospital in an emergency even if they are unable to pay, they still use police, fire, and other municipal services, and their children (regardless of status) are eligible for public primary and secondary education. A few state-level studies have found that immigrants pay more in taxes than they receive in government services and benefits. A study in Arizona, for example, found that Arizona immigrants generate $2.4 billion in taxes while the state spends $1.4 billion on education, healthcare, and law enforcement on immigrants.[24] In Florida, another study found that the average immigrant paid almost $1,500 more in taxes than they received in public benefits.[25]

Researchers Michael Fix and Jeffrey Passel have found, in a survey of several studies conducted at various levels of government throughout the United States, that

Most national studies suggest that immigrants are not an overall fiscal burden on the native population. At the state level the picture is mixed, resulting in part from the differing responsibilities assumed by different state governments. At the local level, analyses . . . have invariably found immigrants to be a net fiscal burden.[26]

In fact, a study by Stephen Moore, an economist who has worked for the Heritage Foundation and the Cato Institute, suggests that the average immigrant (regardless of legal status) pays about $80,000 more in taxes than they receive in benefits over a lifetime. That net benefit to the government, though, is the result of paying $105,000 more over a lifetime than the benefits received to the *federal* government, while receiving $25,000 in benefits more than what is paid to *state* and *local* governments.[27]

While the economic benefits of having immigrant labor are most obvious at the national level, local communities often spend resources supporting the workforce and not feeling the benefits of immigrants. The federal government has recognized this mismatch of resources and flow of benefits, and Congress has introduced measures to direct national resources to help states deal with the costs of illegal immigration, but the disparity persists. Nevertheless, immigrants have a generally positive economic effect on public resources and the national economy.

WHAT IS THE IMPACT ON NATIVE WORKERS?

Another common economic concern is that immigrants take jobs from native-born US citizens. While some economists do believe that undocumented immigrants depress the wages of unskilled native-born workers, others note that in some cases businesses that employ immigrants would not exist in the United States if it were not for immigrant labor, since they would be undercut by cheaper imports from abroad. These businesses would either close out completely or move their operations elsewhere. For example, strawberry pickers in California are not necessarily competing against native workers but against pickers in Mexico and other countries. One farmer, Steve Sarconi, who owns Valley Harvesting and Packing in California, said he invested $1 million in research on mechanization and found that machines could still not tell good crops from bad crops. "I'm as American red-blooded as it gets," he states, "but I'm tired of fighting the fight on the immigration issue."[28] He eventually moved his operations to Mexico because the workforce was more reliable and he did not have to worry about immigration raids.

Additionally, immigrants can stimulate wage growth in other ways. Immigrants are highly concentrated in metropolitan areas, and greater density results in reduced transportation costs, increased labor market efficiencies, increases in knowledge spillover, and general positive effects on productivity.[29] Because immigrants are highly entrepreneurial, immigrants in their self-employment often generate local employment opportunities for native workers.

Local productivity is generated by immigrants as well, which generates positive local effects on growth and wages. As one example, foreign-born workers are concentrated in science, technology, engineering, and math (STEM) occupations. A national study found that foreign college-educated STEM workers have had a significantly positive impact on Americans' wages, as much as 5 percent for those with a college education and 2 percent for those without, through local technological growth and adoption from 1990 to 2010.[30] This greater productivity because of immigrant workers is due to the fact that immigrant workers are more likely to patent and thus innovate than natives in ways that could produce positive productivity spillovers.[31]

Immigrants contribute to the economy not just as workers but as consumers as well. Their presence creates new markets (such as for grocery stores specializing in Mexican, Polish, or Korean foods) and expands existing markets. Immigrants often fuel local businesses and invest in the communities they live in, buying houses, clothes, and food. In many parts of the country, a fast-food restaurant, for example, is very likely to employ immigrant workers, but immigrants also likely make up many of its customers. In this way, immigrants supply their labor to the market but also, by their purchases, add to the demand for more workers.

In September 2016, the National Academies of Sciences, Engineering, and Medicine released one of the most comprehensive reports on the impact of immigration on the labor market and wages over the past twenty years, and the fiscal impact the local, state, and national levels. They found that immigration has an overall positive impact on long-run economic growth in the United States. Although first-generation immigrants are costlier at the state and local levels than the native-born, mostly due to the education of their children, the children of immigrants are among the strongest economic contributors in the US population, contributing more in taxes than their parents or the native-born population.[32] In terms of wages, they found that the impact of immigration on the wages of native-born workers is "very small."

The possibly slight negative impact of immigrants on native, low-skilled workers should not be glossed over. Instead, policymakers have a responsibility to make sure that immigrants who are here in the shadows are regularized in a system so US workers can compete fairly. Having immigrant workers is not necessarily what hurts native-born workers: what may hurt native workers in some cases is the fact that these workers are here illegally. Having undocumented immigrants, who do not have equal rights and protection under the law, allows employers an unfair competitive advantage in hiring cheap immigrant labor over native workers. This is unfair to US-citizen workers and law-abiding employers and puts immigrant workers at risk of exploitation by unscrupulous employers.

THE NEXUS BETWEEN IMMIGRATION AND HUMAN TRAFFICKING

Immigrants, especially those who are undocumented, are uniquely vulnerable to human trafficking, a form of modern-day slavery defined as any situation where an individual is made to work (either in labor or in commercial sex acts) by force, fraud, or coercion. While human trafficking affects both native-born US citizens and immigrants, the US Department of Justice has estimated that the number of foreign-born individuals trafficked into the US each year may be as high as 17,500.[33]

A 2014 analysis of US Department of Justice prosecution data by the Faith Alliance Against Slavery and Trafficking found that roughly 95 percent of labor trafficking victims in recent years have been non-citizens, most of them undocumented.[34] Undocumented immigrants are also disproportionately victims of sex trafficking: about 13 percent of sex trafficking victims were undocumented immigrants, though undocumented immigrants make up only about 4 percent of the overall US population.

The lack of legal status is not incidental. Those who are present unlawfully in the country tend to fear law enforcement and are thus wary of speaking up—even when they are victims of or witnesses to trafficking crimes. In some cases, though *smuggling* and *trafficking* are not synonymous, they can be related: an immigrant who contracts a smuggler to illegally bring her or him into the country sometimes begins their American "dream" in a nightmarish cycle of indebtedness. As their smuggler-turned-trafficker compels them to work either in manual labor or by being prostituted, victims of trafficking will also pay "rent" for inhumane living conditions that exceed their income in order to pay back their debt.

One example of the nexus between human trafficking and immigration status is among tomato harvesters, 80 percent of whom are estimated to be undocumented.[35] Since 1997, the Department of Justice has freed over one thousand women and men from beatings, debt bondage, and starvation wages.[36] To address this injustice, the Coalition of Immokalee Workers created the Fair Food Program, which enlists the top tomato buyers in the United States, including Walmart, McDonald's, Subway, and Whole Foods, to buy tomatoes only from growers who adhere to a code of conduct, committing to provide workers tents for shade, time to eat, higher wages, and basic education.

While progress has made in this particular area through decades of sustained advocacy, immigrants will remain vulnerable to human trafficking in agriculture and other contexts so long as their lack of legal status keeps them afraid to report labor abuses. Recognizing the economic benefits of having immigrant workers in the economy needs to be coupled with providing legal status and rights for these workers, such as the freedom to switch jobs or to join a union. We cannot concurrently express compassion for victims of human trafficking and disdain for "illegal immigrants"—because they're very often the same people. Nor can we ethically benefit from immigrants' labor if we do not pursue policies that recognize their basic rights as human beings, made in God's image.

COMPETITION OR COMPLEMENTS?

Many have argued that immigrants compete with American workers and take their jobs. In many situations, though, immigrants complement native workers, rather than competing with them. Immigrants often are entrepreneurs and startup businesses that would otherwise not exist, offering services in communities, employing other workers, and overall increasing the Gross Domestic Product of the US economy.

It is easy to blame immigrants when our families, our communities, or the nation as a whole face economic hardship. When the country faces a recession, particular companies lay off thousands of American workers, or many Americans' wages are stagnant for years, we point to what we see as the obvious change—immigrants in a previously homogeneous community—and think that they, rather than unseen economic forces, are causing our maladies. Many factors other than immigration, though, may cause a decline in wages, such as trade policy, the advance of technology, and the erosion of the minimum wage's buying power.[37] Immigrants often respond to these changes in the economy rather than cause them.

Many people incorrectly assume that there are a fixed number of jobs in the economy. This is simply not true. The US labor market has an incredible ability to absorb new workers. Immigrants do not further split up the economic pie; they enlarge it.[38] Immigrants often do not have the same skill sets as native-born workers. Rather than taking jobs from the native workforce, they create their own job opportunities and fill jobs in which they have a specific skill set. Immigrants thus choose different occupations in which they have a specialized skill set rather than copy the work of US workers. For example, the foreign born constitute 54 percent of tailors in the United States and 44 percent of plaster-stucco masons. However, they make up less than 1 percent of crane operators and sewer-pipe cleaners.[39]

Jobs that immigrants and natives have are often interdependent, which increases the productivity of natives. The addition of immigrant workers to the labor force also stimulates new investment in the economy, which in turn increases the demand for labor, exerting upward pressure on wages.[40]

Even within the same professions, complementary differences allow for more business opportunities. For example, Chinese cooks differ from American cooks in their traditional fare, while Italian tailors and American tailors will sew clothes differently according to their trade. This idea of complementarity also allows Americans to earn more in the occupations they currently have. For example, a doctor who hires an immigrant landscaping business to take care of his lawn can then spend more time at the hospital taking care of patients. More construction workers also means more jobs and higher wages for architects, plumbers, electricians, and contractors, since their work is dependent on new construction projects, which in turn is dependent on the availability of construction workers.

New York City is a prime example of a community where immigrants are adding richly to its economic vitality. New York City alone is home to more than three million immigrants, who make up nearly 40 percent of the city's population. As former mayor Michael Bloomberg notes,

> About 500,000 came to our City—and continue to come—illegally. . . . Although they broke the law by illegally crossing our borders or overstaying their visas, our City's economy would be a shell of itself had they not, and it would collapse if they were deported. The same holds true for the nation.[41]

Many cities and towns are welcoming immigrants in recognition of the demographic realities that present economic challenges for declining economies. Michigan is the only state that lost population between 2000 and 2010. They also found that while immigrants make up 6 percent of the population, they founded one-third of the high-tech companies in the state over the past decade and were three times more likely to start a business.[42] Through its "Welcoming Michigan" initiative, they have tried to build immigrant-friendly environments to continue to attract immigrants to the state.[43] Other cities such as Baltimore, Maryland, and Dayton, Ohio, have sought to welcome immigrants to revitalize core areas of the city.[44]

Entrepreneurship has made the United States an economic powerhouse and will continue to help the country quickly adapt to changing market conditions. The United States benefits from the entrepreneurial spirit, hard work ethic, and innovation of immigrants who often find themselves unable to prosper in their homelands due to the lack of infrastructure or robust financial markets, but who flourish with the opportunities in a relatively stable US economy. The fact that immigrants move from their homes characterizes their willingness to take risks to succeed in the United States. In 2014, immigrants were about twice as likely as the native-born to be entrepreneurs, according to the Kaufmann Index of Entrepreneurial Activity.[45] More than $775 billion in revenue, $125 billion in payroll, and $100 billion in income is generated by immigrant-owned businesses, and those businesses employ one out of every ten workers.[46] Also, in 2014, immigrants made up 28.5 percent of all new entrepreneurs, which is up from 13.3 percent in 1996.[47]

Immigrant entrepreneurs have founded thousands of businesses, from engineering companies and cleaning services to restaurants and medical practices, and these businesses often revitalize neighborhoods that were struggling. Immigrants thus play a central role in job creation through small and larger businesses. In fact, 18 percent of business owners in the United States are foreign born, higher than their share of either the population (13 percent) or the labor force (16 percent). Among Fortune 500 companies, ninety were founded by immigrants. Sergey Brin, cofounder of Google, came to the United States from Russia with his family when they felt they could not fully thrive in a society that regularly discriminated against Jews. Once here, Sergey advanced through his classes and went on to a doctoral program at Stanford University, though he eventually quit the program to start his business out of a garage. Google is now a multibillion-dollar company and has made Sergey Brin very wealthy, but he also has a desire to give back to the community: "In general, I think our mission is to use technology to really change the world for the better."[48]

John Tu, another immigrant entrepreneur, was born in Taiwan. He founded Kingston Technology in Fountain Valley, California, with fellow Taiwanese immigrant David Sun. Tu sold the company for $1 billion and gave $100 million of the sale's proceeds to his American employees. Gary

McDonald, a Kingston employee, said, "Kingston's success came from a philosophy of treating employees, suppliers and customers like family, this being
based upon the Asian family values of trust, loyalty and mutual support
practiced by John and David."[49]

Immigrants often arrive in the United States without the educational and
financial characteristics that would necessarily portend success once here. Their
initial starting place in life, however, should not discount their ability to succeed
in the future. Dr. Alfred Quinones-Hinojosa, a neurosurgeon at Johns Hopkins
University, was an undocumented immigrant who picked tomatoes in the fields
of California, where the farmer's son would look down on him with disdain.
He worked his way through school and eventually went to Harvard Medical
School, where he gave his class's commencement speech. "The last thing I was
thinking was that I was going to break the law," he says. "I felt what my father
felt, not being able to put food on the table for my family, but I had a dream."[50]

Refugees, who have overcome significant hardships to resettle to the
United States, are some of the most resilient immigrants who contribute
significantly to the US economy. Refugees in the United States have been
found to more than triple their income over decades of living in the United
States, with the median income of those in the country at least twenty-five
years reaching $67,000, $14,000 more than the median income of US households overall.[51] Refugees are committed to laying down roots in their new
homes, and around 57 percent of refugee households own their own homes,
similar to the homeownership rate of US residents overall.[52]

More than 180,000 refugee entrepreneurs have made their home in
the United States as of 2015, which means that 13 percent of refugees are
entrepreneurs, compared to 9 percent of the US born population.[53] These
refugee-owned businesses generated $4.6 billion in business income in
2015.[54] And while refugees (unlike most other immigrants) receive some
limited monetary assistance from the government when they first arrive,
they more than make up for these initial resettlement costs: a US Department of Health and Human Services internal study published in the
New York Times found that, between 2005 and 2014, refugees had paid in
$63 billion more in taxes than the total cost of benefits they received.[55]

HIGH-TECH JOBS

As several of the stories we have already shared illustrate, immigrants are not just concentrated in low-skilled jobs but also in high-skilled jobs. While about one-third of immigrants who are twenty-five years and older do not have a high school degree, 30 percent have a college degree or higher.[56] This heavy concentration at opposite ends of the employment spectrum reflects the growing polarization of the US labor market, with job growth concentrated most heavily at opposite ends of the spectrum for low-wage (or low-education) labor and high-wage (or high-education) labor at the expense of middle-wage labor, due in part to computerization of work as well as globalization where middle-wage jobs relocate to lower-wage countries.[57] The education and skill set of immigrants will thus fill jobs in industries that are expected to create the most jobs in the future. In computer and mathematical

A BENEFIT OR LOSS FOR THE SENDING COUNTRY?

Brain drain, or the emigration of high-skilled workers from low- and middle-income countries, is often cited as one of the negative effects of immigration, especially on developing countries that invest large amounts of their resources into training and educating their workforce, only to have them leave to work in another country. In Ghana, for example, half of all medical school graduates emigrate within five years of graduation. This large exodus of health-care workers to more developed countries like the United States and Canada has been a major barrier to delivering quality health care at the community level.[58] Where there is a dearth of doctors and nurses, local community health workers are often stepping in and providing the needed medical care.

In other countries, however, the emigration of skilled labor can be seen as a consequence of "brain overflow," as well-educated workers lack job opportunities in their communities after graduation and migrate to countries that will better utilize their skills. In some cases, "replacement migration" has occurred, when professionals from surrounding countries have filled in the vacancies left by the emigrating native workforce. In South Africa, for example, doctors from Tanzania, Kenya, and Nigeria have replaced South African doctors who moved to the United Kingdom or other more developed countries. To further ease the effects of "brain drain," the United Kingdom has developed policies to not actively recruit health-care workers from developing countries.

Skilled migration is also not always a permanent loss to the sending countries. Large, growing networks of transnational links and increased communication flows can provide opportunities for professionals in more developed countries to share their knowledge and skills with those in their home countries.

---

occupations, about 64 percent of jobs requires a bachelor's level degree or more, but only about 19 percent of native-born Americans who hold a bachelor's degree have that degree in STEM versus 32 percent of immigrants, which are most often earned in their home countries.[59]

With state-of-the-art research facilities and some of the best educational institutions in the world, the United States has been the destination of choice for the world's best scientists and researchers. Foreign-born students make up more than 40 percent of master's and doctoral graduates in STEM fields in US universities.[60] The contributions of immigrants to the advancement of science and technology in the United States are unmistakable. Along with Google, Yahoo, Intel, and Sun Microsystems were all founded or cofounded by immigrants who came to the United States to live the American dream. Jerry Yang, the Taiwanese immigrant who founded Yahoo, has said,

> Yahoo would not be an American company today if the United States had not welcomed my family and me almost 30 years ago. We must do all that we can to ensure that the door is open for the next generation of top entrepreneurs, engineers, and scientists from around the world to come to the U.S. and thrive.[61]

Of all Nobel Prizes awarded to US-based laureates between 1901 and 2015, 31 percent were born outside the United States. In 2016 alone, all six winners affiliated with American universities of Nobel Prizes were foreign-born.[62] A recent study profiled eighty-seven US startups valued at $1 billion or more. More than half of these startups were founded or cofounded by immigrants.[63] The group was collectively valued at $168 billion and employed an average of 760 people per company. Another study found that one-third of venture-backed companies that went public between 2006 and 2012 were founded or cofounded by an immigrant in the United States. This is an increase from the 25 percent that were immigrant-started between 1990 and 2005.[64] Immigrants don't just "take jobs"; they also create them.

Currently, there are tight caps on the number of visas granted annually to high-skilled workers. Microsoft Corporation has said that thousands of core technology positions go unfilled every year because of these caps. This has inhibited the productivity of Microsoft so much that Bill Gates has proposed eliminating caps on these visas altogether.[65] Intel Corporation and Motorola have also struggled to find enough US workers with advanced degrees in the sciences to fill positions in their businesses. Instead, these companies have invested heavily in research centers in India and China.

India and China continue to compete with the United States to develop students in science and engineering by investing significantly more in high school education, a threefold increase from 2001 to 2006.[66] The European Union has also stepped up efforts to streamline its education systems, and it now offers more courses in English and has launched campaigns to attract international students. Of the six million first university (or bachelor's) degrees in science and engineering, 23 percent came from students in China, 12 percent from students in the European Union, and 9 percent from the United States.[67] Between 2000 and 2012, the number of first university science and engineering degrees doubled in China, Taiwan, Germany, Turkey, and Mexico, but rose more slowly in the United States.[68] To continue to attract the best talent around the world, the United States continues to draw international students to its schools, which increased by more than 50 percent between 2008 and 2014.[69]

The United States needs to continue to prepare and train its native-born population to pursue higher degrees of education or specialization in the

STEM fields. Jobs in the STEM fields are growing three times faster than other jobs in the economy, but given the slow rate of growth of American students pursuing STEM fields at less than one percent per year, in 2018 there will be more than 230,000 advanced degree STEM jobs that will not be filled.[70] In addition, unemployment for Americans in the STEM field is very low in the United States. For example, the employment rates as petroleum engineers is 0.1 percent, computer network architects is 0.4 percent, nuclear engineers is 0.5 percent, environmental scientists and geoscientists is 1.2 percent, and database administrators is 1.3 percent.[71]

Critics argue that, rather than importing workers, the United States should focus on training its native-born population to pursue higher degrees of education or specialization in specific computer and technology-related fields. This is a challenge that should be met with gusto, and the latest trends suggest there has been a renewed interest in the science, math, and engineering fields. While emphasis on STEM education can often start in college, there is growing emphasis on starting STEM interest and education in elementary and middle school to cultivate more Americans towards the STEM field.

However, in an era of increasing global competition, immigrants and their skills can help the United States maintain a competitive edge over other countries by complementing the native workforce while spurring growth in key fields that have allowed the United States to lead in technological advances. This must be couched in the thinking that immigrants expand the innovative edge of the United States.

High-skilled immigrants whose successes are easy to identify and quantify play an important role in maintaining our economy, but so do low-skilled immigrants who come to work in lesser-known and lesser-paying jobs. Low-skilled immigrants, who often labor in difficult conditions picking our produce, landscaping our lawns, and cleaning our homes and offices, have added dynamically to the US economic landscape and are a part of who we are as America. Their intrinsic worth should not be measured by their capital output, though this may be the world's standard. Rather, we should recognize that they, like high-skilled immigrants and native-born workers, bear the image of God and should be treated with the dignity and respect we would afford our Savior.

GLOBAL DYNAMICS OF IMMIGRATION

The turn of the twenty-first century is marked by a world in which globalization has taken front and center stage. Many argue about the costs and benefits of globalization, but, undoubtedly, free trade and open markets have been touted by most of the industrialized world as engines of strong economies worldwide. A greater flow of goods and capital stream across national boundaries as countries grow more specialized in producing certain goods and services. The increasing global interconnectedness also inevitably leads to an increase in the movement of people who follow these trade flows, whether within countries from rural to urban areas, or between countries as people migrate to find better economic opportunities abroad.

REMITTANCES

If skilled migration may have some negative costs on the sending country, remittances, or monies that immigrants send back to their countries of origin, are a strong benefit for many sending countries. Remittances can also have a significant effect on development in many contexts. Most (about 90 percent) of the money that immigrants earn is circulated back into the local economy where they live.[72] Yet in 2013, Latin American immigrants in the United States still managed to send about $54 billion back to their countries of origin.[73] In countries where a sizable share of the population is unable to buy basic food for a healthy diet, remittances have a direct and immediate impact on the ability of families to meet basic nutritional needs.[74] In fact, a comprehensive study of seventy-one developing countries found that a 10 percent increase in per capita remittances leads to a 3.5 percent decline in the share of people living in poverty.[75] Worldwide, remittances to developing countries accounted for $440 billion, several times the amount that all the world's governments spend on foreign aid *combined*.[76]

Remittances not only supplement income but also allow families to make investments that can serve them in the longer term. Mexico, for example, does not have an adequate financial infrastructure to

The movement of people has marked human existence since creation. The International Organization for Migration (IOM), the leading intergovernmental organization in the field of migration, estimates that there are approximately 224 million migrants in the world today, representing about 3 percent of the world's population.[77] The percentage of migrants in the world today versus the total world population has not changed significantly since the mid-1900s.[78] What has changed in the last fifty years is that a greater number of migrants are now concentrated in the more developed regions of the world. In 1960, Europe, North America, Australia, and Japan hosted about 3.4 percent of the world's migrant population. These developed regions now host about 9.5 percent of the world's migrant population.

provide credit and financing to help people purchase a home. Having a steady income of American dollars saved up can help a family eventually purchase their own home. "Households use international migration as a tool to overcome failed or missing markets at home," explains Douglas Massey, an expert on migration at Princeton University.[79] The government of Mexico also provides matching funds for remittances used for home investments.

Remittances can also be vital when a natural disaster strikes. When a hurricane or earthquake hits, many Americans give generously to ministries and organizations working toward relief efforts, and governments generally provide significant assistance. But immigrants who have personal connections to those who are impacted, including family members, tend to be far more generous, playing a significant role in disaster recovery.[80]

While remittances should not be a substitute for long-term development policy, they can in the short term help alleviate the immediate effects of poverty in the home countries of immigrants who currently work in the United States. Immigrants who work in the United States thus keep the US economy strong but also add enormously to the wealth of their families and community members back in their countries of origin.

This should not be surprising. In the past few decades, inequality between developed and developing countries has increased dramatically. It is estimated that the top 10 percent of adults, by income, now own 85 percent of global household wealth.[81] Even though North America and Europe have 18 percent of the world's adult population, they together account for 67 percent of total household wealth.[82] Immigrants in the developing world who are unable to earn enough to feed their families, cannot find jobs, or do not have infrastructures in their local economies to build assets thus often feel compelled to migrate to these more developed regions of the world, often temporarily, to improve their economic lot. In fact, in Europe, immigration is equally if not more heatedly debated, as they have traditionally been more homogeneous societies.

In addition to the growing inequality and demographic differences between developed and developing countries, regional economic liberalization trade agreements have increased the interdependence among countries, spurring migration between countries that are now more openly engaged in the free trade of goods and services. In the United States, where approximately 56 percent of the undocumented and 31 percent of the total foreign-born population are from Mexico, trade policies like the North American Free Trade Agreement (NAFTA) were expected to stop illegal immigration by developing a more robust Mexican economy. In actuality, illegal immigration increased in the years after it its implementation, though it has slowed in the past decade. NAFTA opened up Mexico's market to American imports—including subsidized agricultural products—and displaced many Mexican farmers who, for years, had worked in the agrarian economy but, now unable to compete with American imports, found themselves migrating north.

Migration is often spurred not only by a lack of economic development but also is due to the onset of development itself. According to Princeton University sociology professor Douglas Massey, "The shift from a peasant or command economy to a market system entails a radical transformation of social structures at all levels; a revolutionary shift that displaces people from traditional ways of life and creates a mobile population on the lookout for alternative ways of making a living."[83]

The forces that drive people to migrate are not just affecting the United States but many countries throughout the world, especially Europe, and they are often outside the control of government. Certainly, structural changes and development are needed in the immigrant-sending countries so migrants do not feel the need to migrate. Still, national migration policies that do not reflect the global reality of economic and social forces will not stop people from coming to the United States who are driven by overriding factors such as job availability or reunion with family. Migration to the United States is also inextricably linked to conditions in countries of origin. Restrictive immigration policies may in fact drive people to take more clandestine routes to get to their destination of choice. Thousands of migrants cross the treacherous seas of the Mediterranean every year to find work in European countries, and many die along the way, just as many die crossing the deserts of the American Southwest.

THE VALUE OF CULTURAL DIVERSITY

Immigration in and of itself is not a panacea to all of our country's economic needs. Nor should immigrants' value be measured only by their economic benefit to our country. Greater questions must be asked about who we are and what we want to become as a country that may be inherently more important when crafting immigration policy than any economic considerations. Indeed, as Christians we must be wary of valuing persons solely on the contributions they can make to our affluence. We should also recognize their inherent dignity as a person made in God's image (Gen 1:27) as well as the personal and cultural contributions they can make to our country. If our measuring stick of success is affluence, we become blinded to or devalue the blessings God has poured on us in other forms.[84]

Immigration to the United States means that the nation will also become more racially and ethnically diverse, with the aggregate minority population projected to become the majority in 2043. A hallmark year in the United States was 2013, as this was the first time more minority babies were born than white babies.[85]

Immigrants add to the diversity of the United States, and God works within cultural differences to bring people to understand who he is. Walking into a church where the beat of African drums reverberates or attending a Hispanic church where songs are sung in Spanish continually pushes our creative imagination to see God, who is infinite and real to people from the world over. According to Richard Mouw, "God intended from the beginning that human beings would 'fill the earth' with the processes, patterns and products of cultural formation."[86] Indeed, our ability to unify through diversity can demonstrate the power of the gospel to transcend cultural differences and national identity. From the beginning of creation, God intended humanity to fill the earth and subdue it (Gen 1:28).[87] When people gathered in Babel to "make a name for ourselves [and not] be scattered over the face of the whole earth," God intervened and created different languages (Gen 11:4, 7-8). It was an act of judgment but also of grace, as a way for the people to return to God's original plan.[88]

In the New Testament, Jesus commanded that his disciples be his witnesses "in Jerusalem, and in all Judea and Samaria, and to the ends of the earth" (Acts 1:8). At Pentecost, the Holy Spirit empowered Jesus' disciples to preach the gospel to people from all nations as the wonders of God were declared in the languages of the nations that were gathered. Pentecost signaled to the world God's purpose in reconciling every tribe, language, people, and nation to himself, and he enables us to do so with the power of the Holy Spirit.

Ethnic diversity can help us connect with communities who often experience God in different ways. In fact, throughout the Bible, we see how God used his servants whose different ethnicities were central to accomplishing their purpose here on earth. Moses was a tricultural Hebrew-Egyptian-Midianite who empathized with the suffering of his fellow Israelites but was able to speak before Pharaoh because of his Egyptian upbringing. Paul was a Jewish-Roman citizen God used to evangelize Gentiles who were previously unclean.

Beyond the diversity that, as Christians, we are guided to value, immigrants also benefit the United States by positively influencing our culture.

Immigrants often come from countries with a strong emphasis on community and family life. Many Asian families live in multigenerational homes, for example, where the grandparents do not live in retirement homes, but take care of children and are cared for by their own children. Many Latino cultures also treat their extended family of cousins, uncles, and aunts as members of their immediate families. Immigrants teach younger generations about the reward of hard work and delayed gratification. Refugees also teach us about the fragility of life and the ability of the human spirit to overcome tremendous obstacles in order to survive. Their testimonies of persecution and suffering allow us to glimpse into the reality of the world around us, and their sheer courage inspires us. Immigrants embody the ideals that have made this country great and remind us that the American dream can still be reached.

Cultural diversity also enhances art and beauty in our midst. Immigrant artists have added tremendously to our music, dance, art, and food. Immigrants often find the challenges of displacement can be expressed through art.[89] Latin music expands our sense of rhythm and movement. In ethnic neighborhoods of a Little Italy or Chinatown, restaurants offer delicious foods that bring the world to our palate. Also many famous immigrants, while working in the United States, have added richly to the world. Fashion designers Oscar de la Renta and Carolina Herrera were both born in Latin America but built their fashion empires in the United States. Audrey Hepburn, Justin Bieber, Rihanna, Elizabeth Taylor, Salma Hayek, and Charlize Theron are all immigrants who have entertained us through movies and television. Yo-Yo Ma and Placido Domingo enrich us with their musical talent. Yao Ming, Patrick Ewing, Mariano Rivera, and Martina Navratilova have excelled in their respective sports. Madeleine Albright and Henry Kissinger speak fondly about how their immigrant upbringings shaped their foreign policy.

Alexis de Tocqueville, in his book *Democracy in America*, recognized early in our country's history the virtues that made America great, among them the spirit of equality embodied in the Declaration of Independence that "all men are created equal and are endowed by their Creator with certain unalienable rights." John F. Kennedy eloquently states in his book *A Nation of Immigrants* that

> Immigration is by definition a gesture of faith in social mobility. [Immigration] gave every old American a standard by which to judge how far he had come and every new American a realization of how far he might go. It reminded every American, old and new, that change is the essence of life, and that American society is a process, not a conclusion.[90]

History teaches us that, over the generations, immigrants have integrated into American society, adopting American values, beliefs, and habits. There are waiting lists for English as a Second Language (ESL) classes across the country today. Second- and third-generation immigrants often intermarry at higher rates than earlier ethnic groups, and by the second generation, most immigrants are speaking English, improving job status, and, consequently, paying more in taxes.[91] We have seen in our country's history that the ability of our country to transcend racial differences and reconstruct our collective national identity, while initially difficult, has made us stronger. These new identities reaffirm our country's commitment to the motto stamped on every US coin, *E Pluribus Unum*, or "out of many, one." Through the unique talents, values, and personalities that immigrants bring with them to the United States, immigrants add value to our country in ways that economic measures might miss.

WHAT IS OUR LIMIT?

Economists agree that immigration is a net good for the US economy, and immigrants also benefit our society in other ways. But if we believe, as most economists do, that legal immigration should be increased, what should be the limits to immigration? What is the capacity of the United States to absorb a large number of immigrants? We have seen through our history that the economic forces of supply and demand, where immigrant workers fill jobs in the United States, as well as social factors like family reunification, often override immigration enforcement. Historically, immigration has generally been a boon that has allowed the United States to thrive economically, even though immigration initially tested the social capacity of communities to receive newcomers. Our government must create responsible, balanced policies that reflect larger market forces so immigration flows can be managed in a manner that both economically and socially benefits the United States.

We as Christians, though, must also answer this question outside of strict market considerations. Our tendency may be to think that we should welcome immigrants only so long as they benefit our financial situation, but this attitude is hard to reconcile with Scripture. After all, the many commands of God to the Israelites to welcome immigrants did not focus on their economic contributions but on emulating the character of God. And Jesus' overarching command to love our neighbors does not apply only if particular neighbors will contribute to our affluence. Immigrants, on the net, are a positive economic force, but Christians would be called to welcome them even if they were not.

Immigration has been and will continue to be a part of the American story. But we must choose how to respond to the immigrants in our communities, whether with disdain and fear or with a warm welcome and trust that God will provide for all. A mindset of abundance must be our framework instead of a mindset of scarcity. We must believe that the God who has provided for our every need is the same God who can provide for the needs of others. As Christians, we are foremost citizens in God's kingdom, and everything we have is "on loan" to us here. Our primary allegiance is to the kingdom of God, not to any flag or country. The best of the United States may be shown in how we treat the immigrants among us.

While our faith need not lead us to support a policy of open borders, and there ought to be reasonable limitations on who is allowed to enter the United States, both the economic needs of our country and the guidelines of our faith lead us to a more generous, welcoming immigration policy, where immigrant laborers are able to enter the United States legally. Yet, as of this writing, there has been no substantial change in immigration policy. In chapter eight, we will look at the politics behind the immigration issue that have stalled any significant reform thus far.

EIGHT

IMMIGRATION POLICIES AND POLITICS

Our national immigration laws have created a moral, economic and political crisis in America. Initiatives to remedy this crisis have led to polarization and name calling in which opponents have misrepresented each other's positions as open borders and amnesty versus deportations of millions. This false choice has led to an unacceptable political stalemate at the federal level at a tragic human cost.

THE EVANGELICAL STATEMENT OF PRINCIPLES FOR IMMIGRATION REFORM[1]

IMMIGRATION WAS THE DEFINING POLITICAL ISSUE on which Donald Trump campaigned and subsequently won the election on November 8, 2016. When President Trump launched his campaign in Trump Tower in New York City on June 2015, he made immigration his signature issue saying that "to fix our immigration system, we must change our leadership in Washington and we must change it quickly. . . . The truth is our immigration system is worse than anybody ever realized." Immigration reform was the only position listed on his campaign website several months after the launch of his campaign.[1] Subsequently in nearly every major campaign stop, he used immigration to drive a contrasting picture of him versus not only his Republican primary opponents but ultimately Hillary Clinton.

The use of immigration as a campaign issue is not new. What was exceptional about the 2016 election was the degree to which Mr. Trump employed generalizations and stereotypes to paint the immigrant population as a largely criminal and problem-causing population—and in doing so galvanized enough political support to win the election. Whether people agreed with his broad statements about immigration or not—and exit polls suggest that even most of those who voted for him did not agree with his most extreme policies, such as his call for the mass deportation of all undocumented immigrants—he tapped into a general discontent within the American populace.[2] For a certain segment of Americans who felt disenfranchised by the American political process, Donald Trump was their answer. Michael Wear, a former adviser to President Barack Obama, observes that the American people on both sides of the political spectrum have placed too much hope in politics, expecting more from elected officials than politics could possibly provide. He argues that the state of our politics was the state of people's souls.[3]

From the day that he launched his campaign, Mr. Trump defied the conventions of American politics. The president said in the speech that launched his campaign, "When Mexico sends its people, they're not sending their best. They're sending people that have lots of problems, and they're bringing those problems with us. They're bringing drugs. They're bringing crime. They're rapists. And some, I assume, are good people."[4]

That this statement was condemned by elected officials in both parties did not stop the future president from doubling down on the messaging. He repeatedly pledged to build a "big, beautiful" border wall—and make Mexico pay for it, campaign rhetoric that continued into his presidency. He would subsequently call for a "total and complete" ban on Muslims entering the country.[5]

Evangelical voters, immigration, and the 2016 elections. Leading up to the November 2016 elections, almost every major poll projected that Hillary Clinton was going to win.[6] In fact, some pundits were conjecturing that Clinton would capture some key Republican solid states like Texas, in part because of the presumption that the Trump campaign's harsh rhetoric regarding immigrants would alienate Latino voters. In August 2016, when candidate Trump defeated sixteen more conventional candidates to become the Republican presidential nominee, many expected him to moderate his position in order to appeal to a wider base for the general election. However, Trump doubled down on his tough immigration positions. He continued to rally large numbers of people against immigration and continually sold the border wall (for which Mexico was going to pay) and new restrictions on Muslim migration.[7]

On election night, I (Jenny) was at church small group. After closing in prayer around 9 that evening, I checked my phone and my jaw dropped. I scrolled through the news notifications to find that Mr. Trump had picked up state after state that few had predicted he would win. From Ohio to Florida to North Carolina, he was steadily gaining steam to win the Electoral College. And early the next day he was declared the president-elect.

The election results exposed a rather stark ethnic divide among evangelical voters. Exit polls found that 80 percent of *white, self-identified* "born-again or evangelical" voters supported President Trump, a higher percentage than voted for George W. Bush or any other recent Republican presidential candidate.[8] In a LifeWay Research poll that identified evangelicals by asking about specific theological beliefs, a slightly lower share of white evangelicals (65 percent) expressed support for candidate Trump.[9] But a nearly equal percentage of Hispanic, Asian, African American, and other nonwhite evangelicals—who, based on a theological definition, not self-identification, make up 40 percent of all American evangelicals—supported Hillary Clinton.[10]

Notably, immigration did not register as a top concern for evangelical voters regardless of ethnicity or which candidate they supported; overall, just 5 percent of voters with evangelical beliefs cited it as the most important issue, well behind the economy (26 percent), national security (22 percent), and personal character (15 percent). Few prioritized Supreme Court nominees (10 percent), religious freedom (7 percent), or abortion (4 percent), either, though these were much higher priorities among polling of evangelical *pastors*.[11] Despite the centrality of immigration rhetoric to the campaign, it was not the most urgent priority for many evangelical voters, whether they voted for Trump or Clinton.

A major point of discussion in party politics has been the growth of and influence of the Latino vote on the future of the Democratic and Republican parties. The number of eligible Latino voters is at a record 27.3 million, representing 12 percent of all eligible voters.[12] This means that one in nine potential voters is Latino, a 40 percent increase since the 2008 elections.[13] Millennials also make up 44 percent of Latino eligible voters.[14] Although about half of eligible Latino voters are concentrated in the non-battleground states of California, Texas, and New York, they also increasingly make up more than 10 percent of eligible voters in key swing states like Arizona (22 percent), Florida (18 percent), and Nevada (17.2 percent).[15]

Because most Latino voters since 2000 have voted for the Democratic presidential candidate, some Republican leaders have cited this Democratic political advantage as a reason to oppose legalizing Latino immigrants. However, a substantial number of Latinos are conservative and will consistently vote for the Republican Party.[16] In the past three elections, approximately 30 percent of Hispanic voters supported the Republican presidential candidate. In the 2016 election, Trump performed roughly on par with Republican Mitt Romney from the 2012 election, capturing 28 percent of the Latino vote.[17] This is a drop from the 44 percent of Latinos who voted for George W. Bush. Mark Hugo Lopez from the Pew Research Center argues there's a possible floor among Latinos for Republicans, around 20 to 25 percent. With the right candidate, he argues, that floor can be adjusted up or down.[18] Pollsters attribute this substantial number of Hispanic voters affiliated with the Republican Party to Hispanics' religious commitments. Family values, social values, and religious freedom are all core values to Hispanic evangelicals. And immigration has remained one of the top priorities for Hispanic voters.[19]

The unconventional election of 2016 has led to hand-wringing in the evangelical church. While most white evangelical voters supported President Trump, many traditional Republicans, including conservative columnists such as Michael Gerson, George Will, and Erick Erickson, and evangelical leaders such as Russell Moore of the Southern Baptist Ethics and Religious Liberty Commission, were vocally opposed to the Trump candidacy, with several citing his views on immigration and racially tinged comments as a disqualifier (several found characteristics that they found disqualifying in Hillary Clinton as well and made clear that they would not support either major party candidate). Author and pastor Brett McCracken argued that "White Christians in America must partner with, listen to, defer to nonwhite & nonwestern Christian leaders. We need humility, hope, revival."[20]

IMMIGRATION POLICY IN THE TRUMP ERA

There were questions swirling during President Trump's first days in office about whether the campaign rhetoric would pan out into concrete policy actions. Since taking office, while (as of this writing) there is still no Mexican-funded border wall, and there has not been a significant increase in the overall rate of deportations compared to the Obama administration, the president has significantly influenced immigration with three key decisions: the suspension and then gutting of the refugee resettlement program and subsequent travel restrictions on certain categories of immigrants, the termination of the Deferred Action for Childhood Arrivals program, and changes to interior enforcement.

The "Muslim Ban." In the beginning of the president's term, it was clear that he wanted to send a message as a follow-through to his campaign rhetoric. One week after inauguration, on January 27, 2017, with a hastily written executive order that was not fully vetted by the Departments of State or Homeland Security, who were immediately tasked with its implementation, President Trump initiated dramatic changes that led to chaos at airports around the country. The order banned visitors and immigrants from seven predominantly Muslim countries (Iran, Iraq, Somalia, Sudan, Libya, Yemen, and Syria) without regard to whether they had previously issued visas. It also suspended the entire US refugee resettlement program for 120 days, restricted refugees from Syria indefinitely, and slashed the total number of refugees who could come to the United States in fiscal year 2017 from the 110,000 set by the Obama administration to just 50,000.[21]

Iranian scientists seeking to return to their jobs at Ivy League labs, Afghan refugees who had assisted US troops abroad and were subsequently persecuted as a result, and Sudanese families waiting to be reunited after years of separation were all turned away at the airports as Department of Homeland Security officers sought clarification on precisely how to implement the order. Some were immediately detained upon entry at US airports for hours of questioning, while others were prevented from boarding flights in the first place.

In an interview with the Christian Broadcasting Network the day that the order was released, President Trump pledged that it would help persecuted Syrian Christians.[22] The executive order had the exact opposite effect: not only were Syrians refugees (whether Christian or not) barred indefinitely by the order, but by significantly reducing the refugee ceiling from 110,000 to 50,000 the order guaranteed fewer Christian refugees (from all countries) would be allowed in than in the previous year.[23] Ultimately, about 27,000 fewer persecuted Christians were allowed into the United States as refugees in the first full year of the Trump administration than in the previous year.[24] Just twenty-six Syrian Christians were allowed in between January 27, 2017, and September 30, 2017, the end of the fiscal year, less than half as many as during the same time period in 2016.[25]

It was confounding to anyone who worked directly with refugees why this executive order was issued. Over three million refugees had been resettled to the United States since 1980, the year the formal refugee program started, but not a single refugee had taken an American life in a terrorist attack since that time; the US refugee resettlement program has an incredible security record. The president cited the attacks on September 11, 2001, when announcing the plan, but none of the hijackers on 9/11 came from the countries included in the suspension. Not only did the executive order create chaos out of a nonexistent threat, but it perpetuated a false narrative about refugees and other immigrants from Muslim-majority countries: that these were individuals who deserved to be excluded because they presented a national security threat to the United States.

Two days after the executive order was issued, the Department of Homeland Security issued a statement clarifying that those with green cards would be admitted.[26] A few days later, a federal judge in Seattle suspended some elements of the ban nationwide, claiming the executive order's focus on Muslim-majority countries violated the First Amendment. After the

Trump administration appealed, the Ninth Circuit Court of Appeals backed up the judge's order halting the ban; they cited the Immigration and Nationality Act's provision that "no person shall . . . be discriminated against in the issuance of an immigrant visa because of the person's race, sex, nationality, place of birth, or place of residence."[27]

Rather than appeal the order up to the Supreme Court, the president issued another executive order on March 6, 2017, rescinding the previous order. In this new, more carefully worded order, the president narrowed the list of suspected countries from seven to six (removing Iraq) but still suspended the refugee program for 120 days and reduced the overall number to fifty thousand per year. The Supreme Court ruled in June 2017 that most of the executive order could go into place on an interim basis, but with an exception for individuals with a close relationship to either a family member or an institution in the United States. Before the Supreme Court could hold a hearing on a final decision, the four-month moratorium expired. In the fall of 2017, the Trump administration issued two new executive orders, halting issuance of new visas for nationals of several mostly Muslim-majority countries, then restricting refugee resettlement from several of the same countries for at least ninety days; both orders faced new court challenges.

These executive orders were not responding to a specific or imminent threat posed by refugees generally or by other individuals of these specific nationalities. In fact, analysts in the intelligence arm of the Department of Homeland Security found that citizenship is an "unlikely indicator" of terrorism threats to the United States and that few individuals from the countries listed in the executive order have carried out or been involved in terrorism in the United States since 2011, the start of the Syrian civil war.[28] Seventy-two percent of refugees that came to the United States in 2016 were women and children.[29]

The initial executive order in particular had a chaotic effect on airports across the country. An Afghan family being resettled through World Relief arrived at LAX, and the father, who had been threatened in his home country because he had served the US military, was promptly detained and separated from his wife and two young children. After five hours of questioning, they were then sent to a local detention facility; the mother and her young children were poised to be flown to a family detention facility in Texas until a local judge intervened. After a few harrowing days in detention, this Afghan family was eventually reunited and was able to fly to Washington state, their final destination.

Americans angered by the initial executive order mobilized in airports all across the country. People held signs protesting the ban, and legal teams worked from airport coffee shops, glued to their phones and computers as they sought to aid detained travelers.

Many in the church shared this frustration. The leadership at World Relief drafted a public statement declaring support for refugees and expressing concern with the new policies. We quickly gathered signatures from pastors in all fifty states and released an open letter as a full-page ad in the *Washington Post* in early February 2017. We took copies of the newspaper up to Capitol Hill and met with legislators that day to voice opposition to the ban. We also opened up the letter for signatures for any church leader in the country, and within three weeks had over six thousand pastors and lay leaders sign on in support of refugees.

Under the authority of the Refugee Act of 1980, the president (in consultation with Congress) sets the maximum number of refugees who will be allowed into the United States in each fiscal year. According to press reports, there was heated debate in the White House in summer 2017 on the refugee admissions ceiling President Trump would set his first year in office. Despite pleas from top former national-security experts and from leaders within "the State Department, the Defense Department, the Joint Chiefs of Staff, the Office of the Vice-President, and the Office of Management and Budget" to set the number closer to the historical norm, President Trump ultimately settled on forty-five thousand for fiscal year 2018, the lowest number since the inception of the refugee resettlement program in 1980.[30]

Of the world's 22.5 million refugees, the UN estimates that 1.2 million are in critical need of resettlement in 2018 because they face extreme vulnerabilities or family reunification needs. With a ceiling of just forty-five thousand, the United States will at most resettle about two-tenths of 1 percent of the world's refugees and less than 4 percent of those who are in urgent need of resettlement. By comparison, in 2016, Canada alone—with a population and economy smaller than the single US state of California—resettled 45,700 refugees.[31]

As of this writing, though, after yet another executive order and dramatically slowed overseas processing of refugees, it is unlikely that the United States will actually reach the ceiling of forty-five thousand set for fiscal year 2018. Furthermore, the administration could set the ceiling even lower in future years. We believe that the program should continue to accept the most vulnerable refugee who are selected for humanitarian and foreign policy interests, and that the United States should be doing more, not less, at a time when the world is facing the greatest refugee crisis in recorded history.

Deferred Action for Childhood Arrivals. Another major immigration policy change within the Trump presidency was the president's decision to rescind President Obama's key immigration initiative, the Deferred Action for Childhood Arrivals program.

As we've already described, the DACA program was created in 2012 under President Obama to protect young undocumented immigrants who came to the United States as young children. The policy was announced at a time, toward the end of President Obama's first term, when he was under significant criticism for the record number of deportations that were occurring under his administration, so many that some called him the "Deporter in Chief." During the Obama administration the Department of Homeland Security focused on two primary immigration-enforcement priorities: targeting immigrants with criminal records for deportation and increasing penalties for recent border crossers, who were put into formal removal proceedings instead of being returned across the border (as a deterrent to those who would consider entering unlawfully).[32] By fiscal year 2016, 85 percent of all removals and returns were of noncitizens who had recently crossed the border unlawfully, and of the remaining 15 percent, more than 90 percent had been convicted of serious crimes. Just in that year, the Department of Homeland Security apprehended over 530,000 individuals and removed over 344,000 individuals.[33]

As the Obama administration identified particular immigrants as high priority for enforcement, though, that also left others as clearly low priority.

Among the lowest priority, President Obama believed, were those who were brought into the United States as children, who had not personally made the decision to migrate but whose lack of legal status generally prevented them from working lawfully and (since they were ineligible for any federal financial aid) usually from pursuing education beyond high school. On the premise that such "Dreamers" should have an opportunity to flourish in a country that they have called home, President Obama's Department of Homeland Security established a program called "Deferred Action for Childhood Arrivals" in 2012, formally recognizing Dreamers who met certain requirements as low priority for enforcement and, as such, giving them access to temporary but renewable work authorization and protections from deportation.

As of March 2017, an estimated 800,000 individuals received such deferred action, which allowed many to go to school, work, and travel abroad. While still ineligible for federal financial aid, individuals who could not afford to go to college previously now could lawfully work to afford tuition. Individuals from Mexico represent the largest number of DACA recipients, followed by El Salvador, Guatemala, Honduras, Peru, and South Korea.[34] DACA was always meant to be a temporary solution, and it did not offer a pathway toward legal residency status or US citizenship.

When President Obama tried to expand such protections to the parents of American-born children in 2014—using the same principle of prosecutorial discretion to defer action for a much larger segment of the undocumented immigrant population—ten states' attorneys general sued the administration and ultimately prevailed in a four-four US Supreme Court decision in 2016. The *expanded* "Deferred Action for Parents of Americans" program never went into effect. The DACA program for young people, though, was never successfully challenged in court.

Since the DACA program was not a matter of law, but created at the discretion of the executive branch, it could also be changed by a new president without consulting Congress, simply by adjusting prosecutorial priorities. Candidate Donald Trump pledged he would do so, calling the DACA program an "illegal executive amnesty" that would be terminated "immediately" when he was elected.[35] Many Dreamers and their families feared he would follow through with that commitment.

Between election night and inauguration day, though, President-elect Trump's rhetoric softened. On the situation of the Dreamers whose status depended on DACA, he told *Time* magazine that "it's a very tough situation. . . . We're going to work something out that's going to make people happy."[36] He and his staff were even more explicit in interactions with Christian leaders: Assemblies of God general superintendent George Wood reported early in January 2017 that several of the denomination's leaders had been assured by the president-elect's transition team that the new administration would "seek to protect children of immigrants by replacing Obama's executive order (DACA) with official legislation."[37]

After inauguration day, though President Trump wasted little time in making other changes to immigration policy, he left the DACA program in place, allowing new applications and renewals to continue to be processed. He spoke publicly of Dreamers as "absolutely incredible kids" and said, without committing to specifics, that "we are going to deal with DACA with heart."[38] Polls suggested he had public support to do so: most Republicans as well as most Democrats wanted the protections left in place; when told that President Trump had thus far maintained the program, fully four out of five Republican voters said they agreed.[39]

In the summer of 2017, though, several of the same state attorneys general who had successfully sued to halt the Obama administration's attempted expansion of the Deferred Action program threatened the new administration that they would sue him by September 5, 2017, if the DACA program remained in place. Stunningly, on September 1, 2017, one of those attorneys general, Herbert Slatery III of Tennessee, pulled out of the lawsuit, writing a letter to Tennessee's two US Senators urging them to pass a legislative solution to the crisis. In the letter, he wrote,

> There is a human element to this . . . that is not lost on me and should
> not be ignored. Many of the DACA recipients, some of whose records
> I reviewed, have outstanding accomplishments and laudable ambitions,

which achieved, will be of great benefit and service to our country. [Dreamers] have an appreciation for the opportunities afforded them by our country.[40]

Nevertheless, with the threat of a lawsuit from the other attorneys general still looming, rumors began swirling that the White House would rescind the DACA program. Evangelical leaders publicly urged the president against doing so, echoing the advocacy of Dreamer and immigrant rights groups, while pressing Congress to pass permanent legislation to resolve the situation; polls showed most evangelical voters shared this perspective, with two-thirds supporting legislation to allow Dreamers to become permanent residents or citizens.[41] Shirley Hoogstra, president of the Council for Christian Colleges and Universities, whose member institutions have many Dreamers among their student bodies, said, "We want to support ambitious, driven, intelligent students who have dreams of contributing to their communities and want to pursue an education. We do not believe they should be disqualified from doing so because of acts they did not commit."[42]

Many on President Trump's evangelical advisory board urged the president not to rescind DACA. In a key meeting the Friday before a decision was announced, Samuel Rodriguez, resident of the National Hispanic Christian Leadership Conference, Georgia pastor Jentezen Franklin, and others pressed the president not to rescind DACA until Congress had taken action.[43] "Hundreds of thousands of Hispanic young people will be overcome with fear and grief," warned Rodriguez.[44] By putting a human face to the issue, they appealed to Trump as a father and grandfather to act with compassion toward undocumented youth.

Nevertheless, on September 5, 2017, Attorney General Jeff Sessions—who had been among the fiercest critics of the DACA program as a US Senator from Alabama—announced the end of DACA on behalf of the Trump administration, echoing the rhetoric of the Trump presidential campaign in calling the program a "unilateral executive amnesty" that he said had robbed American citizens of jobs and "put our nation at risk of crime, violence and even terrorism."[45] The program would be phased out gradually, with new applications halted immediately and renewals allowed only for one additional month for those whose employment authorization would expire before March 5, 2018. Beginning in March 2018, unless Congress passed and the president signed legislation to address the situation, approximately thirty thousand Dreamers per month were expected to lose their work authorization and be at risk, once again, of deportation.[46]

Despite the harsh rhetoric of his Attorney General's statement, however, President Trump said that he actually *wanted* Congress to act legislatively to allow Dreamers to stay in the United States lawfully. The president tweeted, "Congress, get ready to do your job—DACA!" then later, "Congress now has 6 months to legalize DACA," even adding, "If they can't, I will revisit this issue!"[47] These tweets suggest a shift away from his harsh campaign rhetoric, where he downplayed the stories of individuals and made sweeping generalizations, to a more softened, even-handed approach.

As this book goes to press, Congress seems to be considering how they will respond, with several bipartisan bills introduced, including a new version of the DREAM Act that would allow those who qualified for DACA and others in their situation to earn permanent legal status and eventually citizenship if they meet certain requirements. Our fervent prayer is that by the time you read this, a bill will have passed through both houses of Congress and been signed by the president. In a sense, that should be easy politically, given consistent polling showing remarkably bipartisan support, including a *Fox News* poll that found 83 percent of Americans—including 63 percent of Trump voters—support granting Dreamers citizenship.[48]

The reality that versions of the DREAM Act have been introduced repeatedly since 2001 and have never gotten enough votes to become law, though, keeps long-time advocates from being overconfident. In February 2018, a bipartisan amendment that paired a twelve-year path to citizenship for Dreamers with an appropriation of $25 billion to expand the wall along the US-Mexico border and make other improvements to border security failed in the US Senate. Most Republican senators voted against the amendment after the White House threatened a veto, saying the president would sign a bill addressing

DACA only if, in addition to funding a border wall, it made dramatic cuts to legal immigration programs by ending the diversity visa lottery and restricting family reunification petitions to spouses and minor children.[49]

If, despite the rhetoric of his campaign, President Trump ends up signing legislation creating an earned path to citizenship for undocumented immigrants brought to the United States as children, something Presidents George W. Bush and Barack Obama both actively supported but which never reached their respective desks for signature, it will be an ironic twist. But if Congress fails to take action (or the president fails to sign a bill that it sends him), the consequences for hundreds of thousands of young people raised in the United States, and for their families, employers, and churches, will be dramatic.

Dreamers themselves have been active and leading the fight for immigration reform. Organizations founded and led by Dreamers, like United We Dream and Voices of Christian Dreamers, have been game changers in the immigration debate. By attesting to the value of immigrants, fighting for their families, and having courage to share their stories, these Dreamers are forcing our elected officials to grapple with real stories and real families, not just numbers. These Dreamers have organized, protested, and raised their voices in the best of political activism, and they will continue to lead the way.

Changes to immigration enforcement priorities. When asked early in the presidential campaign what he would do with mixed-status immigrant families—generally US-citizen kids living with one or both parents who are undocumented—President Trump's response was, "They have to go," though he insisted their removal would be done in a humane way that would "keep the families together."[50] To "enforce immigration laws against 11 million illegal aliens already in the interior of the United States," the campaign website said, a President Trump would seek to triple the number of officers within Immigration and Customs Enforcement (ICE), the agency within the Department of Homeland Security responsible for enforcing immigration laws within the United States.[51] Later in the campaign, without withdrawing his broader statements, candidate Trump said that his administration's primary focus would be the deportation of "bad *hombres.*"[52]

Ironically, deporting "bad hombres" was, in a sense, the Obama administration's immigration enforcement strategy. While during the first term of the Obama administration many immigrants were deported who were neither recent border crossers nor convicted of serious crimes (the administration's two stated priorities), by the last full fiscal year of President Obama's term, almost all individuals deported fit the stated priorities.[53]

While it would take congressional appropriation to dramatically increase the number of ICE officers, which would likely be necessary to realize a correlating increase in deportations, President Trump did act within his first week in office to change enforcement priorities. In an executive order issued five days after inauguration, the president instructed ICE to dramatically broaden the priorities for enforcement to include not just those convicted of serious crimes but those who, in the assessment of the officer, had "committed acts that constitute a chargeable criminal offense."[54]

In reality, as noted in an analysis by the American Immigration Lawyers Association, this priority would include all undocumented immigrants who had entered the country unlawfully. Even though most undocumented immigrants have never been *convicted* of unlawful entry, it is a chargeable offense.[55] If most Americans think of "bad hombres" as those who have committed violent crimes, this executive order actually makes such individuals less likely to be deported, since limited enforcement resources are now focused on a much broader subset of immigrants.

Since President Trump took office, there have been 43 percent more immigration-related arrests versus the same period in 2016.[56] While more immigrants with criminal records were taken into custody, the fastest-growing category of arrests since Trump's inauguration was for those facing no criminal charges. ICE arrested more than twenty-eight thousand "noncriminal immigration violators" in the first seven months of the Trump administration, a nearly threefold increase over the same period in 2016.

Even as the number of arrests have increased, though, the number of deportations in 2017 was actually slightly fewer than the 240,255 individuals deported in fiscal year 2016.[57] The decrease in deportations could be due to the fact that the number of illegal border crosses dropped dramatically after

President Trump was inaugurated, from around 31,000 apprehensions in January 2017 to 12,197 apprehensions in March 2017.[58] In addition, because of increasing arrests, there are more than six hundred thousand cases in the federal immigration court system awaiting a hearing.[59]

In one case that caught the attention of the country, Noe Carias, pastor of a thriving Assemblies of God congregation called Iglesia Pentecostes Cristo La Roca De Poder in Southern California, was arrested during a routine appointment with an immigration officer while his US-citizen wife waited for him in the lobby.[60] Originally from Guatemala, Pastor Noe is also the father of two US-citizen children, who were five and seven years old at the time of his arrest. Though he has no criminal record, he has three deportation orders from when he tried to enter the country unlawfully twenty-five years ago. Pastor Noe had been granted a stay of removal twice while his case for permanent legal status winds through the courts. However, under the new executive order, his stay of removal has been denied, and he is facing deportation. ICE has said that Pastor Carias is a repeat offender, but his only offense was these deportation orders from when he was under twenty-one years old.

Places that are normally considered safe from immigration enforcement, like hospitals and schools, have proven less safe under the Trump administration. Romulo Avelica-Gonzalez—a Mexican citizen who has lived in the United States for twenty-five years—was arrested by federal agents shortly after dropping his twelve-year-old daughter off at school. His other daughter was sitting in the car sobbing as she filmed the encounter in a video that subsequently went viral.[61] In August 2017, an immigration appeals court threw out his final deportation order, kicking the case back to the local immigration court.[62] When he was released from detention, his family went to church together.

In another case, Rosa Maria Hernandez, a ten-year-old girl with cerebral palsy, was headed to a Corpus Christi, Texas, hospital in an ambulance for an emergency gall-bladder surgery, accompanied by a US-citizen cousin. Customs and Border Protection agents followed the ambulance to the children's hospital and, after the surgery was completed, detained Rosa Maria, who had been in the country illegally since she was three months old. She was taken from to a facility for detained immigrant children in San Antonio and placed in deportation proceedings.[63]

Other incidents include six men picked up after leaving a church-operated hypothermia shelter at a local church, and a twenty-two-year-old mother of two in Kentucky who had been granted DACA and was active in her church.[64] These incidents raise ongoing fear that places traditionally considered safe, including schools, hospitals, and churches, are being targeted for immigration checks and potential deportations. While ICE has stated that "Determinations regarding the manner and location of arrests are made on a case-by-case basis, taking into consideration all aspects of the situation" and that "enforcement actions may occur at sensitive locations in limited circumstances, but will generally be avoided," there has been a chilling effect on immigrants going about their daily lives when incidents like this arise.[65] After speaking with a group of Christian and Missionary Alliance women at their retreat in the spring of 2017, I (Jenny) spoke with two women who told me that several Hispanic women were planning to attend the retreat but feared going on the highway and getting picked up by immigration agents so decided not to come. Those fears are widespread: a World Relief survey of regional denominational leaders in three evangelical denominations found that about a third were concerned that church attendance in immigrant communities was down because of rumors of changes to immigration enforcement. According to a Pew Research Center survey, half of Latino Christians worry that they or someone close to them will get deported, and more than 40 percent have "serious concerns" about their place in America under President Trump.[66]

Despite anecdotal concerns and a slight increase in detention of undocumented immigrants, it is still true that the vast majority of eleven million undocumented immigrants in the United States are not likely to be detained or deported, given limited resources for immigration enforcement. By the estimate of the conservative American Action Forum, to deport all immigrants present unlawfully in the United States would cost about $400 billion in new federal spending, an amount Congress is unlikely to appropriate. President Trump's first budget proposal sought a $2.7 billion increase in border and immigration interior enforcement spending, a significant increase but still far from what would be required to deport all undocumented immigrants.[67]

But spending significant amounts of taxpayer money on immigration enforcement is not a new idea. Since 1986, when President Reagan passed the Immigration Reform and Control Act, which legalized a little over two million immigrants, the federal government has spent nearly $187 billion on immigration enforcement.[68] The United States spends more on federal immigration enforcement than on all other federal criminal law-enforcement agencies combined. The budget for immigration enforcement in fiscal year 2012 was 24 percent higher than the combined spending on the FBI, Drug Enforcement Administration, Secret Service, US Marshals Service, and the Bureau of Alcohol, Tobacco, Firearms, and Explosives. Yet, from 1986 to 2012, the unauthorized population tripled in size to roughly eleven million, though the number has held roughly steady since that time.[69]

Immigration enforcement has also focused on deportations (formally known as removals) from the United States. In fiscal year 1990, there were 30,039 removals, which increased steadily to 188,467 removals in fiscal year 2000 and a record high 409,849 removals in fiscal year 2012. These removals include deportations of those caught at the border after an unlawful entry as well as removals of individuals inside the United States, including both those present unlawfully and those with legal status who have committed a deportable criminal offense. This is a tenfold increase in deportations in twenty years.[70] Since 2012, in the second term of the Obama administration and continuing in the first year of the Trump administration, the overall number of removals has declined, largely because fewer individuals are attempting to enter the country unlawfully and thus deportations of those apprehended at the border are down sharply, but the number of people deported is still many times higher than the historic norm throughout the past three decades.

The use of detention has also increased significantly in the United States. From fiscal year 1995 to fiscal year 2011, the total number of people detained by Immigration and Customs Enforcement (ICE) increased fivefold from 85,730 to 429,247. The purpose of immigrant detention is ostensibly to ensure appearances in administrative law proceedings, not to serve criminal law sentences, but there are more immigrant detainees than there are prisoners in the federal prisons systems.[71]

The growth in immigrant detention has meant that private facilities run by for-profit corporations have grown as well. Currently, 65 percent of immigrant detainees stay in private facilities run by companies that contract with the federal government.[72] Many of these immigrant detention facilities were initially built as federal prisons, which means the structures often impose more restrictions than necessary for immigrant detainees and subject immigrant detainees to treatment as common criminals, even when their only crime was a civil violation of immigration law.[73] In a 2009 report by the Department of Homeland Security, they note that immigration detention is not supposed to be a punishment like criminal incarceration; however, "their design, construction, staffing plans, and population management strategies are based largely upon the principles of command and control," often in "secure facilities with hardened perimeters in remote locations at considerable distances from counsel and/or their communities."[74]

An article in the *Architects Newspaper* indicates that "the shared typological features between prisons and detention centers flatten the important differences between criminal sentencing and migrant detention. Where the two intermingle, the distinction between legal and extralegal, private and federal, detention and incarceration is dangerously elusive."[75] Many immigrant rights groups have argued for alternatives to detention that are more closely tied to principles of population management, not criminal enforcement, and have urged ICE to make special exceptions for families, in particular to not detain young children in such facilities.

After several severe cases of mistreatment in immigrant detention—including the deaths in ICE custody of a Haitian pastor who was seeking asylum in the United States in 2004 and a French woman who overstayed her visa in 2011, both of whom were denied proper medical attention—the Department of Homeland Security created the Office of Detention Policy and Planning in 2011, charged with designing a new civil detention system.[76] The government also simultaneously announced intended reforms that would revise detention standards to improve medical and mental health services and access to legal and religious services.[77] Unfortunately, in 2017 the Trump administration announced plans to close the Office of Detention Policy and Planning and to more rapidly expand the use of detention, signing new jail contracts that do not meet basic regulatory standards, including the use of translation services and the prompt evaluation of medical care requests.[78]

The exponential increase in border security spending and immigrant detention over the past three decades runs counter to the narrative that we are not doing enough on border security or enforcement to stem illegal immigration. The question is not whether the nearly $200 billion the United States has already spent on immigration enforcement is enough to "secure" the border; rather, there are greater dynamics at play that drive immigration that often do not correspond with how much we spend on border security, including economic and security factors in the countries from which people emigrate and the availability of lawful immigration options. Immigration laws that are outdated and do not reflect our economy's need for workers or the desire for immigrants to be with their families will continue to drive unauthorized migration. Immigration enforcement and sensible, updated immigration laws work hand in hand to promote national security.

While most of the border security discussion has focused on the US-Mexico border, it is important to acknowledge that unlawful Mexican migration has slowed dramatically in recent years, with declines every year since the recession that began in 2007.[79] In fact, despite calls to further increase the size of the US Border Patrol, in April 2017 there were actually more Border Patrol agents stationed at the US-Mexico border (approximately 17,000)[80] than there were immigrants apprehended (11,125),[81] meaning the average agent did not apprehend a single person seeking to enter unlawfully in the whole month.

Asians now outpace Mexicans in terms of undocumented growth, with those from India, South Korea, and China representing the largest growth. Asian unauthorized immigration has increased 202 percent from 2000 to 2013, tripling the number of undocumented Asian immigrants, while the number of African undocumented immigrants doubled in the same time period.[82] Ironically, many of these immigrants are coming from countries where incomes are growing, but this means that immigrants are now able to afford to migrate to the United States, both legally and illegally.[83]

The focus on border enforcement has had some impact, but as the former Mexican ambassador to the United States Arturo Sarukhán said recently, a border wall is "a first century B.C. strategy to confront twenty-first century challenges."[84] Building a wall is not going to address the immigrants who come legally through ports of entry, nor is it an insurmountable barrier for those desperate enough to seek to enter between ports of entry.

While we must strive to secure the border through border patrols and effective technology, building a fence or wall along the border of the United States and Mexico should be measured carefully in its effectiveness to stop illegal immigration. Additional fences would separate populations that have long thrived on living between two communities. The United States has spent the past fifty years symbolically and literally tearing down walls between countries, whether it was the Berlin Wall or the Iron Curtain. To erect a wall now between two countries not at war would send a hostile message to our neighbors south of the border and to the rest of the world. Just as important, it would probably not work: past wall-building efforts have only redirected border crossings from large urban areas to the dangerous deserts of the American Southwest, without decreasing the overall number of illegal crossings.

THE WAY FORWARD

Since we wrote the first edition of this book, a lot has changed in terms of American politics and, particularly in the new presidential administration, in terms of particular immigration policies. What has not changed, in our view, is the broader need for a comprehensive reform of our immigration laws, addressing each of the elements of a system that is not functioning optimally, either for immigrants or for our national economic, security, and cultural interests.

While the Bible does not directly tell us which policy to support, general biblical principles and practical considerations can guide us as we call on our elected leaders to create a more just, compassionate immigration system.

Foremost is the biblical principle to welcome the foreigner among us. Biblical scholar Daniel Carroll R., in his book *Christians at the Border*, argues that our hospitality on a personal level should be carried through into our public policy:

> Hospitality functions primarily at the personal and familial level and on an informal basis. Its practice could suggest that a people have an openhandedness about them. A test of this possibility is to examine their laws and the structures of their society to ascertain whether the moral qualities of welcome and kindness toward the outsider find formal expression. Do they impact how the society actually operates?[85]

As we Christians carefully consider our role in the public sphere, the politics and jargon can sidetrack us from seeing that there may be more similarities than differences in the positions between "restrictionists" and those who want a broader, more open policy. For example, most people agree that the border must be secured and regulated so those with proper documents—but not those without—can continue to move back and forth legally. Most people who want a more open immigration policy still support secure, regulated borders, while those who prioritize border security rarely want to deport everyone here unlawfully, though they may be more cautious about the consequences of legalizing the undocumented. In understanding these dynamics, we can begin to forge a civil, thoughtful middle ground on immigration reform that will create a space in which our elected leaders can begin to fix the immigration system.

COMPREHENSIVE IMMIGRATION REFORM

For more than a decade now, comprehensive immigration reform has been the moderate basis for any immigration reform bill. The premise of *comprehensive* immigration reform is that to truly solve the issues around immigration, legislation could not focus on just one element (such as border security or legalization of the undocumented) but had to be comprehensive, addressing each element of the immigration issues simultaneously or at least in coordination. By addressing those already here (the undocumented), facilitating pathways for immigrants to come in the future, plus border security and enforcement, comprehensive immigration reform encompassed all major areas of immigration.

The reality that bipartisan bills following this general approach have failed to become law in 2006, 2007, and 2013 reveals that this is not an easy process politically. However, each of these facets are needed to fix our immigration system and prevent future flows of unauthorized migration. As National Association of Evangelicals president Leith Anderson notes, fixing just one element of a dysfunctional system is like choosing between repairing a flat tire, jumping a dead battery, or filling an empty gas tank: if you do not address them all, the vehicle still will not go.[86] Similarly, efforts to legalize the undocumented without ensuring adequate visas to meet labor demands going forward (as was the case in 1986) will not resolve the problem. Neither will addressing border security without addressing visa overstayers and the undocumented already in the country.

Whether in one bill or multiple bills, each element of the system needs to be reformed. Comprehensive immigration reform basically would make three fundamental changes to our existing immigration laws.

1. Improved enforcement policies consistent with humanitarian values. Though the US-Mexico border is much more secure than it was a decade ago, each year some people are still able to enter without inspection, which is not a good, long-term situation for a sovereign country. Others are able to enter on a temporary visa, but then stay permanently, and far fewer resources have been deployed to halt this process than to address the border. We believe it is appropriate to take measures to make it *harder* to immigrate illegally, whether by unlawful entry or by overstaying a valid visa. Furthermore, we can disincentivize unlawful migration by creating functional, enforceable systems to ensure that employers verify the work-authorization status of their employees, making it harder to work unlawfully.

In protecting the border, though, we also believe in treating all individuals with dignity and respect. Our borders with both Canada and Mexico, as well as our airports and seaports, need to be secure while still allowing the legal flow of goods, services, and people to happen daily. Border security measures must be carefully considered for their effectiveness in increasing our national security and not be used to overly penalize immigrants or simply provide us with a false sense of security. Unaccompanied children and those who are seeking asylum in particular should be given a fair screening to ensure they are not returned to a dangerous situation.

2. Reforms to our visa systems. If we are going to make it harder to immigrate *illegally*, we also must make it *easier* to immigrate legally—not without limit but to ensure that families can be reunited without excessive waits, that our economy can access the labor it needs to thrive, which includes both those considered highly skilled and those categorized as low skilled, and that our nation continues to be a place of refuge for some of the most vulnerable individuals fleeing persecution. If visa systems are adjusted so the supply of visas roughly matches the demand for labor and family reunification (which is difficult to achieve in a dynamic economy with a quota of visas set by statute, rather than a flexible annual determination), we provide viable options for both employers and employees to gain the benefits of migration and significantly reduce the motivation for migrants to cross borders illegally.

3. Earned legalization of undocumented immigrants. We should not try to fix a system without addressing what to do with eleven million undocumented people living in the shadows of our society. This current situation mocks the idea of the rule of law and clearly requires reform, but we also recognize that most of the undocumented are hard-working, contributing members of our society. Immigration reform thus must include an opportunity for immigrants who are already contributing to this country to get right with the law by regularizing their status after satisfying reasonable criteria, and over time to pursue an option to become Lawful Permanent Residents and eventually US citizens. A path to legal status would provide undocumented immigrants with a chance to admit their infraction against the law, pay an appropriate fine as a consequence, and proceed to become fully restored, integrated members of our society if they wish to stay here. This would not be amnesty, because immigrants would have to earn their right to stay in the United States.

To be truly comprehensive, the US immigration system must be couched in a larger, overall strategy to tackle the root causes of poverty in immigrant-sending countries. Immigration is affected by trade pacts, economic development policies, financial flows, intra- and international conflicts, and climate change. While economic development aid and strategies will not necessarily stop immigration to the United States, the function of a legal US immigration system must work in close tandem with trade, development, and environmental and diplomatic policies so the system can work and reflect the values that have made America an economically stable, welcoming country.

Past efforts at comprehensive reform often have been labeled as *amnesty*, which has been a significant factor in the demise of Comprehensive Immigration Reform in recent years. The root of the word *amnesty* comes from the Greek word *amnestia*, "forgetfulness." Webster's dictionary defines amnesty as "the act of an authority (as a government) by which pardon is granted to a large group of individuals."[87] To the contrary, none of the comprehensive bills proposed in Congress over the past several years would provide a path to legal status that would forget or pardon the infraction of unlawful presence in the United States.

To allow an undocumented person who is working and obeying the law the option to pursue legal status—including getting to the back of the line, paying back taxes, paying a penalty fee for having violated the law as well as immigration filing fees, and undergoing medical and criminal background checks—is not a blanket pardon. Instead, the undocumented persons would have to admit their infractions against the law, pay the penalties of those infractions, and earn their right to be in the United States. These would be penalties appropriate to the offenses committed. Deporting individuals who have worked hard and paid taxes, and who often have children here, is unworkable as well as detrimental to the family unit.

In my (Jenny's) work on Capitol Hill, numerous congressional staffers have told me of the inundation of calls whenever any legislation arises that would provide legal status for undocumented immigrants in the country. When the debate is at its peak, one can walk into a congressional office in Washington, DC, and hear the phone ringing off the hook. Staffers fielding the calls speak of how angry many of the callers often are. One Hispanic staffer in a Republican office said he was personally barraged with hate messages because his boss was considering support of the bill. The staffer of a freshman Democrat, who had worked with the congressman for years at the state level but was first exposed to immigration on the national level when his boss took office, said he was amazed at how intense and vitriolic the calls were on this specific issue. He told me that many of the calls bordered on complete bigotry.

Politics is the art of compromise, and Republicans and Democrats must work together in a spirit of give-and-take in order to pass immigration reform. The debate in Congress over the past few years has shown that our leaders will need to hear from those who support a more comprehensive approach in order to balance out and hopefully surpass the voices of those in opposition.

COALITION BUILDING

Bringing unlikely allies together for common cause often gets the attention of our elected officials and provides them political cover to do the right thing. It's often said that you can identify a politician in a crowded room; they're usually the ones sticking one of their fingers in the air, testing the direction of the wind. Our job as constituents is to change the way the wind is blowing.

The Evangelical Immigration Table was launched in 2012 as a response to the divisiveness around immigration. As was discussed earlier in the book, a broad coalition of evangelical groups spanning denominational, ethnic, and political differences provided common ground to push our legislators to action based on common principles.[88] Such coalitions shift paradigms and allow individuals to understand that there is more in common than separates different groups of faith—in particular, how we are to treat immigrants among us. During the Evangelical Immigration Table's three-year anniversary in June 2015, we celebrated the fact that nearly seventeen hundred local and national leaders have signed its statement of principles. In addition, local and national organizers had held hundreds of pastors' meetings, prayer events, press conferences, and fly-ins to meet with legislators in Washington. The Table's documentary film, *The Stranger*, has screened more than three thousand times in forty-six states and Washington, DC, since its June 2014 premiere. The Evangelical

Immigration Table has not only shifted evangelical thinking on immigration but has been a powerful force in the halls of Congress and across the country in mobilizing evangelical support for immigration reform.

Comprehensive immigration reform actually brings together groups that would have a hard time agreeing on much else. Organized labor and big business are now roughly on the same page in supporting a comprehensive approach. Catholics, evangelicals, Mormons, mainline Protestants, and just about every other religious group, for all their significant theological differences, tend to agree on the need for immigration reform.

One particular group that has emerged as key to speaking into the immigration debate in recent years is called "Bibles, Badges and Business." This trifecta is composed of those who are often considered the core constituencies of the Republican Party, including business, faith, and law-enforcement communities. Through events in key cities across the country and Capitol Hill events in Washington, DC, these different constituencies have come together to send a forceful message that it's in our moral, public safety, and economic interests to support comprehensive immigration reform.

Within this unique coalition, pastors have met with their members of Congress, joined by local businesspersons who could speak to the economic benefits of immigrants, and county sheriffs, and together they have testified in support of immigration reform as a matter of public safety. In 2012, I was able to meet with a senator from Idaho with a few Idaho dairymen and pastors. It was a powerful meeting that centered on the moral and business interests of the state, and the senator couldn't ignore the diversity of voices around the table—all asking for his courage and support.

POLITICAL OPPORTUNITY

Opportunities where both political parties can come away with a win are rare in politics. In an increasingly polarized world in which compromise is seen as defeat and any nuance of working with the other side is seen as playing with the enemy, compromise is increasingly seen as a dirty word. Senator John McCain observed in the summer of 2017 that senators traditionally accepted the necessity of compromise in order to make incremental progress on solving America's problems and defend her from her adversaries. Incremental progress, compromises that each side criticize but also accept, just plain muddling through to chip away at problems and keep our enemies from doing their worst isn't glamorous or exciting. It doesn't feel like a political triumph. But it's usually the most we can expect from our system of government.[89]

In a functional political system, there are rare windows of opportunity in which both sides compromise and come away with a win. With immigration, core constituents of each party are pretty much in agreement when it comes to immigration policy. The Republican base of business interests and security hawks have weighed in with the GOP to continue robust immigration levels to ensure a steady, robust labor force, while the Democratic base of labor and immigrant rights has continued the fight as a matter of justice. This means that immigration is not necessarily a policy problem to be solved; it's a political problem. Economically, socially, and politically there could be wins for both the Democratic and Republican parties because the immigration debate reveals an unusual facet of this contentious public debate: the core of commonality is greater than the edges of difference. Leaders from both parties are sensitive to the issue of immigration, and a consensus has emerged that this is the right thing to do for the economy, security, and moral fiber of our country. If the restrictionists and liberals are willing to compromise, this marks a huge opening for a deal.

MESSAGING AND FRAMING IMMIGRATION

In order to continue to fight for the rights and well-being of immigrants, we must create a narrative around the positive benefits of immigration. In a survey of swing voters across the country, voters were asked what first came to mind when they thought about immigrants. While the initial response of many was that immigrants are coming to the United States for a better life, many of these voters then immediately said, "They don't speak English," and "They don't pay taxes." This seeming ambivalence, argues clinical psychologist Drew Westen, means that

Because voters have multiple and often competing associations to "immigrants," successful messaging on immigration reform requires deactivating or uncoupling associations that make people hostile toward immigration and instead linking "immigrant" to networks associated with positive values and emotions.[90]

Voters connect words, images, values, and emotions, and these connections, otherwise known as "networks of association," influence receptiveness to political messages more strongly than facts and rational arguments. Dr. Westen observes that "voters respond less to facts, figures and rational arguments than to the emotions associations created."[91]

The term *immigrant* is a loaded word in which individuals often have a strong positive or a strong negative response. This means that fact-based arguments are important because they clear the clutter of misinformation by correcting myths and offering a foundation to form an opinion. However, values-based arguments are more effective because they often appeal to the conscience of the voter: it's more about the heart than the head. We as sinful human beings have a natural tendency to exclude others perceived to be different from us. But while every voter has certain values, beliefs, and prejudices when they make electoral decisions, unconscious prejudices often do not reflect conscious values that effective messaging can bring to the fore.[92] Avoiding euphemistic language about immigrants and avoiding laboring over facts and data may be helpful to connect to a broader audience on the benefits of immigration. Effective immigration advocacy, especially for those in the church, will also acknowledge people's fears, concerns, and misgivings while speaking to people's values and beliefs, which are a greater common denominator.

A CHRISTIAN VOICE IN THE PUBLIC SQUARE

Conversations about immigration are difficult, and as such they tend to happen on our social media feeds, instead of in the church. The Bible's many teachings on this topic are rarely central to the discussion. With this deficit of discipleship, we have too often lost our mooring as a community and tied our response to critical societal issues on our basest, most natural instincts rather than on Scripture. While connecting with others on an emotional level is essential to shifting individuals toward positive opinions about immigrants, we also need to be truth bearers at a time when we are increasing faced with "fake news." We are inundated with media articles, social media posts, and people's opinions that often leave us confused as to what is correct information. It is especially important to continue to test our information, to follow factual news reporting, and to ensure our opinions are based on correct, not false, information. At the least, we should not spread false information about others made in the image of God.

Engaging politically means we have to move away from the false dichotomy of the secular versus sacred. God's dominion is over everything, including government, and we are called to push back the darkness in every corner of our society. Peter Wehner of the Ethics and Public Policy Center aptly writes,

> Politics is certainly not a place for the pursuit of utopia and moral perfection; rather, at its best, it is about achieving the best approximation of the public good, about protecting human dignity and advancing, even imperfectly, a more just social order. That is why Christians shouldn't exile themselves from politics.[93]

Having a consistent political witness means promoting a consistent prolife ethic, recognizing that all human life, at any stage of development and despite any qualifier, has dignity because each person is made in the image of God (Gen 1:27). Reconciliation and justice go hand in hand because relationships are foundational to overcoming our fears and prejudice, but true justice is achieved when unjust laws are dismantled and new laws created that recognize the inherent dignity and worth of every human life. Martin Luther King Jr. once said, "The church must be reminded that it is not the master or the servant of the state, but rather the conscience of the state."[94]

We live in the aftermath of the greatest political event in history, when Jesus rose from the dead and turned upside down the ideas of power, privilege, goodness, and grace. If Jesus left all of his power and privilege to enter into our brokenness, we have a responsibility to enter into the brokenness of others. As the church, we need to be stewards not just of our resources and time but of our voice and influence to shape the common good, to speak up with the marginalized people with whom God calls us into community. The church has the privilege of continuing Jesus' redemptive and restorative work. "Being political," in this sense, is a mere act of pursuing justice and *shalom* that encompasses the fullness of individual flourishing. Advocacy has to become a core part of our discipleship because Jesus was the ultimate advocate on behalf of humanity.

In reading this book, you have taken the first step toward understanding the reality of the current situation and considering the biblical commands to welcome the stranger. However, with understanding must come action. Grassroots movements mobilized by truth and faith can bear tremendous fruit in advancing just and compassionate policies. While the issue can easily become mired in sound bites, Christians have an obligation to speak to our elected leaders in Congress to ensure that immigrants are not dehumanized and our Christian principles are taken into consideration when forming legislation. We need to call on our leaders to look at the issue with compassion, not fear. Having our government leaders develop workable solutions will help us move beyond the rhetoric to see transformed, whole communities where immigrants are recognized as vital and integrated members of our churches and communities. Immigration indeed has shaped the American church landscape, and chapter nine will explore the church's role in the debate.

NINE

IMMIGRATION AND THE CHURCH TODAY

Eighty-six percent of the immigrant population in North America are likely to either be Christians or become Christians. That's far above the national average. . . . The immigrant population actually presents the greatest hope for Christian renewal in North America. . . . We shouldn't see this as something that threatens us. We should see this a wonderful opportunity.

TIMOTHY TENNENT, PRESIDENT AND
PROFESSOR OF WORLD CHRISTIANITY,
ASBURY THEOLOGICAL SEMINARY

BY 2002, ATTENDANCE AT THE CHURCH OF THE NAZARENE in Iowa City, Iowa, was dwindling even as the community around the church was becoming home to more and more immigrants. Some of the remaining, aging congregants, says Pastor Michael Lynch, were "frightened by the prospect of losing their religious and cultural identity in an increasingly diverse neighborhood."[1]

Under their pastor's leadership, though, the local church gradually went from seeing the increasing number of immigrants in the neighborhood surrounding their church as a threat to recognizing them as a blessing. They began reaching out, selling off the church's parsonage in order to have enough financial space to hire a parish nurse who could help address medical needs both of elderly, white congregants and of the generally younger but often uninsured immigrants in their community. But while the Hispanic immigrants served by the parish nurse were grateful and occasionally visited a church service, few returned.

"Eventually," says Michael, "we realized that the real issue was whether we were willing to embrace the unique cultural expressions of those who were different from our traditional congregation. When we finally relinquished full control of our space in 2007 and learned the art of sharing, a Hispanic church was born!"[2]

The following year, they opened up their space to a Congolese pastor, whose congregation now includes worshipers from at least a half-dozen African nations. Their building is now bustling with activity—and with prayer and praise to God in a variety of languages—throughout the week. "Our African congregation sometimes holds services and events that last all night," Michael says. "The Hispanic congregation enjoys prayer meetings early in the morning as well as multiple service times."[3] Releasing control of their facilities has not always been easy, but Pastor Michael sees God's hand in it and credits immigrant brothers and sisters with saving the once-struggling church.

While immigrants breathe new life into existing congregation, they also are planting new churches. The new congregation planted by Pastor Francisco, whose story we shared in chapter two, is one example: less than two years after launching, the Spanish-speaking congregation now reaches about sixty people each week, and most are new believers. In recent years new church plants have sprouted in various locations throughout the suburban Chicago community where I (Matthew) live, including new congregations led by immigrants from Burma, the Democratic Republic of Congo, Ethiopia, Honduras, Iran, Mexico, Nepal, Nigeria, South Korea, and Sudan, among others.

Even at larger, established churches, immigrants are often fueling much of the growth. Calvary Church, in Naperville, Illinois, was already among the largest Assemblies of God congregations in the country when, in 2004, their senior pastor wanted to help the congregation reach the growing Latino population surrounding the church. Alberto López came on board to help launch Calvary Español, which has grown from a small group of less than twenty people to two services reaching eight hundred adults (and many more children) from seventeen countries each week. Alberto's own background has uniquely equipped him to identify with and effectively serve the immigrants within the congregation he leads, many of whom are undocumented. Alberto was brought to the United States illegally as a teenager but obtained legal status as a result of legislation signed by President Reagan in 1986. He was able to graduate from Bethel University in Minnesota, served for eight years in the US Navy, naturalized as a US citizen, and was ordained as a pastor.

Immigrants and their US-born children are not just impacting individual congregations: they are also dramatically changing the overall demographics of Christianity in the United States. In 2015, the Pew Research Center released an extensive study on religion in the United States.[4] Many of the headlines covering the report summarized its findings as "Christianity Faces Sharp Decline,"[5] noting that overall Christian affiliation declined from 78.4 percent of US adults to 70.6 percent in the span of just seven years.[6] The trend does not look likely to be easily reversed, either, as the younger generations are far less likely to be affiliated with a Christian tradition than older generations.

Some evangelical leaders dug into the data to note that the decline was fueled almost entirely by declines in Roman Catholic and Mainline Protestant populations, while the number and share of American evangelicals had basically been flat.

Deeper still into the survey findings, though, the total number of *white* evangelical adults had declined significantly, while the number of ethnic minority evangelicals had risen sharply, from 19 percent of all evangelicals to 24 percent just over the course of less than a decade, with the greatest positive change among Latino evangelicals, the total number of whom increased by nearly 65 percent in just seven years.[7] Much of that growth was fueled by immigrants and their children, who now account for 16 percent of all evangelical Christians, a 33 percent increase over their share in 2007. Similarly, while the number of white Catholics and mainline Protestants declined overall, the number of ethnic minorities in each tradition increased, with Latinos now accounting for more than one-third of all American Catholics.[8]

The Center for the Study of Global Christianity finds that the fastest growth among Americans evangelicals has been among independent (non-denominational) immigrant congregations.[9] But various denominations are also diversifying and growing as they reach out to immigrant communities.

For example, the Christian and Missionary Alliance—which was founded in 1881 when Canadian-born pastor A. B. Simpson resigned from the pulpit of his Presbyterian congregation in New York City because his congregation frowned on his outreach to poor Italian immigrants—now estimates that about 40 percent of its more than two thousand US congregations are composed primarily of immigrants and their children.[10]

Perhaps reflecting the reality that many immigrants come from regions where Pentecostalism is the most common expression of Protestant Christianity, Pentecostal congregations in the United States have also grown dramatically among immigrant communities. As of 2016, 42 percent of the roughly 3.2 million people in the United States affiliated with the Assemblies of God—the largest Pentecostal denomination in the country and also among the fastest growing—were nonwhite, most of whom are Latino.[11] Even among the majority of the denomination's US adherents who are white, a growing share are immigrants, particularly from the former Soviet Union and Romania.[12]

The largest evangelical denomination in the United States, the Southern Baptist Convention, historically has been an almost entirely white denomination, and its membership and baptism numbers have been declining in recent years.[13] However, as the denomination has publicly repented of racism within the denomination's history, denounced "alt-right white supremacy," and embraced both refugees and immigrants more broadly, the denomination now includes nearly eleven thousand congregations where the majority is nonwhite, accounting for more than one-fifth of all Southern Baptist Convention congregations.[14] More than half of new church plants in recent years are majority nonwhite, and non-English-speaking congregations account for the highest baptism rates within the denomination.[15]

Reflecting on these changing dynamics throughout American Christianity, Wesley Granberg-Michaelson observes, "While millennials are walking out the front door of US congregations, immigrant Christian communities are appearing right around the corner, and sometimes knocking at the back door. And they may hold the key to vitality for American Christianity."[16]

ONE FAMILY

While no one celebrates that fewer white, native-born US citizens are identifying as followers of Jesus than in generations past, we can and should rejoice in what God is doing among immigrants and among ethnic minority communities to revitalize the church in the United States. However, because most local congregations still are largely divided by ethnicity (it's still mostly true, as Dr. Martin Luther King Jr. observed in 1960, that "eleven o'clock on Sunday morning is one of the most segregated hours" of the week),[17] many white Christians simply do not realize the transformation that is occurring in the US church overall as a result of immigration. Zooming out to see the big picture is a first step.

As the American church becomes less white, though, it also requires a shift in posture from those in the majority culture. Believers who are US-born cannot rejoice with the growth that immigration has fueled if we are not concurrently willing to suffer with those who suffer (1 Cor 12:26), as many of our brothers and sisters in Christ face realities of separated families, labor exploitation, and fear of deportation as they interact with the US immigration system. These problems are not an external social reality; they are *our* issues, directly affecting the body we are a part of. Immigrants are not only people outside of the church who need to be *reached* for Jesus (though some fit that description), they are also an integral part of the church itself. As National Association of Evangelicals president Leith Anderson has said, "They are us."[18]

Author and professor Soong-Chan Rah has written several insightful books exploring this shift. In *The Next Evangelicalism*, Rah explores the ways that, as American evangelicalism becomes increasingly diverse, it cannot be wed to a single, Western cultural expression.[19] But that cultural shift will not happen—or at least will lag far behind the changing demographics—so long as the top leadership of multiethnic churches, denominations, and Christian institutions remain almost entirely white, US-born men.

It's not enough, Rah argues, for the church to move from hostility toward immigrants to hospitality, welcoming them in as *guests*. Ultimately, we must live into the biblical vision of the church as the family of God, with brothers and sisters of different backgrounds living within the same household under one Father. "Hospitality only takes us so far," he writes. "How do we move from being simply hospitable to one another to actually becoming a family? . . . You will have kimchi on the table for that one meal when you entertain me as a guest. But what if you have to stock kimchi in your refrigerator every single day?"[20]

"Welcoming the stranger" is an important first step for local churches, but we must then move from seeing *strangers* to recognizing *neighbors* we are called to love as ourselves (Lk 10:27) and ultimately—when these strangers turn out to be (or become) fellow believers—*family*.

That process roughly parallels the integration journey that all immigrants pass through as they become a part of the United States, a process that does not require them to give up their distinct culture, food, or language, but which does invite them to become American (and by doing so to slightly redefine what *American* means).[21] America has been enriched throughout its history by the contributions of various immigrant groups who have added to what it means to be American, while embracing the core Constitutional values that define who we are as a nation. But integration—whether in the church context or within a nation—must be a two-way street: it requires both that newcomers desire to become and that the receiving community will recognize them as an essential, coequal part of the new whole.

As new immigrants are integrated into churches within the United States, it also will have ramifications for our corporate worship. Sandra Van Opstal, who has led ethnically diverse groups in worship for the Urbana Students Missions Conference and in various other contexts, notes the vision in Revelation of people "from every nation, tribe, people and language, standing before the throne and before the Lamb" in worship (Rev 7:9). "Our faith calls us not only to dream and hope for this day," she writes, but to point "to the time that is coming by modeling and living into it today."[22] To do so, she argues, churches in the majority culture must recognize that worship styles that are "normal" to them are culturally influenced just like those of every other culture.[23] "Our music and our worship must be multicultural," says theologian Justo González, "not simply because our society is multicultural, but because the future from which God is calling us is multicultural. We must be multicultural, not just so that those from other cultures may feel at home among us, but also so that we may feel at home in God's future."[24]

Finally, an increasingly diverse US church also is revolutionizing how we live out God's mission. Missiologists increasingly are focused on how God is at work through the migration of people in multiple directions to draw people to himself.

On one level, as those who do not yet know Christ arrive in a country like the United States where many are Christ-followers, local churches have an unprecedented opportunity to "make disciples of all nations" (Mt 28:19) right in our own communities—if we have the eyes to see them. Tragically, though many evangelical churches have prayed for decades for those who are unreached (having never heard the gospel) in other parts of the world, many seem to have missed what we believe is part of God's answer to those prayers: less than half of American evangelicals surveyed told LifeWay Research in 2015 that the arrival of immigrants to their communities presented "an opportunity to introduce them to Jesus," while most (including about 70 percent of white evangelicals) believed the arrival of immigrants presented a "threat" or "burden" of some sort.[25] J. D. Payne, a pastor at the Church at Brook Hills, in Alabama, argues that "something is missionally malignant whenever we are willing to make great sacrifices to travel the world to reach a people group but are not willing to walk across the street."[26]

Immigrants, both those who arrive in the United States with a vibrant Christian faith and those who embrace Jesus after migrating, are on the forefront of reaching both fellow immigrants with the gospel and at ministering crossculturally. Some of the most influential Christian leaders today came to the United States as immigrants, including evangelist Luis Palau (born in Argentina), pastor and author Erwin McManus (El Salvador), pastor and author Eugene Cho (South Korea), Compassion International president and CEO Jimmy Mellado (El Salvador), and World Relief CEO Tim Breene (Northern Ireland).

Some immigrants to the United States ultimately decide to serve as missionaries outside of the United States, whether returning (either short- or long-term) to their country of origin or serving crossculturally in a third country. Pastor Paco Amador, whose congregation, New Life Church, is within a largely Mexican neighborhood of Chicago, notes that short-term missions teams from his church that travel to Mexico are usually able to stay in the homes of relatives of members of their church, many of whom are not yet believers, starting with a level of relational trust that most crosscultural missionaries would require years to develop.

Indeed, immigrant congregations, though they generally have far fewer financial resources than longer-established congregations composed mostly of US citizens, are already (in the words of a 2017 *Christianity Today* cover story) "reshaping American missions," sponsoring partner churches and poverty alleviation efforts in the countries of origins of those immigrants.[27] "Poor Christians around the world never got the memo that you needed money to do missions," observes Juan Martinez of Fuller Theological Seminary.[28]

If the church in the United States welcomes "strangers" well—and "they" truly become a fully integrated part of "us," brothers and sisters within the same family, without paternalism—the implications for God's global mission are phenomenal.

CHURCHES SERVING IMMIGRANTS

For many local churches, the first step in welcoming and building relationships with immigrants will be by serving them, meeting a tangible need.

Leaders at Elmbrook Church, a large nondenominational church in suburban Milwaukee, noticed some years ago that there was a growing immigrant community in Waukesha, a community just down the street from their campus. They tasked staff member Paco Cojon, a recent immigrant from Guatemala, with building relational bridges to the Latino immigrant community and discerning what the "gaps" in services were.

As Paco spent roughly a year building relationships, one theme he heard continually was that there was nowhere in the community immigrants could turn to for affordable, reputable immigration legal advice. Several people he met lamented spending thousands of dollars on attorneys—or, more often, "consultants" or *notarios*[29] without authorization to be practicing law—in efforts to rectify legal status situations or be reunited to family members abroad, without results.

Following Paco's recommendations and in consultation with World Relief, the leadership at Elmbrook set out to launch a legal services ministry called James Place, operating out of a storefront in downtown Waukesha. Paco and three others from the church (one other staff person and a retired missionary couple who would work on a volunteer basis) took part in an intensive, forty-hour course on immigration law that generally serves as the first step for nonattorneys affiliated with a church or other nonprofit organization to be accredited by the US Department of Justice as authorized practitioners of immigration law.

Several months later, after completing the training and a subsequent test, "shadowing" under an existing immigration legal program, and applying for approval with the US Department of Justice, James Places was recognized and its trained staff and volunteers accredited to begin operation. They began consulting with those in need of legal guidance and assisting qualifying individuals to file applications for naturalization, legal status, or sponsoring a relative abroad to migrate to the United States.

Five years after the legal services ministry launched, James Place's immigration legal services ministry has served hundreds of individuals from more than forty countries of origin. They've recently launched a second location, in a neighborhood on the south side of Milwaukee where many refugees have been resettled in recent years. Paco's role has evolved to leading Elmbrook en Español, the church's first Spanish-language service, drawing community members who in many cases first encountered the church through its legal services outreach.

In contrast to Elmbrook, one of the largest churches in Wisconsin, the Bridge Community Church in Logansport, Indiana, was down to about twenty people attending each week when Zach Szmara took over as pastor of the historic but struggling congregation. When Zach heard from leaders at his denomination, The Wesleyan Church, about the opportunity for churches to be trained and authorized to provide immigrant legal services, Zach recognized it as an opportunity for his congregation to serve the surrounding community, which did not have a single immigration attorney but included many immigrants who worked at a nearby pork-processing plant.

After undergoing a similar training and application process as Elmbrook, the Bridge was approved by the US Department of Justice in February 2014, and word spread quickly among the immigrant community in Logansport and even beyond. "This week alone we've done ten consultations, and we have six scheduled for next Monday," he told me (Matthew) less than a year after launching.[30] Less than four years after launching, they have served roughly fifteen hundred immigrants from more than seventy countries.

One day, a young man came into the church and asked Zach, "Are you the people who help immigrants?" He had driven more than twenty miles to seek help.

"I was humbled that our small church had such a reputation," reflects Zach. "Yet I was convicted that it was only very recently that I could answer 'yes' to the burning question of this young immigrant who came to me."[31]

Like Elmbrook, the Bridge has also drawn in new people to its Sunday services through the legal services that Pastor Zach provides on Mondays and Wednesdays. The church is now back up to about one hundred people at its Sunday services each week, which are now offered bilingually in Spanish and English, about half English-speaking native-born US citizens and half Spanish-speaking folks from seven countries. And Zach has been able to help more than a dozen other congregations within his denomination launch similar "Immigrant Connection" ministries throughout the country.

In addition to supporting about fifty local churches nationwide with ongoing technical support to provide low-cost immigration legal services, World Relief also provides these services directly through a network of local offices. Local churches, though, are still a central part of their ministry.

In Aurora, Illinois, where I live, for example, my World Relief colleagues with training in immigration law partner with various local churches to offer informational sessions, particularly after changes to immigration policy are announced, such as the 2012 institution and the 2017 rescission of the Deferred Action for Childhood Arrivals program, as many within our community seek accurate, up-to-date information on how these changes might affect them and their loved ones.

The city of Aurora, where more than one-quarter of the city's approximately two hundred thousand residents are foreign-born, also presents a great example of other ways that local churches are serving immigrant communities. One of the most significant needs is for English language instruction: according to the US Census, more than thirty thousand adults in Aurora report that they speak English less than very well.[32] Many churches have stepped into that gap, expanding opportunities for English language instruction. For example, Iglesia San Pablo, a Lutheran congregation in Aurora's largely Latino east side, has served as many as two hundred students at a time with Tuesday and Thursday evening classes. Each is taught by a volunteer who comes from either Iglesia San Pablo or from other churches in the community.

Across town, in a part of Aurora where many refugees have been resettled in recent years, joining a large Spanish-speaking population, Wesley United Methodist Church hosts four different-level English classes four mornings per week, including a specialized class for those who never had the opportunity to learn to read or write in a native language, which often makes acquiring English literacy all the more challenging. The classroom teachers are certified and are employees of World Relief, but the church helps by providing both facilities and classroom aides. While adults are learning, children too young to be in school are learning as well in special early childhood education programs.

Youth, both immigrants and first-generation American, are a focus of a number of local churches. Community Christian Church, for example, began a mentoring and tutoring program in Aurora through its Community 4:12 outreach ministry before it launched a campus of its multisite church in the community. The programs connect church-based volunteers with students (most are the children of Mexican immigrants) at local elementary schools during and after school and on Saturdays. Community 4:12's programs provide academic and social support for students beyond what is available in the classroom environment. But they also provide a relational connection for volunteers, most of whom attend Community Christian campuses in wealthier, less ethnically diverse parts of Chicagoland, to be introduced in a personal way to the structural injustices that impact many low-income immigrant families. When the church launched a bilingual campus in Aurora several years ago, some of the first families to join had children and youth who had already been served by the church.

A number of local churches in Aurora have also been an active part of welcoming newly arrived refugees, who have fled persecution in their countries of origin and then are invited by the federal government to rebuild their lives in communities throughout the United States, including in Aurora. World Relief is one of nine organizations authorized by the State Department to resettle refugees and integrate them into new communities. Our goal is to work through the church with volunteers to ensure that the newcomers have a furnished apartment ready when they arrive, that they're met at the airport, and then that they have the relational support to adjust to a new culture, learn a new language, find a job, and quickly move to being able to cover their own basic living expenses.

Village Bible Church in Aurora is one of many local churches that are part of that process—and which, in welcoming refugees, have seen their own congregations transformed. When World Relief reached out to pastor Travis Fleming to ask if he would consider opening up their church for English classes, he was eager to partner. "It has been pretty clear to me that God is working in the world and bringing the nations to us," Travis says. "I wanted to be able to reach the world by reaching the neighborhood."

Village Bible has not only provided space for learning English; its congregation has also gone out of its way to welcome refugees into their church. Today, more than sixty individuals who came as refugees, representing six countries in Africa, two in Asia, and one in the Middle East, worship at the church; most were believers in their country of origin, but some have made the decision to follow Jesus since arriving in the United States, and a few attend on a regular basis even though they're not yet believers.

Johnson Ferry Baptist Church in Marietta, Georgia, has similarly embraced refugees. After having ministered to Syrian refugees through ministry partnerships in the Middle East, the church leadership wanted to do what they could to help Syrian refugees coming into the United States, beginning late in 2015. Partnering with World Relief Atlanta, the church equipped ministry teams composed of hundreds of volunteers that have welcomed eight different Syrian families (all Muslims) and two Iranian families (both Christian), helping to identify housing, find jobs, and most importantly ensure that the families knew they had friends as they rebuilt their lives in a new country. The church views such ministry as a biblical mandate: "Peoples previously inaccessible are now not only within our reach; they are our neighbors," notes senior pastor Bryant Wright.[33]

THE CHURCH BEYOND THE UNITED STATES

Migration is not just impacting the US church in significant ways, it is also impacting the global church for the furtherance of the kingdom of God. Understanding the role of the US church as a small part of a global church response is important because many churches around the world are leaning into the opportunity to serve their immigrant neighbors, even at significant risk and cost to themselves.

One pastor in Jordan said he was praying for revival for the Middle East for years. As his church has welcomed Syrian refugees into their midst and tangibly met their physical needs, this pastor realized God was answering his prayer for revival through the refugee crisis. Many of these Syrian refugees had entered the church and met Christians for the first time. As the Jordanian Christian community was loving their refugee neighbors, God was answering their prayer for revival.

In Berlin, Germany, Trinity Lutheran Church has opened its doors to immigrants and is sheltering many within its building, hoping to shield them from deportation.[34] As a church with a few hundred members a few years ago, they grew to over a thousand members now, mostly through Iranian and Afghan immigrants who had converted to Christianity, and held baptisms for over two hundred new believers at one time. Similarly, a pastor in northern Germany says, "Starting an outreach to the refugees was the best thing that happened in this church over the last 50 years and is the most exciting part of our church life right now."[35] Missiologist Sam George, who interviewed various refugees and church leaders in several countries in Europe in 2016, concluded that "one of the ways in which God is reviving Christianity in Europe is through refugees."[36]

In Canada, a unique private sponsorship program allows churches or other community groups to identify specific refugees abroad and then supplement the number of refugees that the government sponsors by providing financial support and volunteers. I (Matthew) recently met a half-dozen local churches in central Alberta that were in the process of bringing several Syrian refugee families to their community. While grateful for the amazing church partners we get to work with through World Relief in the United States, I could not help but observe that the general sentiment toward immigrants among Canadian evangelical churches is qualitatively different, with far fewer fears on the part of Christians and a remarkable amount of sacrifice of both money and time. One small Church of the Nazarene congregation of 120 people had raised more than $60,000 to help with the effort.

Many churches in Africa and the Middle East are also ministering to and welcoming refugees and other immigrants and seeing tremendous spiritual fruit as a result. Indeed, as the center of gravity for the evangelical church has shifted to the Global South, the global church is often leading the response without fear and exclusion of immigrants arriving to their doorstep.

A PROPHETIC VOICE

As local churches seek to minister to immigrants, sooner or later they generally run into the public policy challenges that so often limit immigrants from fully flourishing. As they do so, many have leveraged their influence to speak up for just policies they believe are consistent with biblical principles.

When Johnson Ferry Baptist Church first reached out to World Relief to inquire about welcoming Syrian refugees, refugees were not necessarily a particularly controversial political issue. Several months later when their first family was set to arrive, though, refugee issues were at the center of a media firestorm. A photo of a three-year-old boy, Alan Kurdi, face down on a Turkish beach after a failed attempt to reach safety in Europe, had suddenly focused the world's attention on the horrors of the Syrian civil war and the massive, desperate migration it had fueled. Then, after a terrorist attack in Paris sparked rumors (eventually discredited) that Syrian refugees had been responsible, the governors of more than thirty US states declared their opposition to Syrian refugees being resettled in their states.

Among those states was Georgia, where Governor Nathan Deal went beyond most other governors' opposition by signing an executive order to deny state services to Syrian refugees. Despite the controversy, though, the "Good Neighbor Team" at Johnson Ferry still wanted to welcome the families. Welcoming those who had fled persecution had never been a political statement for those at Johnson Ferry: "For us," says Bryan Hanson, an assistant pastor at the church, "it's a biblical issue."[37]

Indeed, senior pastor Bryant Wright has challenged the large congregation on multiple occasions to think about the arrival of refugees and other immigrants first and foremost as a biblical issue, keeping their focus on "what Christ teaches us to do" rather than on what they were "hearing on talk radio, or on the news or from political candidates."[38] Pastor Wright, a past president of the Southern Baptist Convention, brought the same message when interviewed on *60 Minutes* and on *Fox News*.[39]

While making clear that his biblical convictions were driving his views on public policy, rather than the other way around, Pastor Wright also advocated against policies he believed were short-sighted and could harm vulnerable refugees like those his church had embraced. He sent a letter to Governor Deal (for whom, he noted, he had voted) respectfully urging him to reconsider his executive order barring Syrian refugees from accessing state services. (The governor did not respond immediately, but ultimately abandoned the effort when the state's attorney general determined it was not lawful).[40]

About a year later, when President Trump enacted an executive order placing an indefinite moratorium on the resettlement of Syrian refugees and a four-month halt to refugee resettlement from all countries, Wright joined hundreds of other evangelical pastors from every state in the country—along with prominent national leaders, including Tim and Kathy Keller, Bill and Lynne Hybels, Max Lucado, Ann Voskamp, and Ed Stetzer—in a public letter published in the *Washington Post*, urging the president to reconsider his refugee policy.[41]

By leveraging their influence to urge those in positions of governmental authority to take into account God's instruction and particularly his concern for those who are vulnerable as they set public policies, these leaders are following in the prophetic tradition of biblical heroes such as Moses, Nehemiah, Esther, Isaiah, Jeremiah, Amos, and John the Baptist.

In the decade since we wrote the first edition of this book, we've seen a sea change in terms of evangelical advocacy for immigrants. At the time, while the US bishops of the Roman Catholic Church and many mainline Protestant denominations (including the United Methodist Church, the Evangelical Lutheran Church of America, the Episcopal Church, and the Presbyterian Church USA) were actively advocating for immigration reform, evangelical Christians, whether at the level of national leaders, local pastors, or laypeople, were largely silent on the issue, with a few notable exceptions.

The most notable exception was Hispanic evangelicals, who lamented—sometimes publicly—the general absence of white evangelicals in speaking up for the plight of immigrants. In an open letter, Reverend Luis Cortes, the president of Esperanza, called on "our evangelical brothers and sisters to denounce unChristian policy reform and to stand for reform that reflects the values expressed in our history as followers of Christ," specifically urging fellow evangelical leaders "to speak out on behalf of comprehensive immigration reform and support us in this struggle for a Christlike face to this problem."[42] Samuel Rodriguez of the National Hispanic Christian Leadership Conference asked in 2006,

Why they [white evangelical leaders] came down in favor exclusively of enforcement without any mention of the compassionate side? So down the road, when the white evangelical community calls us and says, "We want to partner with you on marriage. We want to partner on family issues," my first question will be: "Where were you when 12 million of our brothers and sisters were about to be deported and 12 million families disenfranchised?"[43]

In early 2009, when the first edition of this book was published, we highlighted the few prominent non-Hispanic evangelicals who had spoken out (some explicitly, some a bit more indirectly) on the need for immigration policy reforms, including National Association of Evangelicals president Leith Anderson (who wrote the foreword to this book, though the NAE had not yet taken a formal position on this issue), David Neff (at the time, editor-in-chief of *Christianity Today*), Dr. Richard Land (who led the Southern Baptist Convention's Ethics and Religious Liberty Commission), Sojourners president Jim Wallis, Prison Fellowship founder Chuck Colson, and Christian Community Development Association founder John Perkins. In some ways, though, these early evangelical advocates proved the exception to the general rule: most evangelical Christian institutions and national leaders had no position on the topic (at least that they were ready to state publicly), and it did not seem to be on the radar of many local pastors.

That has changed rather remarkably in the past decade, a shift we thank God for, while acknowledging that there is still much work to do. In October 2009, after several working sessions of discussion and exploration of biblical teaching and immigration policy, the board of the National Association of Evangelicals—which includes more than one hundred leaders from forty evangelical denominations and many individual congregations, colleges, seminaries, and parachurch ministries—passed a strong resolution urging evangelical Christians to love their immigrant neighbors in tangible ways, and the government to pursue just immigration reforms, including establishing an equitable legalization process for undocumented immigrants.[44]

In 2011, the Southern Baptist Convention gathered in Phoenix, Arizona, and enacted a similar resolution, "On Immigration and the Gospel," including language urging policymakers to enact "a just and compassionate path to legal status, with appropriate restitutionary measures, for those undocumented immigrants already living in our country."[45] Other denominations have weighed in publicly as well, some simply publicly affirming the National Association of Evangelicals' resolution, and others, such as the Evangelical Covenant Church and the Free Methodist Church, have subsequently released their own denominational positions urging immigration reform.[46]

In 2012, several of these national Christian entities came together to launch the Evangelical Immigration Table, uniting around an "Evangelical Statement of Principles for Immigration Reform," including a call for an earned legalization process for undocumented immigrants, that was affirmed by scores of evangelical denominational executives, pastors of influential churches throughout the country, presidents of Christian colleges, universities, and seminaries, and executives of parachurch ministries including Focus on the Family, Prison Fellowship, InterVarsity Christian Fellowship, and the Navigators.

Though the Statement of Principles was not a call for any specific bill or policy, it helped create the political space for policy change to happen in a polarized political environment. The greatest force behind the Obama administration's decision to announce the Deferred Action for Childhood Arrivals policy on June 15, 2012, was the courageous advocacy of "Dreamers" themselves. But "both political sides and the media said that the statement from such a unified and influential group of evangelicals," just three days before the White House's announcement, had "made an 'enormous' difference and created the 'space' and 'support' for political leaders" to act.[47]

That advocacy continued as a bipartisan, comprehensive immigration reform bill worked its way through the Senate in 2013, with the Evangelical Immigration Table even running a series of radio ads on Christian radio stations throughout the country urging a biblically informed, compassionate public policy solution. Republican senator Lindsey Graham of South Carolina, a cosponsor of the bill from a conservative state, said evangelical support had been a "game-changer" and "incredibly positive" in the bill's success.[48] Unfortunately, though, there was not enough pressure to persuade the US House of Representatives to pass a companion bill.

Despite the sea change in evangelical leaders' public views toward immigration policy in the past decade, evangelicals in the pews tend to have more mixed views. On a policy level, a LifeWay Research poll in 2015 found that 68 percent of evangelical Christians would support a bill (such as the Senate's 2013 effort) that combines increased border security and an earned pathway to citizenship for undocumented immigrants.[49] However, on a values level, the same poll found that most evangelicals think of immigrants as a "threat" or a "burden" of some sort, and that (by their own admission) they were significantly more likely to take their cues on immigration primarily from the media than from the Bible.[50]

To address these realities, the Evangelical Immigration Table has focused its efforts in recent years on providing discipleship tools to encourage distinctively biblical thinking about immigration issues. Among the most popular has been their "I Was a Stranger" Challenge, a simple Bible-reading guide, available either as a bookmark to place in a Bible or in digital form through YouVersion's Bible app, highlighting forty Scripture passages related to the topic of immigration. They also prepared a website with resources for pastors preparing to preach on the topic (videos of sermons, sample sermon outlines, relevant illustrations and quotations) and a forty-minute documentary, *The Stranger*, that profiles three Christian immigrant families' stories.

The Evangelical Immigration Table has also worked with dozens of local leaders in various communities to call together local pastors, speak in local churches, and help encourage advocacy. Alan Cross, who for about a decade served as the pastor of a Southern Baptist church in Montgomery, Alabama, is now one of these local "church mobilizers." In 2011, Alan says, he basically thought of immigration as a simple issue: if people were here illegally, they should be deported.[51] But when the Alabama legislature passed a tough immigration bill that drew protests from immigrant activists, he wanted to understand the protestors' perspective, particularly because he was deeply acquainted with the history of civil rights protests in Montgomery and of the complacency of most white evangelicals at the time.[52] When he took the time to listen to protesters and then to study the issue more carefully, he learned that many of his presumptions about US immigration law were inaccurate. He began to see the missional opportunity for the church in the United States as it welcomed immigrants. And he was also startled by the religious liberty implications of his state's bill, which could arguably have made some elements of Christian ministry to undocumented immigrants unlawful. (Most of the bill was eventually struck down by the US Supreme Court.) Alan became a strong advocate for immigration reform, so passionate that he eventually resigned his role as a senior pastor to work with churches throughout the Southeastern United States to encourage distinctly biblical perspectives on immigration.

Brenda Kirk serves in a similar role. Brenda served for many years in a public policy role with the Cherokee Nation, then later used her educational background in nutrition as the executive director of the Houston Food Bank. Her own family's history of forced displacement along the Trail of Tears in the mid-nineteenth century and her concern for those facing food scarcity, along with her Christian faith, have long given her a particular empathy for those forced to migrate today, whether because of conflict or hunger. Today, she dedicates part of her time to working with churches throughout Texas, Oklahoma, and Arkansas to encourage churches to advocate for immigrants.

These on-the-ground efforts are making a difference, as local churches throughout the country are increasingly speaking up. Among the most prominent and earliest churches to do so was Willow Creek Community Church, a multisite church with its largest campus in South Barrington, Illinois. As has been the case in many other local churches who have followed a similar path to advocacy, Willow Creek did not begin their engagement with immigrants as a political issue: they launched a Spanish-language service a number of years ago in an effort to reach the growing immigrant population in their community, and they also noticed more Latino immigrants among those being served by the church's Care Center, it's local outreach ministry. They did all they could to help meet the spiritual and physical needs of the immigrants who came to them, but they eventually concluded (after consulting with various attorneys) that they could not resolve the legal status problems that, for many, were at the root of many other challenges. That would require a change in governmental policy.

Before ever engaging in public policy advocacy, though, the church leadership—led by senior pastor Bill Hybels, in consultation with the church's elders—charted a deliberate process of helping to make sure the members of the church were viewing the topic from an informed, biblical perspective. That process included focusing one of the church's regular midweek services on the topic of immigration, developing a series of classes on the topic, highlighting the issue in the church's weekend services, and engaging with the leadership of Casa de Luz, the church's Spanish-language community.

With that foundation, most in the church concluded that public policies needed to change. "I hate politics," Bill confessed to his congregation in 2014, but he determined that he needed to engage in advocacy on the issue of immigration when he concluded that "only the government can solve this at this point."[53] He's leveraged his influence by visiting Washington, DC, to meet with members of Congress, speaking at an Evangelical Immigration Table press conference, authoring op-eds for local newspapers, and also challenging other pastors throughout the nation to engage the issue, leading with the Scriptures. Many others at Willow have followed his lead, making phone calls to their legislators, writing letters, and using social media to urge them to act.

To have a church as prominent as Willow Creek advocating so boldly for immigrants, including the many within their congregation, is a significant shift from a decade ago, and it's being duplicated at local churches large and small across the country. We are grateful for churches that have pressed into this complex issue, welcoming immigrants into their congregations and their communities, doing the hard work of pursuing church unity despite cultural and linguistic differences, serving sacrificially, and advocating for just policies.

Still, though, there is much more to do. We turn in the final chapter to specific ways that both churches and individual Christ-followers can respond holistically to the challenges and opportunities of immigration.

TEN

A CHRISTIAN RESPONSE TO THE IMMIGRATION DILEMMA

> Do not merely listen to the word, and so deceive yourselves. Do what it says.
>
> **JAMES 1:22**

THE GOAL OF THIS BOOK has been to bring others along on the journey that we have both embarked on personally, of understanding the immigration issue, reflecting on how our Christian faith should inform our opinions, and analyzing the various ways that the church and the US government have responded and are responding. We hope, though, that your own interaction with this important issue will not stop at understanding, information, and analysis: we believe that this thinking ought to inspire appropriate and prayerful action.

Fortunately, there are many ways to respond: some big and some small, but all with the potential for significance. We can begin by bringing immigrants and the immigration situation before God in prayer. From there, we move to action: we can serve our immigrant neighbors through volunteering, allowing us to know them personally and learn from them, as well as financially supporting ministries that facilitate such service. As we better understand the immigration issue through interaction with immigrant neighbors, we can help to educate others in our churches and communities. From there, we can advocate together on behalf of immigrants and refugees. Finally, if we wish to address the root issues behind migration, we will need to begin to address poverty, unemployment, conflict, and environmental degradation in other parts of the world. This final chapter should help guide you to take the first steps toward a Christian response to the immigration issue.

We have argued that Scripture makes repeated and clear calls for us to take special concern for the stranger, to love them as ourselves, and to welcome them as if serving Jesus himself. God commands us to obey, which is primary if we are to truly follow Christ. "There is no other road to faith or discipleship," Dietrich Bonhoeffer writes, except "obedience to the call of Jesus."[1] We dare not dismiss God's instructions to us, but rather should move from reflection to prayerful action. Serving and loving immigrants can take on different expressions, and each are vitally important in the broader Christian witness.

PRAYER

The biblical mandate to care for the foreign-born requires action, but as Christians we dare not attempt that action without prayer. "Prayer," Henri Nouwen writes, "must be our first concern [because] as disciples, we find not some but all of our strength, hope, courage, and confidence in God. . . . Prayer challenges us to be fully aware of the world in which we live and to present it with all its needs and pains to God. It is this compassionate prayer that calls for compassionate action."[2]

As we begin to know our immigrant neighbors, and to share in what they have suffered through the trauma of displacement and perhaps the challenges of their present situations, we can present that suffering to God in prayer, asking him, our heavenly Father, to provide, protect, and guide them. Immigrants often feel insecure about the future or have fears about the potential of deportation and the separation of families. Asking God to watch over our immigrant neighbors and express his care and concern for them in ways only he can is crucial.

We can also pray for our elected officials and for policies that honor God and reflect his justice. None of us, individually, has the authority to change immigration laws, and though we believe we are called to advocacy, the challenge of addressing structural issues can be daunting and frustrating. In prayer, we are reminded "that we can do nothing at all, but that God can do everything through us."[3] We are commanded specifically to pray for our political leaders. Paul exhorts Timothy "that petitions, prayers, intercession and thanksgiving be made for all people," but particularly "for kings and all those in authority" (1 Tim 2:1-2). Whether or not we voted for and support a particular president, senator, or representative, we have the responsibility to pray for them, asking God to grant them wisdom as they make important decisions that affect millions of families. Many of our elected officials are people of faith themselves and are in positions of making incredibly difficult decisions that affect many people. They need godly wisdom, guidance, and counsel to make the best decisions for the common good.

We can also pray beyond the needs of the immigrants in our own communities and pray for the communities that immigrants come from, many of which face desperate poverty and conflict. Scott Arbeiter, president of World Relief, says that prayer is an act of rebellion where we "refuse to accept what might seem unchangeable in our own hearts or the world around us." Prayer is an act of building faith and also professing to God that we cannot do things on our own, an acknowledgement that in some of the most difficult places on earth, where strongholds and bondage exist, and evil flourishes, that God is the only one able to break the chains of injustice and set the captives free. We acknowledge God's sovereignty over kings, dictators, presidents, and prime ministers, and intercede for peace and flourishing in the midst of situations that compel immigrants to cross borders. As we pray, God expands our love for these neighbors we do not know personally. Prayer is not just listening and talking to God but having ourselves be formed to be more like him through such intimate communication. Nouwen writes,

> In the intimacy of prayer, God reveals himself to us as the God who loves all members of the human family just as personally and uniquely as he loves us. Therefore, a growing intimacy with God deepens our sense of responsibility for others. It evokes in us an always increasing desire to bring the whole world with all its suffering and pains

around the divine fire in our heart and to share the revitalizing heat with all who want to come.[4]

This love for others born in times of prayer is not a substitute for action but the fuel that sustains it. As we seek to live God's commands to care for the immigrant and refugee, we ought to begin with prayer and, without ceasing to pray, move into action.

In the past several years we have seen a movement of prayer for immigrants and for immigration reform grow within the United States. In 2014, local churches in various parts of the country hosted prayer gatherings to pray for immigration reform. The Evangelical Immigration Table began a monthly email of prayer guidance, which has continued to encourage people to pray. Late in 2017, various Christian groups organized prayer rallies for Dreamers. The Christian Community Development Association encouraged its members to write prayers for Dreamers, which were then delivered to members of Congress along with prayers written by Dreamers themselves, whose fate in the country was hanging in the balance as Congress debated legislation. As we pray, we can join God in action.

KNOWING AND LEARNING FROM OUR IMMIGRANT NEIGHBORS

Building relationships is foundational to engagement on any issue. We cannot speak about, represent, or take actions "on behalf" of a community without actually knowing those in the community. True justice is not just meeting the material or physical needs of individuals but restoring right relationships. We can begin to act by being involved in our own communities. Almost anywhere you might live within the United States, you now probably have immigrant neighbors within your community, though you might not (yet) interact with them regularly. Our society is structured in such a way that you can live in the same community as thousands of immigrants and never know any of their names, with barriers of language, culture, race, and economic status dividing us. Only when we begin to personally know our immigrant neighbors can we begin to contemplate the biblical mandate to love them. Psychologist Mary Pipher explains that as we begin to interact personally with these individuals we had considered aliens, "that person stops being a stereotype and becomes a complex human being like oneself."[5] The immigration policy debate then becomes less about statistics and more about human faces, about laws that have dramatic effects on families we know.

One of the best ways to begin to know the immigrants in our communities is to serve them. Volunteering can lead to beautifully reciprocal relationships: we can help a recently arrived immigrant to adjust to a new society, while they can help us to understand their culture as well as our own through a new lens.

I (Matthew) have been blessed in many ways through my friendships with my immigrant neighbors, most of whom were born in Mexico. I often feel that I receive much more than I gain. I am able to help my neighbors understand a piece of mail or help their kids with their homework—but I am more than compensated when I am invited over for a delicious Mexican meal, not to mention the enjoyment of the company of good friends. In the process I have also gained new insights into the immigrant experience, the countries and cultures that my neighbors have come from, and even into my own culture, which I can see a bit differently from an outsider's perspective.

I (Jenny) also live in a neighborhood of many immigrants from Southeast Asia. I've enjoyed getting to know them as our kids play together and the parents easily strike up conversation with each other. There is a sense of ownership among us as we look out for each other's kids and spend hours conversing on the streets of our neighborhoods. We often leave our garages open so kids can play with each other's toys. There is a real sense of community outside the walls of our homes.

There is mutuality in getting to know our immigrant neighbors. The challenges and difficulties they have learning a new language, understanding a new culture, and building a new home life are not easy, but their resilience and tenacity teach us much about the human spirit.

SERVING

A natural way to begin such reciprocal relationships is through volunteering. World Relief and many other organizations have a constant need for volunteers to help with English as a Second Language classes or tutoring, to care for the children of those in ESL classes, to assist newcomers in navigating the complexities of life in an entirely new culture, and above all just to serve as a friend. Good Neighbor Teams are the model through which World Relief partners refugees with a team of volunteers from a local church. These volunteers go through training in which they learn about cultural differences, understand the needs of refugees when they first arrive, and coordinate help with other volunteers. These Good Neighbor Teams are critical to help refugees transition to their new homes.

I (Jenny) was part of a group of church volunteers helping a local Syrian refugee family resettle to Baltimore. A mother, father, and four children had lived in Jordan for a few years but were resettled in the United States because the mother and two children had a life-threatening medical disorder. When they first arrived, they lived in a transition home provided by a local church. The mother and two children had a few emergency visits to the hospital where another church volunteer who was a physician stayed with them as their advocate, making sure they understood what was going on. They also have regular English tutors come to their house, and several other volunteers who speak Arabic come and help explain their bills. Every time I visit them, they receive other visitors. Their four kids are generous in sharing their toys with my son David, and the father often runs into their home to bring out a bike for David to play with. When I invited the family to my church's Christmas party, they couldn't make it because several other churches had signed up to take the family to their own Christmas parties. They were in busy holiday mode! While this particular Syrian family is surrounded by many volunteers, though, many other refugees and other immigrants are never welcomed into an American home.

Serving immigrants can take a variety of forms, but how to serve can be answered by asking the simple question, What can I do to love my neighbor well and help them flourish? Anticipating their needs by spending time with them or just simply asking them if there's anything you can do to help is what's often needed for an immigrant neighbor (or anyone) to feel welcomed and loved.

GIVING

As with any ministry, those working with immigrants are often limited by financial resources. Many organizations and ministries that serve the poor are prohibited from serving undocumented immigrants, even if they would like to, because their funding sources—especially governmental grants—specifically state that funds should not be used to provide services to undocumented individuals. As a result, undocumented immigrants often have many serious needs but few places to turn for assistance.

Churches, though, and the individuals who make up the church, are not bound by limitations about who they can serve. Churches and Christian ministries could be providing the practical assistance and social services that the government often cannot provide—if individual Christians were to invest the resources to serve these subclasses of our communities. Churches and organizations partnering with the church have a unique opportunity to provide these services in Christ's name. While some would rather not go near the controversial issue, we believe that, like the lepers of the New Testament era, undocumented immigrants are a stigmatized population God calls us to love and serve. We can do so, as the church, when we as individuals are willing to back up such work with a portion of the money God has entrusted to us.

World Relief's ministries with immigrants in the United States (including refugees, undocumented immigrants, foreign-born victims of human trafficking, and others) are sustained by a number of local churches as well as individuals who give sacrificially. We have even seen children find creative ways to raise funds to welcome immigrants into their communities.

EDUCATING OUR CHURCHES AND COMMUNITIES

Churches will more readily heed the biblical call to care for immigrants—regardless of legal status—only with a substantial increase of education and awareness among individual followers of Christ. As we educate ourselves—through personal interaction with immigrants and refugees and through our own investigation into the issue—we can then help educate others in our churches and communities.[6]

Perhaps the greatest need in terms of education is having Christians develop a biblical worldview on immigration. An individual's understanding of what the Bible teaches on immigration and biblical values of hospitality and love for our neighbor are foundational to Christian engagement. A 2015 Lifeway Research study found that the media has more influence on the average evangelical's thinking on immigration than the Bible or the local church.[7] Even still, 68 percent of evangelicals said they would value hearing a sermon that taught how biblical principles and examples can be applied to immigration.[8] A pastor preaching from the pulpit about the theology and missiology of migration will help deepen the church's understanding of the issue.

In addition to preaching from the pulpit, churches could focus a Sunday school class or small group discussion on the issue of immigration from a Christian perspective; we have provided discussion questions in appendix one to help you use this book as a guide. We have also developed a six-week curriculum to complement this book for use in a small group study.[9] You could also invite a speaker from an organization serving immigrants and refugees, or from an immigrant church in your community, to speak at a service or Sunday school class. Further, we can encourage immigrant involvement and leadership at all levels of our own local churches.

One of the simplest ways to help educate others is by speaking up whenever we hear comments that we know to be untrue about immigrants. Nineteenth-century Baptist preacher Charles Spurgeon remarked, "A lie travels round the world while Truth is putting on her boots."[10] The truth never catches up unless we have the courage to gently and lovingly challenge false or prejudiced statements. When we hear or receive by email a derogatory joke or rumor, we can remind our sisters and brothers in Christ that immigrants, whatever their legal status, are human beings made in the image of God. Correcting misinformation and sharing stories of immigrants themselves are ways to generate light in the immigration debate.

ADVOCACY

While getting to know immigrants and refugees through service is an important start, compassion and justice run deeper than individual acts of service. Advocacy is crucial because transformation should be about the whole of society by meeting immediate needs but also changing the societal structures that inhibit human flourishing. Advocacy can be defined as amplifying the voices of those who are marginalized, standing in the gap to present the realities of injustice around the world to those in positions of influence who can help change the situation.

Scripture specifically calls us to this task. Proverbs 31:8 commands us: "Speak up for those who cannot speak for themselves." It is a biblical imperative to advocate for justice, and most immigrants who are not naturalized citizens cannot vote and are often discounted by our elected officials as a result. Despite their lack of legal status, many immigrants are choosing to bravely share their stories and be a critical part of the American political system. Their stories and voices are helping share the immigration debate. The Dreamers in particular have led the movement, creating various organizations to share their own stories.

We see repeatedly throughout the Old and New Testaments that God's concern for the poor and for justice are central to his character. God loves justice, but he also *does* justice. From Moses and David to Isaiah and Esther, we see ordinary human beings being used by God to bring his vision of justice to the broken world around them, whether through changes in policy, social structure, or attitudes toward certain groups of people.

We also realize that Jesus was the ultimate advocate. We advocate because Jesus advocates for us daily, acting as our intercessor. Jesus' life and ministry here on earth carried forward God's idea of justice from the Old Testament to the New Testament. He continually advocates on our behalf before God and covers over all our sins (Heb 7:23-25; Rom 8:1). Following Jesus' example, we should be intercessors on behalf of those who are the "least of these" (Mt 25:40). Christians must recover a spirit of social action and participate in God's great agenda, since we are called to advocate on behalf of humanity, particularly the poor and oppressed, knowing that God in the end has victory through Jesus' death on the cross.

Churches traditionally have been reluctant to engage in politics, and understandably so. There are certain principles, however, that can guide us as we engage our elected leaders to craft policies and legislation that reflect our values. In "For the Health of the Nation: An Evangelical Call to Civic Responsibility," the National Association of Evangelicals outlines the basis for evangelical engagement in government, stating,

> We engage in public life because God created our first parents in his image and gave them dominion over the earth (Gen. 1:27-28) . . . [and also] because Jesus is Lord over every area of life. Through him all things were created (Col. 1:16-17) and by him all things will be brought to fullness (Rom. 8:19-21). . . . [Thus,] as Christian citizens, we believe it is our calling to help government live up to its divine mandate to render justice (Rom. 13:1-7; 1 Pet. 2:13-17). . . . Our goal in civic engagement is to bless our neighbors by making good laws.[11]

Advocacy allows God's people to seek the fullness of the kingdom of God, keeping in mind that Christ has the final victory, so we can see God working out his purposes for the whole of his kingdom.

During the summer of 2012, the Evangelical Immigration Table had an advocacy fly-in day where over two hundred pastors came to meet with their legislators. Some of them were meeting their legislators for the first time, and everyone had a common message: pass immigration reform that will provide relief for our immigrant neighbors. In the fall of 2016, World Relief partnered with the ONE Campaign and Save the Children to deliver over 124,000 hand-written and typed postcards to senior advisers to President Obama with personal messages from people who wanted the United States to remain a welcoming country for refugees.

Students at colleges and universities are organizing and leading the way in support of refugees and immigrants as well. Students at John Brown University in Arkansas gathered signatures of 450 students in support of refugees and created a Facebook group to strategize more about opportunities to influence their campus. When their governor came to visit the school, they made sure he could not miss the broad support for refugees among the student body by wearing T-shirts that read "Students for Refugees." They discussed the issue of refugees with the governor and continue to activate their campus in support of refugees.

The following are a few ideas that you and your church, school, or community group can engage in to be a voice for immigrants:

- Find out the position of your local congressperson and senator on immigration issues. You can often find statements, congressional votes, and other general information about their position on the issue on their website.

- Write a letter to your local congressperson stating how you feel about the immigration issue, or call them, highlighting the biblical basis for welcoming the stranger or highlighting some personal relationships you have with immigrants in your community. Appendix five will help you identify and contact your elected representatives.

- Schedule a meeting with your congressperson or a staff person to discuss your position on immigration issues. You can bring others who share a similar viewpoint as yours, including pastors and local business leaders, to the meeting and give their office some relevant information. Make sure you follow up on the meeting with a thank-you email or letter!

- Write an editorial in your local newspaper about your personal experience with immigrants and how you feel they positively affect the United States.

- Identify church leaders in your community who support immigration reform and provide forums for them to speak about their position. Adding their name to the Evangelical Statement of Principles for Immigration Reform—and then even writing a local newspaper editorial or organizing a press conference to share why they have done so—is a good place to start.

- Have an "Immigrant Sunday" at your church: organize a panel discussion at your church on a Sunday and get members of your church to write letters, postcards, or email messages to your local elected officials. You can arrange a panel of speakers and ask people to pray and fast on behalf of immigrants in your local community.

- Stay up-to-date on advocacy issues relating to immigrants and refugees by signing up for World Relief's advocacy updates. To join, simply email: advocacy@wr.org.

The Evangelical Immigration Table often sponsors initiatives throughout the year, including advocacy days on the Hill, a monthly prayer partners' newsletter, and advocacy campaigns that you can plug into.

Jesus asked in the Lord's Prayer that his Father's will be done "on earth as it is in heaven" (Mt 6:10). Injustice plagues us here on earth, but by seeking justice for those who do not have it, we are furthering God's kingdom.

Advocacy is vital, both practically and theologically, to the church's calling to bring about justice, speak out for truth, defend the poor and oppressed, and work toward the redemption of the whole of creation.

ADDRESSING THE ROOT ISSUES

As we begin to know our neighbors and hear their stories, we will realize that immigration is often the consequence of difficult and sometimes unlivable conditions in other parts of the world. As long as the average salary of a worker in Mexico and Central America is a small fraction of what a worker in the United States earns, economic migration will continue, whatever border enforcement techniques we employ. As long as wars and persecution threaten the lives of people, there will be the constant flow of people seeking refuge in the United States and other safe havens. As long as environmental degradation threatens people's ways of life, there will be movement to other communities and then, often, to countries such as the United States. People on all sides of the immigration debate—those who want to welcome more immigrants and those who believe we should seal the borders entirely—can agree that we should address these root issues that motivate migration.

We strongly believe, guided by Scripture, that immigrants should be welcomed into our society and treated with dignity and respect. Nevertheless, migration is a difficult, often traumatic event, and people ought to be able to live in dignity in their home countries without being forced to migrate. Many Americans are only vaguely aware of the situations of poverty, conflict, and environmental degradation that threaten the lives of billions of human beings around the world, particularly in Latin America, Africa, the Middle East, and Asia. In a globalizing society, though, we no longer have the excuse of ignorance to keep us from action.

As our new immigrant neighbors tell us about their lives before they came to the United States, we are challenged to think about how our lifestyles—our consumption habits, our use of energy, our country's foreign policies—might affect how others live. Few young men eager to be married, for example, stop to think about where the diamond in their fiancée's engagement ring came from, and if it helped to fund a civil war in West Africa. Most would rather pay $1 less for a bag of coffee than spend the additional money for the assurance that the coffee farmer was paid a reasonable wage. Few of us seriously consider the environmental impact on the poorest nations as we hop into our cars instead of using public transportation, walking, or riding a bicycle. And not many take the time to investigate how US trade policy, foreign aid policy, or support of a particular foreign political leader will affect individuals in other countries, and even fewer take the time to let their elected representatives know what they think.

We can also support churches in these countries who are responding valiantly—often with few financial resources—to these situations of poverty, marginalization, conflict, and environmental degradation that so often compel people to emigrate. At World Relief, we train and equip local churches in some of the poorest countries of the world to work together in what we call a "Church Empowerment Zone" to serve the most vulnerable in their community, recognizing the resources that God has already entrusted to them. Churches and individual believers in the United States make this ministry possible through their financial support, which in turn minimizes the necessity of migration.

Most of us think of ourselves as small, inconsequential actors on the global scene. Indeed, our individual lifestyle choices and small financial contributions to ministries abroad, when viewed in isolation, may not, in themselves, make a significant difference. Collectively, though, the potential for positive change is enormous. We can help to improve the situations in the countries most immigrants come from if we examine and adjust our own lifestyles, advocate for just policies, and support churches and ministries doing important work abroad to support economic development, improve public health, protect and provide for children, increase education, and empower women.

CONCLUSION

This book has been the fruit of a journey for both of us as we have befriended immigrants in our respective neighborhoods, worked on immigration policy issues, and began to learn how God would have us respond. This book was born out of our own questions; we do not claim to have stumbled on the right biblical answers to every question, but we think that we have learned a lot along the journey. Above all, we believe Scripture makes clear that immigrants are to be specifically included in the call to love our neighbors as ourselves. This love must be personal, and that means getting to know our immigrant neighbors.

When we begin to love our immigrant neighbors on a personal level, we will want to advocate for just, merciful, and loving immigration policies as well. As we begin to converse and better understand the difficulties these neighbors left in their home countries, we will also find our hearts stretching to other neighbors in need—the people still living in those places devastated by economic difficulties, war, and environmental disaster—and we might, as the church, begin to do more to bring God's love into those situations as well.

Loving our immigrant neighbors well is not a temporary thing but requires long-term commitment that comes from a heart committed to God's flourishing in the world.

Our prayer as we have embarked on this book has been that the church, particularly the evangelical arm of the church we both strongly identify with, will take up this charge and even lead other faith communities to love our new immigrant neighbors. We believe that obedience to Christ means committing ourselves, not just as a few individuals but united as God's people, to serving the sojourners among us and advocating alongside them, even (perhaps especially) when that is counterculture in our polarized political environment. That movement starts with individuals—with you—and grows through you to entire congregations and denominations until the church here in North America and worldwide is known by its love for the immigrant, whether they are undocumented, a refugee, or any other category of foreigner residing among us. In the process, we have already begun to discover that God has provided his church in this country with a unique privilege to be blessed by our brothers and sisters from other parts of the globe.

ACKNOWLEDGMENTS

'M SO GRATEFUL TO EVERYONE who has helped make this book possible, in both its original form and now in this second edition. More than a decade ago Al Hsu and everyone at InterVarsity Press took a chance on a book on a controversial topic written by two mostly unknown, heretofore unpublished individuals in their mid-twenties. I was thankful then and am thankful now for the invitation to thoroughly update the book, as well as for all the support with editing, refining, and marketing the book.

My colleagues at World Relief DuPage/Aurora, past and present, have taught me most of what I know about immigration law and have also been extraordinarily supportive of this book project since the first edition. World Relief colleagues around the United States and throughout the world do the inspiring work of empowering churches to welcome strangers day after day. The folks at our home office in Baltimore and in our Strategic Engagement Division have been exceptionally supportive of Jenny and me both in writing and in making the space for us to focus our time on the themes of this book. And *Welcoming the Stranger* would probably still be an idea lingering in my mind were it not for Catherine Norquist, whose initial encouragement and assistance have been priceless.

Colleagues and friends within the Evangelical Immigration Table, past and present, have given me hope for the evangelical church when news reports make me want to give up on the label.

A few professors of mine from my time at Wheaton College—particularly Lindy Scott, Sandra Joireman, Jeff Greenberg, Paul Robinson, and Amy Black—have helped me to integrate my Christian faith with the issues facing our world, including the topic of this book. They have taught me much about what it is to seek God's justice, to share with God's people both in joy and suffering, and to charitably engage even with those I disagree with.

My neighbors—whose names are mostly changed to protect their privacy—have contributed in countless ways to this text, both at Parkside in

Glen Ellyn and now in Aurora. Their stories make up the heart of this book. Their courage, perseverance, and faith inspire me.

Thanks also to the local church communities that have supported and grounded me over the past decade: Church of the Resurrection, Community Christian Church, and Iglesia San Pablo.

Three Central American families—the Muñoz Montero family of Pavas, San José, Costa Rica; the Quiñónez Matute family of Ocotal, Nicaragua; and particularly the Pérez Gutiérrez family of Granada, Nicaragua—have taught me a great deal about authentic Christian hospitality by welcoming and embracing me as a member of their own families when I was a stranger in their respective lands. *Gracias por todo su amor para conmigo; nos vemos pronto, si Dios quiere.*

My parents, Dave and Jane Soerens, have nurtured my faith, challenged me to apply it to the difficult situations in our world, and modeled Christlike hospitality and compassion.

Finally, to my wife, Diana, and children, Zipporah, Zephaniah, and Zoë: of all that has happened in the decade since the first edition of this book, nothing could possibly be more important or precious to me than you. I love you!

MATTHEW SOERENS, Aurora, Illinois, January 2018

THANK YOU TO INTERVARSITY PRESS for investing in this book and believing in Matthew and me, as young authors, to be true to our faith, to fact, and to our ministry in writing this book. I also want to thank Matthew for birthing the idea for this book in the first place—I'm continually amazed by your relentless pursuit of love and justice for immigrants, the way you live out your faith with your family, your intellect and rigor, and your utter humility. I'm grateful to count you as a brother, friend, and colleague in this journey together.

Being a part of the World Relief team over the past decade of my life has been formational for me in my faith. I have been educated, inspired, and challenged to follow Jesus more faithfully through my ongoing work for this organization. To the staff of our World Relief offices, both in the United States and international, thank you for being so faithful to the Lord and being the best examples of Christ-followers in the world. To the leadership team at World Relief—Tim, Scott, Emily, James, Kevin, Gil, Kathleen, Rene, and Eeva—thanks for being so exceptional in your respective positions and faithfully and selflessly serving the most vulnerable through your many gifts and talents.

Mark and Vickie Reddy, thank you for creating community wherever you go. You two work together to creatively imagine a place where the pursuit of justice is rooted in real relationships and invite others to come along in the journey. Thanks for being kindred spirits and making it so fun along the way. Thanks also for always pushing me to believe more in myself, encouraging me, and affirming who I am.

Stephan and Belinda Bauman, thanks for being my earliest teachers and pushing the boundaries of what's possible! Your intelligence, creativity, and belief in and encouragement of others have inspired so many to more faithfully follow Jesus.

Sandra Maria Van Opstal, you are a brilliant, passionate, and talented woman whose strength gives strength to others. I'm amazed at who you are and all that you do as a mother, wife, pastor, and community leader. I see how everything you do is rooted out of a deep love and respect for people and for the Lord. Thanks for being so generous with who you are, always lending a listening ear to me, and always encouraging me to lean into my full self. You are a mentor, sister, and friend to me.

Lisa Sharon Harper, you have been a voice that has given space for other women leaders, especially those of color, to rise. Thanks for being so fluid in your advocacy and voice, consistently applying biblical principles to a fuller vision of justice and flourishing for all.

Thanks to Nikki Toyama–Szeto and Kathy Khang for being instigators, thought leaders, sisters, and friends in this journey. I continue to learn from and am inspired by you.

To our current and former partners and friends at the Evangelical Immigration Table and the greater immigrant and refugee rights community, thanks for being a consistent and clarion voice in the public square for reason, compassion, and justice.

To my friends and family at Grace Life Church, I truly believe the local church is the answer to the brokenness of the world. Thanks for living into that call every day through your consistent belief in and practice of the fundamentals of faith—prayer, worship, discipleship, and community. And to my girlfriends from Hopkins and back home in Blue Bell/Philly, thanks for the all the fun group texts, phone calls, and gatherings that make me believe community can be created anywhere despite distance.

To my parents, June and Bob Hwang, you have modeled for me Christlike compassion, love, and service. Words will never be able to fully express how much I love you and am grateful for you. I would not be who I am today without your constant prayers, care, and support. I can never repay you on this side of the earth, but I constantly pray and hope that God will see your good works and reward you here and in heaven. To my brother Charlie, I always thought you were the smarter, kinder, and more selfless sibling—thanks for bearing with me all these years and being the best brother a sister could ask for. And to my dearest husband, Phil, thanks for being a true partner in this journey God has called us to and being a great father to our kids. I love your integrity and pursuit of the Lord and am so glad we're in this together.

And to my two sons, David and baby on the way, thanks for reminding me daily of how amazing and gracious God is. You two are miracles who have brought immeasurable laughter and joy into our lives. Being your mom is the greatest privilege I will ever know!

JENNY YANG, Baltimore, Maryland, January 2018

DISCUSSION QUESTIONS

T HESE QUESTIONS ARE DESIGNED to encourage discussion about and deeper reflection on the complexities surrounding immigration and the integration of this important issue with our Christian faith. We hope that they will be particularly useful for guiding small group discussions.

CHAPTER 1: THE IMMIGRATION DILEMMA

1. Two views were presented in the quotations at the beginning of the chapter. Which of these views have you heard the most?

2. The chapter says, "It is these 'easy' issues that often prove to be the most complex and the hardest to resolve, since our presumptions keep us from hearing the other side." What presumptions have you held regarding the issue of immigration?

3. The authors have shared their backgrounds and experiences with immigrants. Spend some time sharing your own experiences with immigrants.

4. C. S. Lewis says that humans are the "holiest object presented to your senses." How does this quotation help us to begin to treat our neighbors in God's image?

5. Which aspect of the immigration debate either interests or confuses you the most (political, economic, spiritual, etc.)?

6. What is one question concerning immigration that you would like to see answered in your study of this issue?

CHAPTER 2: "ALIENS" AMONG YOU

1. The rhetoric surrounding undocumented immigrants is particularly fierce. How does the emotional rhetoric change the debate?

2. How do the stories of immigrants help us see the image of God in present-day circumstances?

3. Which story stands out as the most interesting story? Why are you drawn to that particular story?

4. In the story of Pedro and Martha, Social Security cards and taxes show the complexity of ethical dimensions in the issue of undocumented immigrants. If most undocumented immigrants pay taxes, what rights should they have under the law?

CHAPTER 3: NATION OF IMMIGRANTS

1. God presents care for immigrants as a justice issue while reminding the Hebrews that he was faithful to redeem their situation. How can the church remember its past in a productive way? How can we rehearse our own immigrant history both in a national and spiritual sense?

2. Historian Roger Daniels has proposed that Americans have a "dualistic" view of immigration. What does he mean? Do you think this is historical or hypocritical?

3. What are two or three goals that you find immigrants of the past and present share?

4. What does the ebb and flow of historical sentiment toward immigrants reveal about our country? Is it an encouragement or a discouragement to read the brief historical immigration summary of our nation?

5. In the section titled "The Church and Immigration History," what surprised you the most about the church's response to immigration in the past?

CHAPTER 4: IMMIGRATING THE LEGAL WAY

1. Before reading this chapter, what were some common misconceptions that you either have heard or held with regard to the current immigration system?

2. Many say that undocumented immigrants should just "wait in line." How does this chapter shed light on this misconception? How has your understanding of the immigration system changed?

3. Have you ever known anyone who struggled with the process of obtaining a visa, whether to visit or to immigrate to the United States? What was their experience?

4. What surprised you the most about the path to legal status in the United States?

5. In your opinion, what role does the US economy have on illegal immigration?

6. Do you believe that the economy and family unity should continue to be the two driving factors for US immigration today?

7. What value do you think family-based immigration has on the United States, either economically or socially?

8. Do you think that economic or environmental hardship should be added to the definition of a refugee? Why or why not?

CHAPTER 5: THINKING BIBLICALLY ABOUT IMMIGRATION

1. Share and reflect on a past experience of turning to Scripture for insight and principles regarding a particular social or political issue. How is the issue of immigration similar or different?

2. How should our heavenly citizenship dictate the way we view and treat immigrants in our churches? How about in our schools and communities?

3. Why do you think that God places special emphasis on the well-being of immigrants?

4. How does Jesus respond when he is asked, "Who is my neighbor?" How does his response inform how we view immigrants?

5. The question of how to respond to immigrants who are present unlawfully in the country is particularly complex for many Christians. How does the Bible inform how you believe we should respond?

6. After reading this chapter, do you agree that there is a biblical mandate to care for immigrants? If so, what is one way you could begin to fulfill this calling during the next week?

CHAPTER 6: CONCERNS ABOUT IMMIGRATION

1. What were some of your primary concerns regarding this debate before reading this book? Who or what was your source for these concerns?

2. Do you think that we have an obligation to the poor living among us that is more important that an obligation to the poor living abroad? What are some possible nuances to that argument?

3. Which argument of those against a more generous immigration policy—poverty already in our communities, national security, cultural identity, etc.—is most persuasive and compelling to you? Why?

4. Describe or reflect on a time when you were a minority. What was the most uncomfortable aspect of this experience?

5. Are there any immigrants or refugees in your daily path? At the end of your time together, take some time to pray for ways to reach out to immigrants and the foreign born in your own neighborhood.

CHAPTER 7: THE VALUE OF IMMIGRANTS TO THE UNITED STATES

1. What do you see as the impact of immigration on your local community? What are the benefits? What are the costs?

2. Do you think God's instructions to "welcome the stranger" trump any negative effect that immigrants might have on the economy? Why or why not?

3. How does recognizing that immigration is a global issue—not just something that is impacting the United States—affect your thinking about this topic?

4. Over the last fifty years, immigrants have increasingly moved to more economically developed countries. What are the implications for the sending and receiving countries as well as for the immigrants themselves?

5. In your personal experience (or in those of your family or community), how have you observed the economic impact of immigrants?

6. Brainstorm together some of the possible root causes of why there are so many undocumented immigrants in America today.

CHAPTER 8: IMMIGRATION POLICIES AND POLITICS

1. Do you think that the issue of immigration has been used for political gain by members of Congress and those running for president?

2. Do you think that a path to earned legalization with appropriate penalties is a fair consequence for the legal infraction of unlawful presence in the United States?

3. How do you think the moral voice of the faith community can shape the immigration debate?

4. What factors have made immigration a hot topic in political circles?

5. After reading about various debates Congress has had on immigration, what are the core elements that you believe immigration reform should include?

6. What further information would you need to know in order to advocate on behalf of immigrants?

CHAPTER 9: IMMIGRATION AND THE CHURCH TODAY

1. How do you see your church ministering to "the least of these" in the United States?

2. How should ethnic-majority churches respond to the rise in immigrant churches?

3. If your church were to create a statement on immigration, what would it say?

4. In his daily life, Jesus showed personal hospitality to outcasts, both ethnically with the Samaritan woman (John 4), religiously with the Roman centurion (Matthew 8), and socially with the woman caught in adultery (John 8). What can we do to show Christlike hospitality both personally and corporately?

5. Do you agree with the authors when they state that God is using cultural diversity to accomplish his greater purposes here on earth?

6. How does the fact that the immigrant church is the fastest growing evangelical church in America change the missions strategy of the church?

7. After reading this chapter, what do you think is essential to God's heart in the midst of the immigration debate? What do you think God may be asking of you as you read this book?

CHAPTER 10: A CHRISTIAN RESPONSE TO THE IMMIGRATION DILEMMA

1. The authors argue that we cannot really understand the immigration issue until we personally know and interact with immigrants in our communities. How could you begin to do this?

2. Is there a church or organization in your community that is actively serving the foreign born? How could you get involved?

3. What could you (individually or as a group) do to help educate your larger church community about this issue?

4. Many Christians are wary of meddling in politics. Why do you think this is? Do you think that there is a place for the church to be involved in political advocacy?

5. How could you (personally and as a church community) help your congressional representatives understand your position(s) on this issue?

6. What do the authors argue are some of the root causes of immigration? Do you agree? What part of the way that you live might contribute, either positively or negatively, to these situations?

7. What response do you believe that God is calling you to with this important and controversial issue? How will you respond to that call?

EVANGELICAL STATEMENT OF PRINCIPLES FOR IMMIGRATION REFORM

Released June 15, 2012, by the Evangelical Immigration Table, www.evangelicalimmigrationtable.com

OUR NATIONAL IMMIGRATION LAWS have created a moral, economic and political crisis in America. Initiatives to remedy this crisis have led to polarization and name calling in which opponents have misrepresented each other's positions as open borders and amnesty versus deportations of millions. This false choice has led to an unacceptable political stalemate at the federal level at a tragic human cost. We urge our nation's leaders to work together with the American people to pass immigration reform that embodies these key principles and that will make our nation proud. As evangelical Christian leaders, we call for a bipartisan solution on immigration that:

- Respects the God-given dignity of every person
- Protects the unity of the immediate family
- Respects the rule of law
- Guarantees secure national borders
- Ensures fairness to taxpayers
- Establishes a path toward legal status and/or citizenship for those who qualify and who wish to become permanent residents

You can personally affirm this statement as well as sign up for monthly prayer requests related to immigrants and immigration at EvangelicalImmigrationTable.com.

ABOUT WORLD RELIEF

WORLD RELIEF—OUR EMPLOYER, a partner in the publication of this book, and the recipient of the authors' portions of the royalties of this book—is the humanitarian arm of the National Association of Evangelicals. Our mission at World Relief is to empower the local church to serve the most vulnerable.

Within the United States, World Relief has office locations throughout the country that partner with local churches to holistically assist refugees and other immigrants to become fully integrated participants in society. You can find specific contact information for all World Relief US office locations at www.worldrelief.org/us. Each office has a website with local volunteer, giving, and church partnership opportunities. We also work directly with churches in locations beyond the vicinity of our US offices to provide training and technical support for immigration legal services programs (see www .worldrelief.org/immigration-legal-services).

Finally, World Relief lives out that same mission of empowering local churches to serve the vulnerable beyond the US, equipping local churches throughout the world to address the root causes of migration, such as poverty, marginalization, conflict, and environmental degradation. You can explore the various countries where World Relief is at work at www .worldrelief.org/international.

Contact us for more information:

World Relief
7 E. Baltimore St.
Baltimore, MD 21202

Telephone: 443-451-1900
or 800-535-5433

Email: worldrelief@wr.org
Facebook: World Relief
Twitter: @WorldRelief
Instagram: @WorldRelief

SELECTED RESOURCES FOR LEARNING MORE ABOUT THE IMMIGRATION ISSUE

ADDITIONAL RESOURCES FROM WORLD RELIEF

- *Church Leader's Guide to Immigration*: A free, downloadable resource addressing some of the most common legal, biblical, and practical questions that pastors and other church leaders have regarding immigration, available at welcomingthestranger.com.

- *"Discovering and Living God's Heart for Immigrants: A Guide to Welcoming the Stranger"*: A free, downloadable curriculum suitable for a small group or adult-education class focused on many of the themes in this book, available at welcomingthestranger.com.

- *Seeking Refuge: On the Shores of the Global Refugee Crisis* (Moody Publishers, 2016): An in-depth look at the global refugee crisis by Matthew Soerens along with Stephan Bauman and Dr. Issam Smeir.

- *Standing with the Vulnerable: A Curriculum for Transforming Lives and Communities* (InterVarsity Press, 2016): Written by our colleague Gil Odendaal, World Relief's senior vice president for Integral Mission, this curriculum explores issues of poverty and vulnerability from a Christian perspective.

- *welcomingthestranger.com:* Additional resources and information.

BOOKS

Christian Perspectives on Immigration

- *A Better Country: Embracing the Refugee in Our Midst,* by Cindy M. Wu (William Carey Library, 2017)

- *Bulls, Bears and Golden Calves: Applying Christian Ethics in Economics,* by John E. Stapleford (InterVarsity Press, 2009) (see particularly chapter sixteen)

- *Christians at the Border: Immigration, the Church, and the Bible,* by M. Daniel Carroll R. (Baker Academic, 2013)

- *Christian Hospitality and Muslim Immigration in an Age of Fear,* by Matthew Kaemingk (Eerdmans, 2018)

- *Diaspora Missiology: Theory, Methodology, and Practice,* by Enoch Wan (Institute of Diaspora Studies, 2011)

- *Faith in the Voting Booth: Practical Wisdom for Voting Well,* by Leith Anderson and Galen Carey (Zondervan, 2016) (see particularly chapter eleven)

- *God and the Illegal Alien: United States Immigration Law and a Theology of Politics,* by Robert W. Heimburger (Cambridge University Press, 2017)

- *God Is Stranger: Finding God in Unexpected Places,* by Krish Kandiah (InterVarsity Press, 2017)

- *Immigrant Neighbors among Us: Immigration across Theological Traditions,* edited by M. Daniel Carroll R. and Leopoldo Sanchez M. (Pickwick Publications, 2015)

- *Immigration: Tough Questions, Direct Answers,* by Dale Hanson Bourke (InterVarsity Press, 2014)

- *Muslims, Christians, and Jesus: Understanding the World of Islam and Overcoming the Fears That Divide Us,* by Carl Medearis (Bethany House, 2017)

- *The Next Evangelicalism: Freeing the Church from Western Cultural Captivity,* by Soong-Chan Rah (InterVarsity Press, 2009)

- *The New Pilgrims: How Immigrants Are Renewing America's Faith and Values,* by Joseph Castleberry (Worthy Publishing, 2015)

- *Santa Biblia: The Bible Through Hispanic Eyes*, by Justo González (Abingdon Press, 1996) (see particularly chapter four)

- *Strangers Next Door: Immigration, Migration and Mission*, by J. D. Payne (InterVarsity Press, 2012)

- *You Welcomed Me: Loving Refugees and Immigrants Because God First Loved Us*, by Kent Annan (InterVarsity Press, 2018)

Immigrant and Refugee Stories

- *Brother, I'm Dying*, by Edwidge Danticat (Alfred A. Knopf, 2007)

- *Enrique's Journey*, by Sonia Nazario (Random House, 2006)

- *Just Like Us: The True Story of Four Mexican Girls Coming of Age in America*, by Helen Thorpe (Scribner, 2011)

- *Love Undocumented: Risking Trust in a Fearful World*, by Sarah Quezada (Herald Press, 2018)

- *The New Americans: Seven Families Journey to Another Country*, by Rubén Martínez (New Press, 2004)

- *Of Beetles & Angels: A Boy's Remarkable Journey from a Refugee Camp to Harvard*, by Mawi Asegdom (Little, Brown and Company, 2001)

- *The Story of My Life: An Afghan Girl on the Other Side of the Sky*, by Farah Ahmedi and Tamim Ansary (Simon Spotlight Entertainment, 2005)

- *Where the Wind Leads*, by Vinh Chung and Tim Downs (W Publishing, 2014)

On Serving and Advocating with Immigrants and Refugees

- *Assimilate or Go Home: Notes from a Failed Missionary on Rediscovering Faith*, by D. L. Mayfield (HarperOne, 2016)

- *At Home in Exile: Finding Jesus among My Ancestors and Refugee Neighbors*, by Russell Jeung (Zondervan, 2016)

- *Faith-Rooted Organizing: Mobilizing the Church in Service to the World*, by Alexia Salvatierra and Peter Heltzel (InterVarsity Press, 2014)

- *Many Colors: Cultural Intelligence for a Changing Church,* by Soong-Chan Rah (Moody Publishers, 2010)

- *The Middle of Everywhere: Helping Refugees Enter the American Community,* by Mary Pipher (Harvest Books, 2003)

- *The Power of Proximity: Moving Beyond Awareness to Action,* by Michelle Ferrigno Warren (InterVarsity Press, 2017)

- *There Goes the Neighborhood: How Communities Overcome Prejudice and Meet the Challenge of American Immigration,* by Ali Noorani (Prometheus Books, 2017)

- *This Flowing Toward Me: A Story of God Arriving in Strangers,* by Marilyn Lacey (Ave Maria Press, 2009)

- *Where the Cross Meets the Street: What Happens to the Neighborhood When God is at the Center,* by Noel Castellanos (InterVarsity Press, 2015)

History of Immigration to the United States

- *Driven Out: The Forgotten War against Chinese Americans,* by Jean Pfaelzer (Random House, 2007)

- *Guarding the Golden Door: American Immigration Policy and Immigrants since 1882,* by Roger Daniels (Hill and Wang, 2004)

- *Harvest of Empire: The History of Latinos in America,* by Juan Gonzalez (Viking Penguin, 2000)

- *Immigrants, Baptists, and the Protestant Mind in America,* by Lawrence B. Davis (University of Illinois Press, 1973).

- *Not Fit for Our Society: Immigration and Nativism in America,* by Peter Schrag (University of California Press, 2010)

- *Strangers in the Land: Patterns of American Nativism, 1860–1925,* by John Higham (Rutgers University Press, 2002)

WEBSITES

- American Immigration Council, www.americanimmigrationcouncil.org

- America's Voice, www.americasvoiceonline.org

- Evangelical Immigration Table, www.evangelicalimmigrationtable.org
- FWD.us, www.fwd.us
- Immigration Advocates Network, www.immigrationadvocates.org
- Immigration Policy Center, www.immigrationpolicy.org
- Interfaith Immigration Coalition, www.interfaithimmigration.org
- Migration Policy Institute, www.migrationpolicy.org
- National Immigration Forum, www.immigrationforum.org
- New American Economy, www.newamericaneconomy.org
- Pew Hispanic Center, www.pewhispanic.org
- Refugee Council USA, www.rcusa.org
- US Catholic Bishops' "Justice For Immigrants" Campaign, www.justiceforimmigrants.org
- US Chamber of Commerce, www.uschamber.com/immigration
- United States Citizenship and Immigration Services, www.uscis.gov
- United We Dream, https://unitedwedream.org
- Voices of Christian Dreamers, www.christiandreamers.us
- We Welcome Refugees, www.wewelcomerefugees.com
- World Relief, www.worldrelief.org

FILMS

Note: Some films may contain language or other content that some may find offensive.

- *All Saints*, directed by Steve Gomer (Sony Pictures, 2017)
- *Dying to Live: A Migrant's Journey,* directed by William Groody (Groody River Films, 2005)
- *God Grew Tired of Us,* directed by Christopher Dillon Quinn and Tommy Walker (NewMarket Films, 2006)
- *The Good Lie*, directed by Philippe Falardeau (Warner Brothers, 2014)

- *How Democracy Works Now*, directed by Shari Robertson and Michael Camerini (Filmakers Library, 2013), available at howdemocracyworksnow.com

- *McFarland, USA*, directed by Niki Caro (Walt Disney Studios, 2015)

- *Rain in a Dry Land*, directed by Anne Makepeace (Anne Makepeace Productions, 2006)

- *The Stranger*, directed by Linda Midgett (Evangelical Immigration Table, 2014), available at thestrangerfilm.org

- *Under the Same Moon*, directed by Patricia Riggen (Fox Searchlight, 2007)

- *Underwater Dreams*, directed by Mary Mazzio (50Eggs, Inc., 2014)

- *The Visitor*, directed by Tom McCarthy (Overture Films, 2007)

TOOLS FOR
POLITICAL ADVOCACY

E LECTED OFFICIALS REALLY DO TAKE SERIOUSLY the concerns of their constituents—if they know what they are. The debate over immigration policy in the United States over the past several years has been driven by a group of relatively small but committed, persistent anti-immigration activists, who diligently have called their US representatives and senators whenever legislation was being considered. Contacting your legislators is very important in order to ask for their support on a particular issue or piece of legislation, including writing letters, making phone calls, sending emails, and tagging your member on social media. You can contact your members to thank them for their voice or to ask them for their support on a particular issue.

Contacting your elected officials is easy. The first step is to know who they are. Each citizen of the United States is represented in Washington by one representative, who represents a congressional district, and by two senators, who each represent the entire state. To find your representative and senators, call the congressional switchboard at 202-224-3121 or check online at house. gov and senate.gov. To contact the White House, visit whitehouse.gov. World Relief also has online tools to determine which elected officials represent you and to send them an email message at worldrelief.org/advocate.

When you call, state your name, where you are calling from, and then express your opinion. If there is a particular bill that you would like your elected representative to support or not support, be sure to mention the bill name or number.

Writing a letter, which can either be mailed or faxed to your elected officials, can also be an effective way to let them know what you think about a particular issue. The mailing address for each official should be available on their website. When you write, be sure to include your name and address, express clearly the position or specific legislation that you would like your representative to support or not support, and perhaps provide some of the reasons that you would like them to take this position. For example, you may want to explain how your faith motivates you or about how a particular issue personally affects you, a neighbor, or a member of your church community. Though a personalized letter is more likely to get noticed, emails are also helpful. And social media—tagging your member of Congress on Twitter, Facebook, or Instagram—is also increasingly an influential way to get the attention of your elected officials.

You can also ask in your telephone call or letter to meet with your congressperson or their staffer who focuses specifically on an issue. Be flexible in scheduling an appointment, and do your research beforehand! Know how the issue specifically affects your community and bring along materials that represent your viewpoint. You may also consider bringing to the meeting other people or leaders in your community who have a position similar to yours. Make sure to write a follow-up thank-you email or letter after the meeting, and try to keep in touch.

Finally, visit worldrelief.org/advocate for up-to-date resources on advocacy opportunities related to immigration.

NOTES

CHAPTER 1: THE IMMIGRATION DILEMMA

[1]Campaign flier, quoted in Alex Kotlowitz, "Our Town," *New York Times Magazine*, August 5, 2007.

[2]Elvira Arellano, "Statement of Elvira Arellano on August 15, 2007," Los Angeles Independent Media Center, August 21, 2007, la.indymedia.org/news/2007/08/205070.php.

[3]Amy E. Black, *Beyond Left and Right: Helping Christians Make Sense of American Politics* (Grand Rapids: Baker, 2008), 160.

[4]Here and throughout this book we have, in some cases, changed names and identifying details of those whose stories we include to maintain their privacy. Anyone whose story is told in this book has given us permission to use it.

[5]C. S. Lewis, "The Weight of Glory," in *The Weight of Glory and Other Addresses* (New York: HarperCollins, 2001), 45.

[6]That said, even murderers, rapists, and kidnappers are made in the image of God, so we should not dehumanize them either.

CHAPTER 2: "ALIENS" AMONG YOU

[1]Jeffrey S. Passel and D'Vera Cohn, "As Mexican Share Declined, U.S. Unauthorized Immigrant Population Fell in 2015 Below Recession Level," Pew Research Center, April 25, 2017, www.pewresearch.org/fact-tank/2017/04/25/as-mexican-share-declined-u-s-unauthorized-immigrant-population-fell-in-2015-below-recession-level; Center for Migration Studies, "State-Level Unauthorized Population and Eligible-to-Naturalize Estimates," accessed August 17, 2017, http://data.cmsny.org; Bryan Baker and Nancy Rytina, "Estimates of the Unauthorized Immigrant Population Residing in the United States: January 2012," U.S. Department of Homeland Security Office of Immigration Statistics, March 2013, www.dhs.gov/sites/default/files/publications/Unauthorized%20Immigrant%20Population%20Estimates%20in%20the%20US%20January%202012_0.pdf.

[2]Email about illegal immigrants, quoted in Chuck Colson, "Defending the Strangers in Our Midst," Townhall.com, June 6, 2006, www.townhall.com/columnists/ChuckColson/2006/06/09/defending_the_strangers_in_our_midst-n1005801.

[3]Ibid.

[4]Malia Zimmerman, "Elusive Crime Wave Data Shows Frightening Toll of Illegal Immigrant Criminals," Fox News, September 16, 2015, www.foxnews.com/us/2015/09/16/crime-wave-elusive-data-shows-frightening-toll-of-illegal-immigrant-criminals.html.

[5]Alex Nowrasteh, "You Know Trump's Immigrant Crime Wave? It Doesn't Exist," *Newsweek*, July 10, 2017, www.newsweek.com/you-know-trumps-immigrant-crime -wave-doesnt-exist-634438?amp=1.

[6]Ibid.

[7]Ibid.

[8]Amy Goodman, "Dobbs Needs to Follow His Own Advice," *Seattle Post-Intelligencer*, December 6, 2007, B6.

[9]James C. Russell, *Breach of Faith: American Churches and the Immigration Crisis* (Raleigh, NC: Representative Government Press, 2004), 3-5.

[10]Ed Stetzer, "The Immigration Crisis and the Great Commission," *Facts & Trends*, Winter 2016, 51.

[11]Mario H. Lopez, "Hijacking Immigration," *Human Life Review*, October 28, 2012, www.humanlifereview.com/hijacking-immigration.

[12]J. C. Derrick, "Friend or Foe?," *World*, March 9, 2013, world.wng.org/2013/02/ friend_or_foe; and John Tanton, "Topic 9: Demographic Momentum," interview by George Colburn, May 2, 2008, www.youtube.com/watch?v=htw2b4iXCEc.

[13]"About One-in-Four U.S. Immigrants Are Unauthorized," Pew Research Center, May 1, 2017, www.pewhispanic.org/2017/05/03/facts-on-U-S-immigrants/ph_stat -portraits_foreign-born-2015_key-charts_foreign-born-breakdown. See also Jie Zong and Jeanne Batalova, "Frequently Requested Statistics on Immigrants and Immigration in the United States," Migration Policy Institute, March 8, 2017, www. migrationpolicy.org/article/frequently-requested-statistics-immigrants-and- immigration-united-states; and James Lee and Bryan Baker, "Estimates of the Lawful Permanent Resident Population in the United States: January 2014," U.S. Department of Homeland Security Office of Government Statistics, June 2017, www. dhs.gov/sites/default/files/publications/LPR%20Population%20Estimates%20 January%202014.pdf.

[14]Passel and Cohn, "As Mexican Share Declined"; Zong and Batalova, "Frequently Requested Statistics"; and Baker and Rytina, "Estimates of the Unauthorized Im- migrant Population."

[15]"DataBank: Poverty & Equity," World Bank, accessed August 15, 2017, http://data bank.worldbank.org/data/reports.aspx?source=poverty-and-equity-database.

[16]Muzaffar Chishti, Sarah Pierce, and Jessica Bolter, "The Obama Record on Deportations: Deporter in Chief or Not?," Migration Policy Institute, January 26, 2017, www.migrationpolicy.org/article/obama-record-deportations-deporter- chief-or-not.

[17]Ibid.

[18]"Profile of the Unauthorized Population: United States," Migration Policy Institute, accessed August 21, 2017, www.migrationpolicy.org/data/unauthorized-immigrant -population/state/US#.

[19]Lisa Christensen Gee, Matthew Gardner, and Meg Wiehe, "Undocumented Immigrants' State and Local Tax Contributions," Institute on Taxation & Economic Policy, February 2016, https://itep.org/wp-content/uploads/immigration2016.pdf.

[20]Ibid.

[21]"Profile of the Unauthorized Population."

[22]Stephen Goss et al., "Effects of Unauthorized Immigration on the Actuarial Status of the Social Security Trust Funds," Social Security Administration Office of the Chief Actuary, actuarial n. 151, April 2013, www.ssa.gov/oact/NOTES/pdf_notes/note151.pdf, 2, 4.

[23]Ibid, 3.

[24]Ibid.

[25]"2016 Annual Report to Congress," vol. 1, Internal Revenue Service National Taxpayer Advocate, accessed August 21, 2017, https://taxpayeradvocate.irs.gov/Media/Default/Documents/2016-ARC/ARC16_Volume1_MSP_18_ITINS.pdf, 239.

[26]Mark Everson, quoted in Nina Bernstein, "Tax Filings Rise for Immigrants in U.S. Illegally," New York Times, April 16, 2007, A1.

[27]Michael E. Fix and Jeffrey Passel, "The Scope and Impact of Welfare Reform's Immigrant Provisions," The Urban Institute, January 15, 2002, www.urban.org/UploadedPDF/410412_discussion02-03.pdf, 6; and "Questions and Answers for Undocumented Immigrants Regarding FEMA Assistance," Federal Emergency Management Agency, June 17, 2004, www.fema.gov/news-release/2004/06/17/questions-and-answers-undocumented-immigrants-regarding-fema-assistance.

[28]Rachel Fabi and Brendan Saloner, "Covering Undocumented Immigrants—State Innovation in California," New England Journal of Medicine, November 17, 2016, www.nejm.org/doi/full/10.1056/NEJMp1609468#t=article.

[29]Leighton Ku and Brian Bruen, "Poor Immigrants Use Public Benefits at a Lower Rate than Poor Native-Born Citizens," Cato Institute, Economic Development Bulletin 17, March 4, 2013, www.cato.org/publications/economic-development-bulletin/poor-immigrants-use-public-benefits-lower-rate-poor.

[30]"Foreign-Born Workers: Labor Force Characteristics—2016," U.S. Department of Labor Bureau of Labor Statistics, May 18, 2017, www.bls.gov/news.release/pdf/forbrn.pdf; and Jeffrey S. Passel, written testimony submitted to the U.S. Senate Committee on Homeland Security and Governmental Affairs, "Securing the Border: Defining the Current Population Living in the Shadows and Addressing Future Flows," March 26, 2015, www.hsgac.senate.gov/hearings/securing-the-border-defining-the-current-population-living-in-the-shadows-and-addressing-future-flows.

[31]The Border Patrol's practice of returning those apprehended at the border was quite common for many years; now, beginning under the Obama administration and continued under the Trump administration, those apprehended are much more

likely to be formally deported, sometimes after being criminally charged for unlawful entry and jailed.

[32]"Southwest Border Deaths by Fiscal Year," US Border Patrol, October 14, 2016, www.cbp.gov/sites/default/files/assets/documents/2016-Oct/BP%20Southwest%20Border%20Sector%20Deaths%20FY1998%20-%20FY2016.pdf.

[33]Annette Bernhardt et al, "Broken Laws: Unprotected Workers: Violation of Employment and Labor Laws in America's Cities," University of California Los Angeles Labor Center, 2009, www.labor.ucla.edu/publication/broken-laws-unprotected-workers, 42, 46.

[34]"Profile of the Unauthorized Population."

[35]Ibid; and Jeffrey S. Passel and D'Vera Cohn, "Number of Babies Born in U.S. to Unauthorized Immigrants Declines," Pew Research Center, September 11, 2015, www.pewresearch.org/fact-tank/2015/09/11/number-of-babies-born-in-u-s-to-unauthorized-immigrants-declines.

[36]Gilberto Mendoza, "States Offering Driver's Licenses to Immigrants," National Conference of State Legislatures, November 30, 2016, www.ncsl.org/research/immigration/states-offering-driver-s-licenses-to-immigrants.aspx.

[37]While Francisco and Alison's frustrating experience was with an attorney, these sort of situations are even more common with individuals who are *not* actually attorneys but who may present themselves as "*notarios*" or "immigration specialists." In order to avoid receiving inaccurate and possibly unethical legal advice, immigrants should not accept immigration advice from anyone other than an immigration attorney (preferably a member of the American Immigration Lawyers Association) or a nonprofit organization that is recognized by the US Department of Justice, which includes most World Relief offices. A list of Department of Justice–recognized organizations and accredited individuals at those organizations is maintained by the Executive Office for Immigration Review of the US Department of Justice and can be found at www.justice.gov/eoir/recognition-accreditation-roster-reports. Churches and other nonprofit organizations that want to assist immigrants with immigration legal services should undergo the training necessary to become recognized by the Department of Justice, because without adequate knowledge, wellmeaning people can actually do irrevocable harm to an immigrant seeking advice.

[38]Jens Manuel Krogstad, Jeffrey S. Passel, and D'Vera Cohn, "5 Facts About Illegal Immigration in the U.S.," Pew Research Center, April 27, 2017, www.pewresearch.org/fact-tank/2017/04/27/5-facts-about-illegal-immigration-in-the-u-s.

[39]Ana Gonzalez-Barrera, "More Mexicans Leaving Than Coming to the U.S.," Pew Research Center, November 19, 2015, www.pewhispanic.org/2015/11/19/more-mexicans-leaving-than-coming-to-the-u-s.

[40]"Unauthorized Immigrant Population Trends for States, Birth Countries, and Regions," Pew Research Center, November 3, 2016, www.pewhispanic.org/interactives/unauthorized-trends.

[41]"Intentional Homicide Rate per 100,000 Population," United Nations Office of Drugs and Crime, accessed August 23, 2017, https://data.unodc.org.

[42]I (Matthew) first heard the history of Salvadoran migration to the United States described in the three distinct waves described here by Ron Bueno of Enlace, San Salvador, El Salvador, May 23, 2017.

[43]Roger Waldinger, "Between Here and There: How Attached Are Latino Immigrants to Their Native Country?," Pew Research Center, October 25, 2007, www.pewhispanic.org/2007/10/25/between-here-and-there-how-attached-are-latino-immigrants-to-their-native-country.

[44]"United States Border Patrol Southwest Family Unit Subject and Unaccompanied Alien Children Apprehensions Fiscal Year 2016," US Customs and Border Protection, October 18, 2016, www.cbp.gov/newsroom/stats/southwest-border-unaccompanied-children/fy-2016; note that these figures are for the federal fiscal year 2016, which began on October 1, 2015.

[45]Current law treats unaccompanied children from non-contiguous countries slightly differently than those from Mexico or Canada.

[46]Robert Warren and Donald Kerwin, "The 2,000 Mile Wall in Search of a Purpose: Since 2007, Visa Overstayers Have Outnumbered Border Crossers by Half a Million," *Journal on Migration and Human Security* 5, no. 1 (2017): 125.

[47]Robert Warren and Donald Kerwin, "Beyond DAPA and DACA: Revisiting Legislative Reform in Light of Long-term Trends in Unauthorized Immigration to the United States," *Journal on Migration and Human Security* 3, no. 1 (2015): 94.

[48]For a more comprehensive understanding of refugee issues, we suggest a book written by Matthew and two other World Relief colleagues, *Seeking Refuge: On the Shores of the Global Refugee Crisis* (Moody Publishers, 2016).

[49]US State Department Refugee Processing Center, accessed August 24, 2017, www.wrapsnet.org.

[50]Ibid.

[51]Adam Babiker, quoted in Scott Cooper, "Adam Babiker: Veteran +," *Human Rights First*, July 4, 2017, www.humanrightsfirst.org/blog/adam-babiker-veteran.

[52]"Number of Form I-821D, Consideration of Deferred Action for Childhood Arrivals, by Fiscal Year, Quarter, Intake, Biometrics, and Case Status, Fiscal Year 2012-2017," United States Citizenship and Immigration Services, March 31, 2017, www.uscis.gov/sites/default/files/USCIS/Resources/Reports%20and%20Studies/Immigration%20Forms%20Data/All%20Form%20Types/DACA/daca_performancedata_fy2017_qtr2.pdf.

CHAPTER 3: NATION OF IMMIGRANTS

[1]Nancy Foner, *From Ellis Island to JFK: New York's Two Great Waves of Immigration* (New Haven, CT: Yale University Press, 2000), 3.

[2]Roger Daniels, *Guarding the Golden Door: American Immigration Policy and Immigrants Since 1882* (New York: Hill and Wang, 2004), 6.

[3]Benjamin Franklin, *Franklin: Writings*, ed. J. A. Leo Lemay (New York: Library of America, 1987), 374.

[4]Emma Lazarus, *Selected Poems*, ed. John Hollander (New York: Library of America, 2005), 58.

[5]See Gerald Neuman, "The Lost Century of American Immigration Law: 1776-1875," *Columbia Law Review* 93, no. 8 (December 1993): 1859.

[6]Immigrant Legal Resource Center, *A Guide for Immigration Advocates* (San Francisco: Immigrant Legal Resource Center, 2006), 2:21-22.

[7]Appendix four suggests a variety of books and other resources about the history of immigration to the United States for those interested in delving deeper.

[8]George Washington, quoted in Daniels, *Guarding the Golden Door*, 7.

[9]Daniel Kanstroom, *Deportation Nation: Outsiders in American History* (Cambridge, MA: Harvard University Press, 2007), 52.

[10]Stephen Behrendt, "Transatlantic Slavetrade," in *Africana: The Encyclopedia of the African and African American Experience*, ed. Kwame Anthony Appiah and Henry Louis Gates Jr. (New York: Basic Civitas Books, 1999), 1867.

[11]Marcus Lee Hanson, *The Immigrant in American History* (Cambridge, MA: Harvard University Press, 1940), 162.

[12]James Ciment, ed., *Encyclopedia of American Immigration* (Armonk, NY: Sharpe Reference, 2001), 1:67-68.

[13]Brian N. Fry, *Nativism and Immigration: Regulating the American Dream* (New York: LFB Scholarly, 2007), 39.

[14]Daniels, *Guarding the Golden Door*, 5.

[15]William Craig Brownlee, *Popery, an Enemy to Civil and Religious Liberty; And Dangerous to Our Republic* (New York: Charles K. Moore, 1839), 4.

[16]Fry, *Nativism and Immigration*, 39.

[17]Ibid., 41. The "Know Nothing" party acquired that name because, as a secret society, members were instructed to respond to outside questions about their organization with "I know nothing."

[18]"Primary Documents in American History: Indian Removal Act," Library of Congress, accessed November 3, 2017, www.loc.gov/rr/program/bib/ourdocs/Indian.html.

[19]John A. Andrew III, *From Revivals to Removal: Jeremiah Evarts, the Cherokee Nation, and the Search for the Soul of America* (Athens: University of Georgia Press, 1992), 220.

[20]"Primary Documents in American History."

[21]Daniels, *Guarding the Golden Door*, 178.

[22]Ibid.

[23]Orlando Crespo, *Being Latino in Christ: Finding Wholeness in Your Ethnic Identity* (Downers Grove, IL: InterVarsity Press, 2003), 147.

[24]Ulysses S. Grant, quoted in Juan Gonzalez, *Harvest of Empire: A History of Latinos in America* (New York: Penguin Books, 2001), 44.

[25]Abraham Lincoln, quoted in David Herbert Donald, *Lincoln* (New York: Touchstone, 1996), 123-24.

[26]The term *Hispanic*, which we use here interchangeably with the term *Latino*, includes individuals of Mexican descent but also those from Spanish-speaking countries in Central America, South America, and the Caribbean.

[27]"Sex by Age by Nativity and Citizenship Status (Hispanic or Latino)," US Census Bureau, accessed October 24, 2017, https://factfinder.census.gov/faces/tableservices/jsf/pages/productview.xhtml?src=bkmk.

[28]Jean Pfaelzer, *Driven Out: The Forgotten War Against Chinese Americans* (New York: Random House, 2007), 3-4.

[29]Advertisement quoted in Pfaelzer, *Driven Out*, 4-5.

[30]Daniels, *Guarding the Golden Door*, 12.

[31]Ibid.

[32]Ibid.

[33]Pfaelzer, *Driven Out*, 256, 259-64, 268-73.

[34]Ibid., 257.

[35]Ibid.

[36]Congressional report quoted in Daniels, *Guarding the Golden Door*, 17-18.

[37]Daniels, *Guarding the Golden Door*, 19.

[38]Ibid., 3.

[39]Ibid., 92-93.

[40]Ibid., 24.

[41]Fred Tsao, "Making Sense of the Immigration Debate," Wheaton College, Wheaton, IL, October 19, 2006, https://wheaton.account.box.com/login?redirect_url=%2Ffile%2F243571903719.

[42]Daniels, *Guarding the Golden Door*, 5, 30. In 2013, based on census data, an estimated 13 percent of the US population was foreign born, less than at the turn of the previous century, despite popular perception to the contrary.

[43]Foner, *From Ellis Island to JFK*, 19.

[44]Ibid., 20.

[45]Ibid., 22.

[46]Foner, *From Ellis Island to JFK*, 23.

[47]Ibid., 22.

[48]"Ellis Island History," Ellis Island Foundation, accessed November 3, 2017, www.libertyellisfoundation.org/ellis-island-history.

[49]"The Immigrant Journey," OhRanger.com, accessed November 3, 2017, www.ohranger.com/ellis-island/immigration-journey.

[50]"Ellis Island History."

51Drew Keeling, "Mass Migration as a Travel Business," BusinessofMigration.com, April 15, 2015, www.business-of-migration.com/immigrant-ancestors/how-many -today-have-ancestors-who-immigrated-during-1900-1914.

52Daniels, *Guarding the Golden Door*, 31.

53Michael C. LeMay, *Guarding the Gates: Immigration and National Security* (Westport, CT: Praeger Security International, 2006), 22.

54Immigration Commission, *Reports of the Immigration Commission: Emigration Conditions in Europe* (Washington, DC: Government Printing Office, 1911), 209; Toni Young, *Becoming American, Remaining Jewish: The Story of Wilmington, Delaware's First Jewish Community, 1879–1924* (Cranbury, NJ: Associated University Presses, 1999), 189.

55Immigration Commission, *Brief Statement of the Investigations of the Immigration Commission, with Conclusions and Recommendations and Views of the Minority* (Washington, DC: Government Printing Office, 1911), 48.

56Daniels, *Guarding the Golden Door*, 46.

57Ibid., 51-52.

58Stefan Kuhl, *The Nazi Connection: Eugenics, American Racism, and German National Socialism* (New York: Oxford University Press, 1994), 86.

59Paul Lombardo, "Eugenics Laws Restricting Immigration," Cold Spring Harbor Laboratory, accessed November 3, 2017, www.eugenicsarchive.org/html/eugenics/ essay9text.html.

60Ibid.

61Ibid.

62Daniels, *Guarding the Golden Door*, 52.

63Ibid., 53.

64Chapter four provides a summary of the rules governing who can immigrate to the United States under current immigration and nationality law.

65Fry, *Nativism and Immigration*, 39.

66Robert Seager II, "Some Denominational Reactions to Chinese Immigration to California, 1856–1892," *Pacific Historical Review* 28, no. 1 (February 1959): 65.

67Lawrence B. Davis, *Immigrants, Baptists, and the Protestant Mind in America* (Urbana: University of Illinois Press, 1973), 42.

68Ibid., 90-94.

69Ibid., 127-28.

70Howard B. Grose, *The Incoming Millions* (New York: Fleming H. Revell, 1906), 106-7.

71Davis, *Immigrants, Baptists, and the Protestant Mind*, 189.

72The National Association of Evangelicals (NAE) represents a number of evangelical denominations and churches and is the parent organization of World Relief, our employer and a partner in the publication of this book. While World Relief was in existence at the time of the NAE's statement, it was not involved in ministry to refugees and immigrants until the 1970s. It seems that, as was the case with the generation of American evangelicals who lived a century ago, a closer proximity to immigrants and refugees may have changed our perspective on immigration policy.

[73]"Immigration Laws of 1965," National Association of Evangelicals, accessed January 3, 2018, www.nae.net/immigration-laws-1965.

[74]Douglas A. Sweeney, *The American Evangelical Story: A History of a Movement* (Grand Rapids: Baker Academic, 2005), 182.

[75]Gonzalez, *Harvest of Empire*, 103; and Daniels, *Guarding the Golden Door*, 143.

[76]Eric Schlosser, "In the Strawberry Fields," *Atlantic*, November 1995, www.theatlantic.com/magazine/archive/1995/11/in-the-strawberry-fields/305754.

[77]G. Mark Hendrickson, "U.S. Department of Labor," in *Poverty in the United States: An Encyclopedia of History, Politics and Policy*, ed. Gwendolyn Mink and Alice O'Connor (Santa Barbara, CA: ABC-CLIO, 2004), 753.

[78]Richard Griswold del Castillo and Richard A. Garcia, *Cesar Chavez: A Triumph of the Spirit* (Norman: University of Oklahoma Press, 1995), 29.

[79]Harry Truman, quoted in David M. Reimers, *Still the Golden Door: The Third World Comes to America* (New York: Columbia University Press, 1985), 63.

[80]Ibid., 68.

[81]John F. Kennedy, *A Nation of Immigrants* (New York: Harper Torchbooks, 1964), 82.

[82]Reimers, *Still the Golden Door*, 67.

[83]Lyndon B. Johnson, "Remarks at the Signing of the Immigration Bill," New York: October 3, 1965, www.lbjlib.utexas.edu/Johnson/archives.hom/speeches.hom/651003.asp.

[84]"U.S. Annual Refugee Resettlement Ceilings and Number of Refugees Admitted, 1980-Present," Migration Policy Institute, September 26, 2017, www.migrationpolicy.org/programs/data-hub/charts/us-annual-refugee-resettlement-ceilings-and-number-refugees-admitted-united.

[85]Faye Hipsman and Doris Meisner, "Immigration in the United States: New Economic, Social, Political Landscapes with Legislative Reform on the Horizon," Migration Policy Institute, April 16, 2013, www.migrationpolicy.org/article/immigration-united-states-new-economic-social-political-landscapes-legislative-reform.

[86]Pear, Robert. "President Signs Landmark Bill on Immigration." *New York Times*, November 7, 1986. www.nytimes.com/1986/11/07/us/president-signs-landmark-bill-on-immigration.html.

[87]"George H. W. Bush and Ronald Reagan Debate on Immigration in 1980," *USA TODAY*, accessed November 3, 2017, www.usatoday.com/videos/news/2017/01/28/george-h.-w.-bush-and-ronald-reagan-debate-immigration-1980/97184364.

[88]Ibid.

[89]Ibid.

[90]Ronald Reagan, "Statement on Signing the Immigration Reform and Control Act of 1986," Ronald Reagan Presidential Library, November 6, 1986, https://reaganlibrary .archives.gov/archives/speeches/1986/110686b.htm.

[91]Ronald Reagan, "Statement on United States Immigration and Refugee Policy," American Presidency Project, July 30, 1981, www.presidency.ucsb.edu/ws/?pid=44128.

[92]Ron Elving, "For Every President Since Reagan, Immigration Has Been One More Minefield," NPR, October 15, 2017, www.npr.org/2017/10/15/557863705/for-every -president-since-reagan-immigration-has-been-one-more-minefield.

[93]Reagan, "Statement on Signing the Immigration Reform and Control Act of 1986."

[94]Donald Kerwin, "More than IRCA: US Legalization Programs and the Current Policy Debate," Migration Policy Institute, December 2010, www.migrationpolicy .org/research/us-legalization-programs-by-the-numbers.

[95]Mary Powers, Ellen Percy Kraly, and William Seltzer, "IRCA: Lessons of the Last US Legalization Program," Migration Policy Institute, July 1, 2004, www.migrationpolicy .org/article/irca-lessons-last-us-legalization-program.

[96]Ibid.

[97]Bill Clinton, quoted in Elving, "For Every President Since Reagan."

[98]George W. Bush, quoted in Massimo Calabresi, "Family Values and Immigration," Time, May 18, 2007, http://content.time.com/time/magazine/article/0,9171,1622573,00 .html.

[99]Jason De Leon, quoted in "Anthropologist Jason De Leon Awarded MacArthur Genius Grant," interviewed by Kelly McEvers, NPR, October 11, 2017. www .npr.org/2017/10/11/557198050/anthropologist-jason-de-leon-awarded-macarthur -genius-grant.

CHAPTER 4: IMMIGRATING THE LEGAL WAY

[1]"Ellis Island," National Park Service, June 28, 2006, www.nps.gov/archive/stli/ serv02.htm#Ellis.

[2]Technically, refugees cannot apply to become Lawful Permanent Residents until one year after their arrival in the United States, so they could be considered as having a fourth category of legal status. In practical terms, almost all refugees eventually become Lawful Permanent Residents, so their refugee status is an interim classification.

[3]Immigration and Nationality Act INA § 212, US Citizenship and Immigration Services, accessed November 3, 2017, www.uscis.gov/laws/immigration-and- nationality-act.

[4]Robert Warren and Donald Kerwin, "The 2,000 Mile Wall in Search of a Purpose: Since 2007, Visa Overstayers Have Outnumbered Border Crossers by Half a Million," Journal on Migration and Human Security 5, no. 1 (2017): 125.

[5]INA § 237.

[6]Brian Greene, "Study: One-in-Three Americans Fails Naturalization Civics Test," *U.S. News & World Report*, April 30, 2012, www.usnews.com/news/blogs/washington -whispers/2012/04/30/study-one-in-three-americans-fails-naturalization-civics-test.

[7]"2015 Yearbook of Immigration Statistics," US Department of Homeland Security Office of Immigration Statistics, December 2016, www.dhs.gov/sites/default/files/ publications/Yearbook_Immigration_Statistics_2015.pdf, 58.

[8]There are a few other categories of legal statuses, such as those paroled into the United States (mostly from a few specific countries, such as Cuba), refugees or asylees who have not yet adjusted their status to Lawful Permanent Resident, and certain individuals given temporary legal status. But these constitute a relatively small number of the total foreign-born population.

[9]"Number of Form I-821, Consideration of Deferred Action for Childhood Arrivals," US Citizenship and Immigration Services, March 31, 2017, www.uscis.gov/sites/ default/files/USCIS/Resources/Reports%20and%20Studies/Immigration%20 Forms%20Data/All%20Form%20Types/DACA/daca_performancedata_fy2017_ qtr2.pdf.

[10]Joe Caraccio, "Every President Since 1956 Has Granted a Form of Deferred Action Like DACA/DAPA," November 12, 2015, www.nyimmigrationlawyers.org/single -post/2015/11/12/Every-President-Since-1956-Has-Granted-A-Form-of-Deferred -Action-Like-DACADAPA.

[11]The Obama administration subsequently sought to expand Deferred Action status to an even larger number of undocumented immigrants, those with a US citizen or Lawful Permanent Resident child, but several states filed suit to block the move, and a divided Supreme Court ultimately prevented the "Deferred Action for Parents of Americans" program from going into place.

[12]Maria Sacchetti, "Their Lives Were Transformed by DACA. Here's What Will Happen If It Disappears," *Washington Post*, September 4, 2017, www.washingtonpost.com/local/ immigration/their-lives-were-transformed-by-daca-heres-what-will-happen-if-it -disappears/2017/09/04/a1a34574-8c75-11e7-91d5-ab4e4bb76a3a_story.html.

[13]INA § 203(b)(5); and Tracy Jan, "'Everyone in China Has the American Dream'—and a Popular Path to It May Disappear," *Washington Post*, July 7, 2017, www.washingtonpost .com/business/economy/everyone-in-china-has-the-american-dream—and-a-popular -path-to-it-may-disappear/2017/07/07/37617510-5c4c-11e7-9b7d-14576dc0f39d _story.html.

[14]INA § 201(d).

[15]INA § 203(b).

[16]Rob Paral, "No Way In: U.S. Immigration Policy Leaves Few Legal Options for Mexican Workers," *Immigration Policy in Focus* 4, no. 5 (July 2005), http://robparal .com/downloads/nowayin.htm.

[17]INA § 201(c).

[18]INA § 202(a)(2).

[19]"Visa Bulletin for July 2017," US Department of State, https://travel.state.gov/content/visas/en/law-and-policy/bulletin/2017/visa-bulletin-for-july-2017.html.

[20]Ibid.

[21]A person's "child" status is in some cases preserved beyond the twenty-first birthday through a series of complicated calculations, based on the reasoning that immigrants should not be penalized by the government's processing delays, as was often the case prior to the passage of the Child Status Protection Act in 2002.

[22]Ibid.

[23]Ibid.

[24]"Our Fees," United States Citizenship and Immigration Services, January 5, 2017, www.uscis.gov/forms/our-fees.

[25]Ibid.; Kevin McCoy, "Complaints Cause Delays in Increased INS Fees," *Daily News* (New York), August 7, 1998, 38.

[26]Some people in this situation may be eligible to apply for a waiver, which an officer has the discretion to approve or deny. To be eligible for a waiver in this case, though, a person would need to demonstrate that their absence would cause extreme hardship to a US-citizen spouse or parent. Elena has neither, and the effect on her US-citizen children is not considered under the law.

[27]Philip Connor, "Applications for U.S. Lottery Program More than Doubled since 2007," Pew Research Center, March 24, 2017, www.pewresearch.org/fact-tank/2017/03/24/applications-for-u-s-visa-lottery-more-than-doubled-since-2007.

[28]"Instructions of the 2018 Diversity Immigrant Visa Program," US Department of State, October 4, 2016, https://travel.state.gov/content/dam/visas/Diversity-Visa/DV-Instructions-Translations/DV-2018-Instructions-Translations/DV-2018%20Instructions%20English.pdf.

[29]"Convention and Protocol Relating to the Status of Refugees," United Nations High Commissioner for Refugees, December 14, 1950, www.unhcr.org/en-us/3b66c2aa10; and INA § 101(a)(42).

[30]"Global Trends: Forced Displacement in 2016," United Nations High Commissioner for Refugees, accessed November 3, 2017, www.unhcr.org/5943e8a34, 2.

[31]"U.S. Annual Refugee Ceilings and Number of Refugees Admitted, 1980-Present," Migration Policy Institute, September 26, 2017, www.migrationpolicy.org/programs/data-hub/charts/us-annual-refugee-resettlement-ceilings-and-number-refugees-admitted-united; and "Historical Arrivals Broken Down by Region," U.S. State Department Refugee Processing Center, accessed July 11, 2017, www.wrapsnet.org/s/Graph-Refugee-Admissions-since-19757317.xls.

[32]Kuang Keng Kuek Ser, "Map: Here Are the Countries with the World's Highest Murder Rates," Public Radio International, June 27, 2016, www.pri.org/stories/2016-06-27/map-here-are-countries-worlds-highest-murder-rates.

[33]The largest exception would be those who were previously undocumented but were granted Lawful Permanent Resident status through the Immigration Reform and Control Act, commonly known as the amnesty, which was signed by President Ronald Reagan in 1986.

[34]The fee to apply for a nonimmigrant visa at foreign consulates has since increased beyond $100.

CHAPTER 5: THINKING BIBLICALLY ABOUT IMMIGRATION

[1]R. J. D. Knauth, "Alien, Foreign Resident," in *Dictionary of the Old Testament: Pentateuch*, ed. David W. Baker and T. Desmond Alexander (Downers Grove, IL: IVP Academic, 2003), 29.

[2]Stevie J. Swanson, "Slavery Then and Now: The Trans-Atlantic Slave Trade and Modern Day Human Trafficking: What Can We Learn from Our Past?" *Florida A&M University Law Review* 11, no. 1 (fall 2015): 128-29.

[3]Justo L. González, *Santa Biblia: The Bible Through Hispanic Eyes* (Nashville: Abingdon, 1996), 96-97.

[4]Stuart Anderson, "40 Percent of Fortune 500 Companies Founded by Immigrants or Their Children," *Forbes*, June 19, 2011, www.forbes.com/sites/stuartanderson/ 2011/06/19/40-percent-of-fortune-500-companies-founded-by-immigrants-or -their-children.

[5]M. Daniel Carroll R., *Christians at the Border: Immigration, the Church, and the Bible* (Grand Rapids: Baker Academic, 2008), 102.

[6]Biblical scholars debate whether Jesus' words in this passage refer to *all* who are in need or, given his reference to his "brothers and sisters" (Mt 25:40), whether he is referring only to those who are followers of Jesus or even a smaller subset thereof. Given that the significant majority of immigrants to the United States in recent years profess to be Christians, this passage is applicable to our context in either case.

[7]Translation by George Grant, *The Micah Mandate: Balancing the Christian Life* (Nashville: Cumberland House, 1999), 8, 10.

[8]James Edwards, "Seeking Biblical Principles to Inform Immigration Policy," *Christianity Today*, September 2006, www.christianitytoday.com/ct/2006/septemberweb -only/138-32.0.html.

[9]"For the Health of the Nation: An Evangelical Call to Civic Responsibility," National Association of Evangelicals, 2004, http://nae.net/wp-content/uploads/2015/06/For -the-Health-of-the-Nation.pdf, 8, 10.

[10]"Views About Abortion Among Evangelical Protestants by Race/Ethnicity," Pew Research Center, 2014, www.pewforum.org/religious-landscape-study/compare/ views-about-abortion/by/racial-and-ethnic-composition/among/religious-tradition/ evangelical-protestant.

[11]Shane Claiborne, "Welcoming the Stranger, Even If It's Against the Law," *Washington Post*, October 2, 2014, www.washingtonpost.com/national/religion/welcoming-the -stranger-even-if-its-against-the-law-commentary/2014/10/02/82f6bc5c-4a6a-11e4 -a4bf-794ab74e90f0_story.html.

[12]For a more thorough explanation of the legal issues surrounding ministry to immigrants, our World Relief colleagues have prepared a useful, free guide downloadable at http://welcomingthestranger.com/sites/default/files/page/files/ChurchLeader GuideToImmigration.pdf.

[13]H.R. 4437, "The Border Protection, Anti-Terrorism, and Illegal Immigration Control Act of 2005," §274(a)(1)(C), December 17, 2005, www.congress.gov/109/ bills/hr4437/BILLS-109hr4437rfs.pdf.

[14]Rick Warren, quoted in in Cathy Lynn Grossman, "Rick Warren Speaks Up on Compassion, Politics, 'Big' Churches," *USA TODAY*, September 21, 2009, http:// content.usatoday.com/communities/Religion/post/2009/09/rick-warren-lords -prayer-compassion-illegal-immigration/1.

[15]John Piper, "What Should We Do About Illegal Immigration?," *DesiringGod*, March 10, 2008, www.desiringgod.org/interviews/what-should-we-do-about -illegal-immigration.

[16]We will explore more in chapter nine how the immigrant church is growing in the United States.

CHAPTER 6: CONCERNS ABOUT IMMIGRATION

[1]Deut 15:11; Ps 82:3; Prov 14:31; Amos 5:12; Mt 19:21; Lk 12:33; and Gal 2:10, among many others.

[2]Carol Swain, "Love Thy Neighbor: Main Issues in Contemporary Immigration Debates" (Center for Applied Christian Ethics Spring 2006 Conference, Wheaton College, Wheaton, IL, March 23, 2006).

[3]As we will explore below and further in chapter seven, the economics are actually more complicated than this, and most economists think any negative impact on wages of native-born citizens is minimal.

[4]James Edwards, "Seeking Biblical Principles to Inform Immigration Policy," *Christianity Today*, September 20, 2006, www.christianitytoday.com/ct/2006/ septemberweb-only/138-32.0.html.

[5]We would also do well to note that the reasons for global poverty are complex and multifaceted, and that US policies in some cases may have directly contributed to the economic situation of those outside of our borders.

[6]Matthew Soerens, "The Reasons Why the Travel Ban Is So Misguided," *Relevant*, July 7, 2017, https://relevantmagazine.com/article/the-reason-why-the-travel-ban -is-so-misguided.

[7]Tim Annett, "Illegal Immigrants and the Economy," *Wall Street Journal*, April 13, 2006, www.wsj.com/articles/SB114477669441223067.

[8]Madeline Zavodny, "Immigration and American Jobs," American Enterprise Institute for Public Policy Research and the Partnership for a New American Economy, December 2011, www.aei.org/wp-content/uploads/2011/12/-immigration-and -american-jobs_144002688962.pdf, 11.

[9]For example, Gianmarco Ottaviano and Giovani Peri find that the long-term effect of immigrant labor between 1996 and 2006 was a 0.3% increase in the wages of native-born workers without a high school degree ("Immigration and National Wages," National Bureau of Economics Research Working Paper No. 14188, July 2008, www.nber.org/papers/w14188.pdf); and Heidi Shierholz finds a similar result for the same group in a study of the wage impacts of immigration to the United States between 1994 and 2007 ("Immigration and Wages: Methodological Advancements Confirm Modest Gains for Native Workers," EPI Briefing Paper No. 255, Economic Policy Institute, February 4, 2010, www.epi.org/files/page/-/bp255/bp255.pdf).

[10]Though many Americans associate terrorism with extremist Islam, since 2008 there have been more than twice as many terrorist attacks or foiled attacks in the United States fueled by non-Muslim ideologies (white supremacists, "sovereign citizen" movements and other militias, animal rights activists, etc.) than by Islamist ideologies (David Neiwert, Darren Ankrom, Esther Kaplan, and Scott Pham, "Homegrown Terror," Center for Investigative Reporting, June 22, 2017, https:// apps.revealnews.org/homegrown-terror). Even just among jihadist terrorist attacks perpetrated within the United States since 9/11, of the 396 perpetrators for whom citizenship status is known, more than half have been native-born US citizens (Peter Bergen, Albert Ford, Alyssa Sims, and David Sterman, "Terrorism in America after 9/11," *New America*, accessed September 15, 2017, www.newamerica .org/in-depth/terrorism-in-america).

[11]Warren Richey, "Are Terrorists Crossing the US-Mexico Border? Excerpts from the Case File," *Christian Science Monitor*, January 15, 2017, www.csmonitor.com/USA /Justice/2017/0115/Are-terrorists-crossing-the-US-Mexico-border-Excerpts-from -the-case-file.

[12]"Efforts by DHS to Estimate Southwest Border Security Between Ports of Entry," US Department of Homeland Security Office of Immigration Statistics, September 2017, www.dhs.gov/sites/default/files/publications/17_0914_estimates-of-border -security.pdf, 19.

[13]Alex Nowrasteh, "Terrorism and Immigration: A Risk Analysis," Cato Institute, September 13, 2016, https://object.cato.org/sites/cato.org/files/pubs/pdf/pa798_2 .pdf.

[14]Calculated from ibid.; and "Facts & Statistics: Mortality Risks," Insurance Information Institute, 2014, www.iii.org/fact-statistic/facts-statistics-mortality-risk.

[15]Seth Freed Wessler, "Primary Data: Deportations of Parents of U.S. Citizen Kids," *Colorlines*, December 17, 2012, www.colorlines.com/articles/primary-data

-deportations-parents-us-citizen-kids. This number (92,000) was as of October 22, 2012. The information was obtained by a Freedom of Information Act Request filed by Colorlines.com, and came from "Number of Removals of Aliens Who Claim to Have US-Born Children by Category of Removal," Immigration and Customs Enforcement.

[16]Seth Freed Wessler, "Shattered Families: The Perilous Intersection of Immigration Enforcement and the Child Welfare System," Applied Research Center, November 2011, www.asph.sc.edu/cli/word_pdf/ARC_Report_Nov2011.pdf.

[17]Immigration and Nationality Act INA§ 212(a)(9)(B)(i)(II).

[18]Jeffrey S. Passel and D'Vera Cohn, "Number of Babies Born to Unauthorized Immigrants in the U.S. Continues to Decline," Pew Research Center, October 26, 2016, www.pewresearch.org/fact-tank/2016/10/26/number-of-babies-born-to-unauthorized-immigrants-in-u-s-continues-to-decline.

[19]"Family Economics," Family Research Council, accessed January 3, 2018, www.frc.org/family-economics.

[20]Jason Richwine, "More Immigration Would Mean More Democrats," National Review, October 3, 2017, www.nationalreview.com/article/452140/democrats-immigration-more-it-helps-them.

[21]Latino and Asian evangelicals, interestingly, have been swing voting blocs, more evenly divided between support for the two major parties than either white evangelicals or nonevangelical Latinos and Asians.

[22]"Latino Voters and the 2014 Midterm Elections," Pew Research Center, October 16, 2014, www.pewhispanic.org/2014/10/16/latino-voters-and-the-2014-midterm-elections/ph-2014-10-latino-voters-2014-midterm-election-02-03.

[23]Ibid.

[24]Mathew Staver and Samuel Rodriguez, "The Evangelical, Latino Case for Immigration Reform," FoxNews.com, June 11, 2013, www.foxnews.com/opinion/2013/06/11/latino-evangelical-case-for-immigration-reform.html.

[25]William F. Buckley, quoted in Alex Nowrasteh, "Proposition 187 Turned California Blue," Cato at Liberty, July 20, 2016, www.cato.org/blog/proposition-187-turned-california-blue.

[26]Ibid; B. Drummond Ayres Jr., "The Expanding Hispanic Vote Shakes Republican Strongholds," New York Times, November 10, 1996, www.nytimes.com/1996/11/10/us/the-expanding-hispanic-vote-shakes-republican-strongholds.html.

[27]Nowrasteh, "Proposition 187 Turned California Blue."

[28]Robert Suro, Richard Fry, and Jeffrey S. Passel, "How Latinos Voted in 2004," Pew Research Center, June 27, 2005, www.pewhispanic.org/2005/06/27/iv-how-latinos-voted-in-2004.

[29]Brett Snider, "Is Illegal Immigration a Crime? Improper Entry v. Unlawful Presence," FindLaw Blotter, July 9, 2014, http://blogs.findlaw.com/blotter/2014/07/is-illegal-immigration-a-crime-improper-entry-v-unlawful-presence.html.

[30]"Voters Measure Illegal Immigration in Major Crime, More Tax Dollars," *Rasmussen Reports*, March 29, 2017, www.rasmussenreports.com/public_content/politics /current_events/immigration/march_2017/voters_measure_illegal_immigration_in _major_crime_more_tax_dollars.

[31]Michelangelo Landgrave and Alex Nowrastch, "Criminal Immigrants: Their Numbers, Demographics, and Countries of Origin," Cato Institute, March 15, 2017, www.cato.org/publications/immigration-reform-bulletin/criminal-immigrants -their-numbers-demographics-countries.

[32]Walter Ewing, Daniel Martinez, and Ruben Rumbaut, "The Criminalization of Immigration in the United States," American Immigration Council, July 2015, www .americanimmigrationcouncil.org/sites/default/files/research/the_criminalization _of_immigration_in_the_united_states.pdf.

[33]Ibid.

[34]Jacob Stowell, Steven Messner, Kely McGeever, and Lawrence Raffalovich, "Immigration and the Recent Violent Crime Drop in the United States: A Pooled, Cross-Sectional Time-Series Analysis of Metropolitan Areas," *Criminology* 47:3 (2009): 889. Despite politicians' claims of "tremendous danger" on the US-Mexico border and of drug-related violence "spilling over" from Mexico, a *USA TODAY* analysis of FBI and local law enforcement agencies found that US communities within a fifty mile range of the US-Mexico border consistently had lower violent crime rates than both other cities within their states *and* lower than the national average (Alan Gomez, Jack Gillum, and Kevin Johnson, "U.S. Border Cities Prove Haven from Mexico's Drug Violence," August 18, 2011, https://usatoday30.usa today.com/news/washington/2011-07-15-border-violence-main_n.htm).

[35]As an illustration of how complex the intersection of criminal and immigration law can be—and a warning not to dispense legal advice if you are not authorized to do so: had the candy bar been stolen in neighboring Illinois, the immigrant shoplifter would be eligible for a "petty offense exception," despite having committed the exact same offense.

[36]Chris Magnus, quoted in Magen Wetmore, "Law Enforcement Leaders Condemn 'Sanctuary Cities' Order," National Immigration Forum, January 26, 2017, http:// immigrationforum.org/blog/law-enforcement-leaders-condemn-sanctuary-cities -executive-order.

[37]Ibid. Though not directly related, these policing policies are sometimes confused with "sanctuary churches," local congregations (mostly mainline Protestant) that shielded Central American immigrants from being deported back to a war zone in the 1970s and 1980s. In the current environment, some churches have embraced that moniker once again as they seek to shelter immigrants from deportation. This strategy is not a legal strategy per se, because the federal government could obtain a warrant to enter the church with just cause, but it has worked in some cases because, largely for public

relations reasons, federal immigration agents will generally avoid entering into "sensitive locations" like churches to pick up immigrants from deportation.

[38]Mike Glover, "Buchanan Names New Campaign Head," *Associated Press Wire*, April 28, 1999.

[39]"By 2055, the U.S. Will Have No Racial or Ethnic Majority Group," Pew Research Center, September 23, 2015, www.pewhispanic.org/2015/09/28/modern-immigration -wave-brings-59-million-to-u-s-driving-population-growth-and-change-through -2065/ph_2015-09-28_immigration-through-2065-17.

[40]Patrick Buchanan, *State of Emergency: The Third World Invasion and Conquest of America* (New York: St. Martin's Press, 2006), 146.

[41]Patrick Buchanan, quoted in Jonathan Alter and Michael Isikoff, "The Beltway Populist," *Newsweek*, March 4, 1996, 26.

[42]Steve Bannon, quoted in Sarah Posner, "How Donald Trump's New Campaign Chief Created an Online Haven for White Supremacists," *Mother Jones*, August 22, 2016, www.motherjones.com/politics/2016/08/stephen-bannon-donald-trump-alt -right-breitbart-news.

[43]Steve Bannon, quoted in "Steve Bannon Says Catholic Church Has 'Economic Interest' in 'Unlimited Illegal Immigration,'" *CBS News*, September 7, 2017, www .cbsnews.com/news/steve-bannon-on-trump-daca-decision-60-minutes.

[44]"Response from U.S. Conference of Catholic Bishops on Care for Migrants and Refugees," US Conference of Catholic Bishops, September 7, 2017, www.usccb.org /news/2017/17-159.cfm.

[45]Besheer Mohamed, "A New Estimate of the U.S. Muslim Population," Pew Research Center, January 6, 2016, www.pewresearch.org/fact-tank/2016/01/06/a-new-estimate -of-the-u-s-muslim-population.

[46]Ibid.

[47]David Neiwert, Darren Ankrom, Esther Kaplan, and Scott Pham, "Homegrown Terror," Center for Investigative Reporting, June 22, 2017, https://apps.revealnews .org/homegrown-terror.

[48]Michael Lipka, "Muslims and Islam: Key Findings in the U.S. and around the World," Pew Research Center, August 9, 2017, www.pewresearch.org/fact-tank/2017/08/09 /muslims-and-islam-key-findings-in-the-u-s-and-around-the-world.

[49]Manal Omar, "Islam Is a Religion of Peace," *Foreign Policy*, November 9, 2015, http://foreignpolicy.com/2015/11/09/islam-is-a-religion-of-peace-manal-omar -debate-islamic-state.

[50]Kate Shellnutt, "Most White Evangelicals Don't Believe Muslims Belong in America," *Christianity Today*, July 26, 2017, www.christianitytoday.com/news/2017 /july/pew-how-white-evangelicals-view-us-muslims-islam.html.

[51]Matthew Soerens, "The Reason Why the Travel Ban Is So Misguided," *Relevant*, July 7, 2017, https://relevantmagazine.com/article/the-reason-why-the-travel-ban -is-so-misguided.

CHAPTER 7: THE VALUE OF IMMIGRANTS
TO THE UNITED STATES

[1]Gustavo Lopez and Kristin Bialek, "Key Findings about U.S. Immigrants," Pew Research Center, May 3, 2017, www.pewresearch.org/fact-tank/2017/05/03/key-findings-about-u-s-immigrants; Tobin Grant, "SBC Vote Reveals Delicate Evangelical Support for Immigration Reform," *Christianity Today*, June 29, 2011, www.christianitytoday.com/news/2011/june/sbc-vote-reveals-delicate-evangelical-support-for.html.

[2]Ashley Kirk, "Mapped: Which Country Has the Most Immigrants?" *Telegraph*, January 21, 2016, www.telegraph.co.uk/news/worldnews/middleeast/12111108/mapped-which-country-has-the-most-immigrants.html.

[3]"Migration to Australia: A Quick Guide to the Statistics," Parliament of Australia, January 18, 2017, www.aph.gov.au/About_Parliament/Parliamentary_Departments/Parliamentary_Library/pubs/rp/rp1617/Quick_Guides/MigrationStatistics; and "Immigration and Ethnocultural Diversity in Canada," Statistics Canada, September 15, 2016, www12.statcan.gc.ca/nhs-enm/2011/as-sa/99-010-x/99-010-x2011001-eng.cfm.

[4]Doris Meissner, *Immigration and America's Future: A New Chapter* (Washington, DC: Migration Policy Institute, 2006), 1.

[5]Susan B. Carter and Richard Sutch, "Historical Perspectives on the Economic Consequences of Immigration into the United States," in *The Handbook of International Migration: The American Experience*, ed. Charles Hirschman, Philip Kasinitz, and Josh DeWind (New York: Russell Sage Foundation, 1999), 319.

[6]"The U.S. Economy to 2024," Bureau of Labor Statistics, December 2015, www.bls.gov/opub/mlr/2015/article/the-us-economy-to-2024.htm.

[7]Jeffrey Passel and D'Vera Cohn, "U.S. Population Projections: 2005–2050," Pew Research Center, February 11, 2008. www.pewhispanic.org/2008/02/11/us-population-projections-2005-2050/#fn-85-2.

[8]Ibid.

[9]"Futurework: Trends and Challenges for Work in the 21st Century," US Department of Labor, accessed November 3, 2017, www.dol.gov/dol/aboutdol/history/herman/reports/futurework/report/chapter1/main.htm.

[10]Sandra L. Colby and Jennifer M. Ortman, "The Baby Boom Cohort in the United States: 2012 to 2060," US Census Bureau, May 2014, www.census.gov/prod/2014pubs/p25-1141.pdf.

[11]Gretchen Livingston, "5 Facts about Immigrant Mothers and US Fertility Trends," Pew Research Center, October 26, 2016, www.pewresearch.org/fact-tank/2016/10/26/5-facts-about-immigrant-mothers-and-u-s-fertility-trends.

[12]"Labor Force Projections to 2024: The Labor Force Is Growing, but Slowly," Bureau of Labor Statistics, December 2015, www.bls.gov/opub/mlr/2015/article/labor-force-projections-to-2024.htm.

[13]Passel and Cohn, "U.S. Population Projections: 2005–2050."

[14]US Department of Labor, "Futurework."

[15]"Occupational Employment Projections to 2022," US Department of Labor, December 2013. www.bls.gov/opub/mlr/2013/article/occupational-employment -projections-to-2022.htm.

[16]Ibid.

[17]"Immigrant Workers in the Construction Labor Force," National Association of Home Builders, February 3, 2015, www.nahbclassic.org/generic.aspx?generic ContentID=241345.

[18]Hugh Morton, "Housing Short-Handed Without Immigrant Workers," *Nation's Building News,* July 31, 2006, www.nahb.org/news_details.aspx?newsID=3010.

[19]Jie Zong and Jeanne Batalova, "College-Educated Immigrants in the United States," Migration Policy Institute, February 3, 2016, www.migrationpolicy.org /article/college-educated-immigrants-united-states.

[20]Jeffrey Passel and D'Vera Cohn, "Share of Unauthorized Immigrant Workers in Production, Construction Jobs Falls Since 2007," Pew Research Center, March 26, 2015, www.pewhispanic.org/2015/03/26/share-of-unauthorized-immigrant-workers -in-production-construction-jobs-falls-since-2007.

[21]Tim Annett, "Illegal Immigrants and the Economy," *Wall Street Journal,* April 13, 2006, www.wsj.com/articles/SB114477669441223067.

[22]Roger Lowenstein, "The Immigration Equation," *New York Times Magazine,* July 9, 2006, 36.

[23]Stephen Goss et al, "Effects of Unauthorized Immigration on the Actuarial Status of the Social Security Trust Funds," Social Security Administration Office of the Chief Actuary, actuarial n. 151, April 2013, www.ssa.gov/oact/notes/pdf_notes /note151.pdf, 3.

[24]Judith Gans, "Immigrants in Arizona: Fiscal and Economic Impacts," University of Arizona, June 2008, www.udallcenter.arizona.edu/immigration/publications /impactofimmigrants08.pdf, 3.

[25]Emily Eisenhauer, et al., "Immigrants in Florida: Characteristics and Contribu- tions" (Florida International University, May 2007), 7, 34.

[26]Michael Fix and Jeffrey S. Passel, *Immigration and Immigrants: Setting the Record Straight* (Washington, DC: Urban Institute, 1994), 58.

[27]Stephen Moore, *A Fiscal Portrait of the Newest Americans* (Washington, DC: Cato Institute and the National Immigration Forum, 1998), 20.

[28]Steve Sarconi, quoted in Julia Preston, "Short on Labor, Farmers in U.S. Shift to Mexico," *New York Times,* September 5, 2007, A1.

[29]Michael Greenstone, Richard Hornbeck, and Enrico Moretti, "Identifying Ag- glomeration Spillovers: Evidence from Winners and Losers of Large Plant Openings," *Journal of Political Economy* 118, no. 3 (June 2010): 536-98.

[30]Giovanni Peri, Kevin Shih, and Chad Sparber, "STEM Workers, H-1B Visas, and Productivity in U.S. Cities," *Journal of Labor Economics* 33, no. S1 (July 2015): S225-55.

[31]Robert Fairlie, "Minority and Immigrant Entrepreneurs: Access to Financial Capital," in *International Handbook on the Economics of Migration*, ed. Amelie Constant and Klaus Zimmerman (Cheltenham, UK: Edward Elgar), 153.

[32]"Immigration's Long-Term Impacts on Overall Wages and Employment of Native-Born US Workers Very Small, Although Low-Skilled Workers May Be Affected, New Report Finds; Impacts on Economic Growth Positive, While Effects on Government Budgets Mixed," National Academies of Sciences, Engineering, Medicine, September 21, 2016, www8.nationalacademies.org/onpinews/newsitem.aspx?RecordID=23550.

[33]Faith Alliance Against Slavery and Trafficking, "Uniquely Vulnerable: The Nexus Between Human Trafficking and Immigration," June 2014, https://s3.amazon aws.com/media.cloversites.com/33/336bad01-3ae4-41f0-aaab-dde25ca8746f /documents/Uniquely_Vulnerable_the_nexus_between_human_trafficking_and _immigration.pdf, 2.

[34]Ibid.

[35]Eric Schlosser, "Penny Foolish," *New York Times*, November 29, 2007, www.nytimes .com/2007/11/29/opinion/29schlosser.html.

[36]Holly Burkhalter, "Fair Food Program Helps End the Use of Slavery in the Tomato Fields," *Washington Post*, September 2, 2012, www.washingtonpost.com/opinions /fair-food-program-helps-end-the-use-of-slavery-in-the-tomato-fields/2012 /09/02/788f1a1a-f39c-11e1-892d-bc92fee603a7_story.html.

[37]Eduardo Porter, "Cost of Illegal Immigration May Be Less Than Meets the Eye," *New York Times*, April 16, 2006, www.nytimes.com/2006/04/16/business/yourmoney /cost-of-illegal-immigration-may-be-less-than-meets-the.html.

[38]Tamar Jacoby, "Immigrant Nation," *Foreign Affairs*, November-December 2006.

[39]I. P. Giammarco and Giovanni Peri, "Rethinking the Gains from Immigration: Theory and Evidence from the U.S.," National Bureau of Economic Research Working Paper 11672 (September 2005): 12-13.

[40]"Immigration Myths and Facts," US Chamber of Commerce Labor, Immigration and Employee Benefits, April 14, 2016, www.uschamber.com/sites/default/files /documents/files/022851_mythsfacts_2016_report_final.pdf.

[41]Michael R. Bloomberg, testimony before the Committee on the Judiciary, United States Senate, July 5, 2006, http://judiciary.senate.gov/testimony.cfm?id=1983&wit _id=5493.

[42]See the Welcoming Michigan website at www.welcomingmichigan.org.

[43]Tamar Jacoby, "U.S. Economic Competitiveness at Risk: A Midwest Call to Action on Immigration Reform," Chicago Council on Global Affairs, February 28, 2013,

www.thechicagocouncil.org/sites/default/files/2013_ImmigrationTaskForce_Final
.pdf, 69.

[44]Acacia Squires and Lauren Silverman, "Baltimore Says, 'Immigrants Welcome,'"
NPR, December 9, 2012, www.npr.org/2012/12/09/166829186/baltimore-says
-immigrants-welcome.

[45]Robert W. Fairlie et. al., "The Kauffman Index: Startup Activity, National Trends,"
Ewing Marion Kauffman Foundation, June 2015, www.kauffman.org/~/media
/kauffman_org/research%20reports%20and%20covers/2015/05/kauffman_index
_startup_activity_national_trends_2015.pdf, 6.

[46]Robert W. Fairlie, "Open for Business: How Immigrants Are Driving Small
Business Creation in the United States," Partnership for a New American Economy,
August 2012, www.renewoureconomy.org/sites/all/themes/pnae/openforbusiness
.pdf, 3.

[47]Fairlie, "Kauffman Index," 6.

[48]Sergey Brin, quoted in Stephen Shankland, "How Google Is Becoming an Ex-
tension of Your Mind," CNET.com, July 16, 2012, www.cnet.com/news/how-google
-is-becoming-an-extension-of-your-mind.

[49]Gary D. MacDonald, testimony before the Immigration Subcommittee, United
States Senate, Washington, DC, April 15, 1997.

[50]Alfred Quinones-Hinojosa, quoted in Max Alexander, "An Illegal Immigrant
Turned Brain Surgeon—with His Own Two Hands," *Reader's Digest*, February 2008,
www.readersdigest.com.au/true-stories-lifestyle/inspirational/illegal-immigrant
-turned-brain-surgeon.

[51]"From Struggle to Resilience: The Economic Impact of Refugees in America,"
New American Economy, June 2017, www.newamericaneconomy.org/wp-content
/uploads/2017/06/NAE_Refugees_V5.pdf.

[52]Ibid.

[53]Ibid.

[54]Ibid.

[55]Julie Hirschfield Davis and Somini Sengupta, "Trump Administration Rejects Study
Showing Positive Impact of Refugees," *New York Times*, September 18, 2017, www
.nytimes.com/2017/09/18/us/politics/refugees-revenue-cost-report-trump.html.

[56]"The State of the World's Children 2008: Child Survival," United Nations Children's Fund, December 2007, 76.

[57]"Immigrants and Education," Public Policy Institute of California, April 2011,
www.ppic.org/publication/immigrants-and-education.

[58]Laurent Cavenaile, "Offshoring, Computerization, Labor Market Polarization and
Top Income Inequality," New York University, October 28, 2016, https://sites
.google.com/site/cavenailelaurent/polarization.pdf.

[59]U.S. Census Bureau, 2009-2011 American Community Survey data; See also
Gordon H. Hanson and Matthew J. Slaughter, "Talent, Immigration, and U.S.

Economic Competitiveness," Compete America, May 2013, https://gps.ucsd
.edu/_files/faculty/hanson/hanson_publication_immigration_talent.pdf.

[60]"Help Wanted: The Role of Foreign Workers in the Innovation Economy," Information
Technology Industry Council, accessed January 29, 2018, www.newamericaneconomy
.org/sites/all/themes/pnae/stem-report.pdf, 21.

[61]Jerry Yang, quoted in Jessica Seid Dickler, "Immigrant Entrepreneurs Spur Ren-
aissance," *CNN Money*, November 15, 2006, http://money.cnn.com/2006/11/15
/smbusiness/immigrant_entrepreneur/index.htm. www.workpermit.com/news
/2006_11_27/us/ immigrant_business_venture_capital.htm.

[62]Elizabeth Redden, "America's Immigration Laureates," *Inside Higher Ed*, October
11, 2016, www.insidehighered.com/news/2016/10/11/foreign-born-professors
-account-us-nobel-haul.

[63]Stuart Anderson, "Immigrants and Billion Dollar Startups," National Foundation
for American Policy, March 2016, http://nfap.com/wp-content/uploads/2016/03
/Immigrants-and-Billion-Dollar-Startups.NFAP-Policy-Brief.March-2016.pdf.

[64]Ibid.

[65]William H. Gates, testimony before the Committee on Health, Education, Labor,
and Pensions, United States Senate, Washington, DC, March 7, 2007.

[66]Kelsey Sheehy, "High School Grads in China, India Are Better Prepared for
College," *US News and World Report*, August 27, 2012, www.usnews.com/education
/blogs/high-school-notes/2012/08/27/high-school-grads-in-china-india-are
-better-prepared-for-college.

[67]"Science and Engineering Indicators 2016," National Science Board, January 2016,
www.nsf.gov/statistics/2016/nsb20161/#/report/chapter-2.

[68]Ibid.

[69]Ibid.

[70]"Not Coming to America: Why the U.S. Is Falling Behind in the Global Race for
Talent," May 2012, Partnership for a New American Economy and the Partnership
for New York City, www.newamericaneconomy.org/sites/all/themes/pnae/not
-coming-to-america.pdf, 2.

[71]"Help Wanted: The Role of Foreign Workers in the Innovation Economy," Information Technology Industry Council, Partnership for a New American Economy,
and U.S. Chamber of Commerce, November 2012, www.renewoureconomy.org
/sites/all/themes/pnae/stem-report.pdf.

[72]Inter-American Development Bank, *Sending Money Home: Leveraging the Development Impact of Remittances* (Washington, DC: Inter-American Bank, 2004), 4.

[73]D'Vera Cohn, Ana Gonzalez-Barrera, and Danielle Cuddington, "Remittances to
Latin America Recover—But Not to Mexico," Pew Research Center, November
15, 2013, www.pewhispanic.org/2013/11/15/remittances-to-latin-america-recover
-but-not-to-mexico.

[74]"Income Generation and Social Protection for the Poor," World Bank (World Bank, 2004), 150.

[75]Richard H. Adams Jr. and John Page, "Do International Migration and Remittances Reduce Poverty in Developing Countries?," *World Development* 33, no. 10 (2005): 1645.

[76]Ade Daramy, "Remittances Are Three Times Greater Than Aid—How Can They Go Even Further?," *Guardian*, May 11, 2016, www.theguardian.com/global-development -professionals-network/2016/may/11/remittances-three-times-greater-aid-sdgs.

[77]Douglas Massey, "Five Myths About Immigration: Common Misconceptions Underlying U.S. Border-Enforcement Policy," *Immigration Policy in Focus* 4, no. 6 (August 2005): 5.

[78]"Haiti Remittances Key to Earthquake Recovery," World Bank, May 17, 2017, www .worldbank.org/en/news/feature/2010/05/17/haiti-remittances-key-to-earthquake -recovery.

[79]International Organization for Migration, "International Migration Trends" (Geneva, Switzerland: International Organization for Migration, 2005), 380.

[80]Phillip Connor, "International Migration: Key Findings from the US, Europe and the World," Pew Research Center, December 15, 2016, www.pewresearch.org/fact -tank/2016/12/15/international-migration-key-findings-from-the-u-s-europe -and-the-world.

[81]James B. Davies, Susanna Sandstrom, Anthony Shorrocks, and Edward N. Wolff, "The World Distribution of Household Wealth," International Association of Research in Income and Wealth, December 5, 2006, www.iariw.org/papers/2006 /davies.pdf, 26.

[82]"Global Wealth Report," CreditSuisse, accessed November 3, 2017, www.credit -suisse.com/corporate/en/research/research-institute/global-wealth-report.html.

[83]Douglas Massey, "Five Myths About Immigration: Common Misconceptions Underlying U.S. Border-Enforcement Policy," *Immigration Policy in Focus* 4, no. 6 (August 2005): 5.

[84]Tim Amstutz, *A Church Leader's Guide to Immigration* (Baltimore: World Relief National Immigration Resource Network, 2003), 3.

[85]D'Vera Cohn, "It's Official: Minority Babies Are the Majority Among the Nation's Infants, but Only Just," Pew Research Center, June 23, 2016, www.pewresearch .org/fact-tank/2016/06/23/its-official-minority-babies-are-the-majority-among -the-nations-infants-but-only-just.

[86]Richard Mouw, *When the Kings Come Marching In* (Grand Rapids: Eerdmans, 2002), 11.

[87]Orlando Crespo, "Our Transnational Anthem," *Christianity Today* 50, no. 8 (2006): 32.

[88]Ibid.

[89]Richard Beattie, "Immigrant Art Exhibitions: Insights of Passage," *New York Times*, May 19, 2006, F2.

[90]John F. Kennedy, *A Nation of Immigrants* (New York: Harper Perennial, 2008), 36.

[91]Meissner, *Immigration and America's Future*, 13.

CHAPTER 8: IMMIGRATION POLICIES AND POLITICS

[1]Archive of Donald Trump's campaign website, accessed November 3, 2017, http://web.archive.org/web/20150824010152/https://www.donaldjtrump.com/positions/immigration-reform.

[2]Max Ehrenfreund, "The Odd Thing That Happens When You Actually Ask Trump's Supporters About Mass Deportation," November 9, 2016, www.washingtonpost.com/news/wonk/wp/2016/11/09/trumps-voters-dont-actually-support-mass-deportation.

[3]Michael Wear, cited in Amber Strong, "'We Have a Whole Bunch of Folks Who Have Been Looking for Hope in All the Wrong Places,' Former White House Faith Director on the State of Politics," CBN, August 20, 2017, www1.cbn.com/cbnnews/politics/2017/august/lsquo-we-have-a-whole-bunch-of-folks-who-have-been-looking-for-hope-in-all-the-wrong-places-rsquo-fmr-wh-faith-dir-on-the-state-of-politics.

[4]"Here Is Donald Trump's Presidential Announcement Speech," *Time*, June 16, 2015, http://time.com/3923128/donald-trump-announcement-speech.

[5]Jenna Johnson and David Weigel, "Donald Trump Calls for 'Total' Ban on Muslims Entering United States," *Washington Post*, December 8, 2015, www.washingtonpost.com/politics/2015/12/07/e56266f6-9d2b-11e5-8728-1af6af208198_story.html.

[6]Josh Katz, "Who Will Be President?," *New York Times*, November, 8, 2017, www.nytimes.com/interactive/2016/upshot/presidential-polls-forecast.html?_r=0.

[7]Donald Trump, Phoenix, Arizona, August 31, 2016, www.politico.com/story/2016/08/donald-trump-immigration-address-transcript-227614.

[8]"Exit Polls 2016," CNN, November 23, 2017, http://edition.cnn.com/election/results/exit-polls/national/president.

[9]Bob Smietana, "2016 Election Exposes Evangelical Divides," LifeWay Research, October 14, 2016, http://blog.lifeway.com/newsroom/2016/10/14/2016-election-exposes-evangelical-divides.

[10]Ibid.

[11]Ibid; see also "Pastor Views on 2016 Election Campaign," LifeWay Research, September 2016, http://lifewayresearch.com/wp-content/uploads/2016/10/Sept-2016-Pastor-Views-on-Presidential-Election.pdf.

[12]Jens Manuel Krogstad, "Key Facts About the Latino Vote in 2016," October 14, 2016, www.pewresearch.org/fact-tank/2016/10/14/key-facts-about-the-latino-vote-in-2016.

[13]Mickey Ibarra, "Getting Out the Latino Vote: America's Future at Stake," *The Hill*, May 11, 2016, http://thehill.com/blogs/congress-blog/presidential-campaign/279321-getting-out-the-latino-vote-americas-future-at.

[14]Jens Manuel Krogstad, "Key Facts About the Latino Vote in 2016," Pew Research Center, October 14, 2016, www.pewresearch.org/fact-tank/2016/10/14/key-facts -about-the-latino-vote-in-2016.

[15]Jens Manuel Krogstad, Mark Hugo Lopez, Gustavo Lopez, Jeffrey Passel, and Eileen Patten, "Looking Forward to 2016: The Changing Latino Electorate," Pew Research Center, January 19, 2016, www.pewhispanic.org/2016/01/19/looking -forward-to-2016-the-changing-latino-electorate.

[16]Asma Khalid, "Latinos Will Never Vote for a Republican, and Other Myths About Hispanics from 2016," NPR, December 22, 2016, www.npr.org/2016 /12/22/506347254/latinos-will-never-vote-for-a-republican-and-other-myths -about-hispanics-from-20.

[17]CNN, "Exit Polls 2016."

[18]Khalid, "Latinos Will Never Vote for a Republican."

[19]"Latino Priorities for the Trump Administration and Congress in 2017," Pew Research Center, February 23, 2017, www.pewhispanic.org/2017/02/23/latino -priorities-for-the-trump-administration-and-congress-in-2017.

[20]Brett McCracken, Twitter, November 9, 2016, https://twitter.com/brettmccracken/ status/796243146594058240.

[21]Donald J. Trump, "Executive Order: Protecting the Nation from Foreign Terrorist Entry into the United States," White House, January 27, 2017, www.whitehouse .gov/the-press-office/2017/01/27/executive-order-protecting-nation-foreign -terrorist-entry-united-states.

[22]David Brody, "Trump Says Persecuted Christians Will Be Given Priority as Refugees," CBN News, January 27, 2017, www1.cbn.com/thebrodyfile/archive/2017/01/27/ brody-file-exclusive-president-trump-says-persecuted-christians-will-be-given -priority-as-refugees.

[23]David Curry, Nina Shea, Matthew Soerens, and Jeremy Courtney, "Should America's Refugee Policy Put Persecuted Christians First?," *Christianity Today*, January 31, 2017, www.christianitytoday.com/news/2017/january/should-us-refugee-policy -put-persecuted-christians-first.html.

[24]US State Department Refugee Processing Center, accessed October 30, 2017, www .wrapsnet.org.

[25]Ibid.

[26]"Statement by Secretary John Kelly on the Entry of Lawful Permanent Residents into the United States," Department of Homeland Security, January 29, 2017, www .dhs.gov/news/2017/01/29/statement-secretary-john-kelly-entry-lawful-permanent -residents-united-states.

[27]Immigration and Nationality Act INA §202(a)(1)(A).

[28]Vivian Salama and Alicia Caldwell, "AP Exclusive: DHS Report Disputes Threats from Banned Countries," February 24, 2017, www.apnews.com/39f1f8e4ceed4a30a 4570f693291c866.

[29]US State Department, "Fact Sheet: Fiscal Year 2016 Refugee Admissions," January 20, 2017, www.state.gov/j/prm/releases/factsheets/2017/266365.htm.

[30]Jonathan Blitzer, "How Stephen Miller Single-Handedly Got the U.S. to Accept Fewer Refugees," *New Yorker*, October 13, 2017, www.newyorker.com/news/news-desk/how-stephen-miller-single-handedly-got-the-us-to-accept-fewer-refugees.

[31]"Canada's 2016 Record High Level of Resettlement Praised by UNHCR," United Nations High Commissioner for Refugees, April 24, 2017, www.unhcr.org/en-us/news/press/2017/4/58fe15464/canadas-2016-record-high-level-resettlement-praised-unhcr.html.

[32]Muzaffar Chishti, Sarah Pierce, and Jessica Bolter, "The Obama Record on Deportations: Deporter in Chief or Not?," Migration Policy Institute, January 26, 2017, www.migrationpolicy.org/article/obama-record-deportations-deporter-chief-or-not.

[33]Ibid.

[34]"Number of Form I-821D, Consideration of Deferred Action for Childhood Arrivals, by Fiscal Year, Quarter, Intake, Biometrics, and Case Status, Fiscal Year 2012–2017," United States Citizenship and Immigration Services, March 31, 2017, www.uscis.gov/sites/default/files/USCIS/Resources/Reports%20and%20Studies/Immigration%20Forms%20Data/All%20Form%20Types/DACA/daca_performancedata_fy2017_qtr2.pdf.

[35]"Full Text: Donald Trump Immigration Speech in Arizona," *Politico*, August 31, 2016, www.politico.com/story/2016/08/donald-trump-immigration-address-transcript-227614.

[36]"Donald Trump on Russia, Advice from Barack Obama and How He Will Lead," *Time*, December 7, 2016, http://time.com/4591183/time-person-of-the-year-2016-donald-trump-interview.

[37]George O. Wood, "All the Gospel to All the World—Next Door," *PE News*, January 3, 2017, https://penews.org/news/all-the-gospel-to-all-the-world-next-door.

[38]"Remarks by President Trump in Press Conference," White House, February 16, 2017, www.whitehouse.gov/the-press-office/2017/02/16/remarks-president-trump-press-conference.

[39]"National Immigration Survey Presentation—May 2007," FWD.US Poll, June 27, 2017, www.fwd.us/wp-content/uploads/2017/07/FWD.us-Polling-072017.pdf.

[40]Herbert H. Slatery III, letter written to Senator Lamar Alexander and Senator Bob Corker, September 1, 2017, http://i2.cdn.turner.com/cnn/2017/images/09/01/dacaletter9-1-2017.pdf.

[41]Kate Shellnutt, "Trump Ends DACA Despite Pleas from Evangelical Advisers," *Christianity Today*, September 5, 2017, www.christianitytoday.com/news/2017/september/trump-ends-daca-dreamers-despite-evangelical-advisers.html.

[42] Shirley Hoogstra, quoted in "Evangelical Leaders Urge White House, Congress to Protect Dreamers," Evangelical Immigration Table, August 30, 2017, http://evangelicalimmigrationtable.com/evangelical-immigration-table-press-release-evangelical-leaders-urge-white-house-congress-to-protect-dreamers.

[43] Shellnutt, "Trump Ends DACA."

[44] Samuel Rodriguez, quoted in Frances Stead Sellers, "Pastors Who Stood by Trump after Charlottesville Plead with Him to Show 'Heart' for 'Dreamer' Immigrants" *Washington Post*, September 4, 2017, www.washingtonpost.com/politics/pastors-who-stood-by-trump-after-charlottesville-plead-for-him-to-show-heart-for-dreamer-immigrants/2017/09/04/0f5c4312-90a2-11e7-8754-d478688d23b4_story.html.

[45] Jeff Sessions, quoted in Ryan Teague Beckwith, "'We Cannot Admit Everyone.' Read a Transcript of Jeff Sessions' Remarks on Ending the DACA Program," *Time*, September 5, 2017, http://time.com/4927426/daca-dreamers-jeff-sessions-transcript.

[46] Alana Abramson, "Ending the 'Dreamers' Program Could Cost Hundreds of Thousands of Jobs," *Fortune*, August 31, 2017, http://fortune.com/2017/08/31/daca-dreamers-jobs-donald-trump.

[47] Donald Trump, Twitter, September 5, 2017, https://twitter.com/realdonaldtrump/status/905038986883850240?lang=en; Donald Trump, Twitter, September 5, 2017, https://twitter.com/realdonaldtrump/status/905228667336499200?lang=en.

[48] Victoria Balara, "Fox News Poll: 83% Support Path to Citizenship for Illegal Immigrants," Fox News, September 28, 2017, www.foxnews.com/politics/2017/09/28/fox-news-poll-83-percent-support-pathway-to-citizenship-for-illegal-immigrants.html.

[49] American Immigration Lawyers Association, "Rounds/King Amendment," February 2018, www.aila.org/File/Related/Rounds_1_pager_Google_Docs.pdf.

[50] Alexandra Jaffe, "Donald Trump: Undocumented Immigrants 'Have to Go,'" NBC News, August 16, 2015, www.nbcnews.com/meet-the-press/donald-trump-undocumented-immigrants-have-go-n410501.

[51] "Immigration Reform That Will Make America Great Again," Donald J. Trump Campaign, accessed October 31, 2017, https://assets.donaldjtrump.com/Immigration-Reform-Trump.pdf.

[52] Donald Trump, quoted in Maya Rhoden, "Donald Trump Raises Eyebrows with 'Bad Hombres' Line," *Time*, October 19, 2016, http://time.com/4537847/donald-trump-bad-hombres.

[53] Chishti, Pierce, and Bolter, "Obama Record on Deportations."

[54] Donald J. Trump, "Executive Order: Enhancing Public Safety in the Interior of the United States," White House, January 25, 2017, www.whitehouse.gov/the-press-office/2017/01/25/presidential-executive-order-enhancing-public-safety-interior-united.

[55]"Summary and Questions/Analysis of Executive Order 'Enhancing Public Safety in the Interior of the United States,'" American Immigration Lawyers Association and American Immigration Council, January 25, 2017, www.aila.org/infonet/summary-brief-analysis-of-trump-executive-orders.

[56]Nick Miroff, "Deportations Slow Under Trump Despite Increase in Arrests by ICE," *Washington Post*, September 28, 2017, www.washingtonpost.com/world/national-security/deportations-fall-under-trump-despite-increase-in-arrests-by-ice/2017/09/28/1648d4ee-a3ba-11e7-8c37-e1d99ad6aa22_story.html.

[57]Ibid.

[58]"Southwest Border Migration," US Customs and Border Protection, November 3, 2017, www.cbp.gov/newsroom/stats/sw-border-migration.

[59]"Immigration Court Backlog Tool," *TRACImmigration*, http://trac.syr.edu/phptools/immigration/court_backlog. Data through August 2017.

[60]Leila Miller, "Religious Leaders Protest LA Pastor's Detention During Routine ICE Appointment," *Los Angeles Times*, July 25, 2017, www.latimes.com/local/california/la-me-pastor-carias-20170724-story.html.

[61]"ICE Arrests Romulo Avelica-Gonzalez in Front of His Family," YouTube, July 31, 2017, www.youtube.com/watch?v=MDHM7Ef59FQ.

[62]Andrea Castillo, "LA Immigrant Detained While Taking His Daughters to School Is Released," *Los Angeles Times*, August 30, 2017, www.latimes.com/local/lanow/la-me-romulo-avelica-release-20170831-story.html.

[63]Marwa Eltagouri, "A 10-Year-Old Immigrant Was Rushed to the Hospital in an Ambulance. She Was Detained on the Way," *Washington Post*, October 27, 2017, www.washingtonpost.com/news/post-nation/wp/2017/10/26/a-10-year-old-immigrant-was-rushed-to-the-hospital-in-an-ambulance-she-was-detained-on-the-way/?utm_term=.e20507d5f7a2.

[64]Arelis R. Hernandez, "ICE Raids Under Trump Spark Fear in Maryland, Virginia," *Washington Post*, February 17, 2017, www.washingtonpost.com/local/ice-raids-under-trump-spark-fear-in-maryland-virginia/2017/02/17/01044db8-f517-11e6-8d72-263470bf0401_story.html.

[65]"FAQ on Sensitive Locations and Courthouse Arrests," Immigration and Customs Enforcement, June 13, 2017, www.ice.gov/ero/enforcement/sensitive-loc.

[66]Kate Shellnut, "Half of Hispanic Christians Worry About Deportation Under Trump," *Christianity Today*, February 24, 2017, www.christianitytoday.com/news/2017/february/half-of-hispanic-christians-worry-deportation-trump-dhs-ice.html.

[67]"The Costs of Mass Deportation," *Wall Street Journal*, March 21, 2016, www.wsj.com/articles/the-costs-of-mass-deportation-1458342018; and Julie Hirschfield Davis and Ron Nixon, "Trump Budget Takes Broad Aim at Undocumented Immigrants," *New York Times*, May 25, 2017, www.nytimes.com/2017/05/25/us/politics/undocumented-immigrants-trump-budget-wall.html.

[68]Doris Meissner, Donald Kerwin, Muzaffar Chishti, and Claire Bergeron, "Immigration Enforcement in the United States: The Rise of a Formidable Machinery," Migration Policy Institute, January 2013, www.migrationpolicy.org/research/immigration-enforcement-united-states-rise-formidable-machinery.

[69]Jeffrey S. Passel and D'Vera Cohn, "Unauthorized Immigrant Totals Rise in 7 States, Fall in 14," Pew Research Center, November 18, 2014, www.pewhispanic.org/files/2014/11/2014-11-18_unauthorized-immigration.pdf.

[70]"FY2016 ICE Immigration Removals," Immigration and Customs Enforcement, February 10, 2017, www.ice.gov/removal-statistics/2016.

[71]Ibid.

[72]Ersela Kripa and Stephen Mueller, "Growing Private Detention Industry Threatens Immigrants' Rights on the US-Mexico Border," *Architects Newspaper*, August 21, 2017, https://archpaper.com/2017/08/private-detention-industry-us-mexico-border/#gallery-0-slide-0.

[73]Dora Schriro, "Immigration Detention Overview and Recommendations," Immigration and Customs Enforcement, October 6, 2009, www.ice.gov/doclib/about/offices/odpp/pdf/ice-detention-rpt.pdf.

[74]Ibid.

[75]Kripa and Mueller, "Growing Private Detention Industry."

[76]"2009 Immigration Detention Reforms," Immigration and Customs Enforcement, December 12, 2011, www.ice.gov/es/factsheets/2009detention-reform.

[77]U.S. Immigration and Customs Enforcement, "2011 Operations Manual: ICE Performance-Based National Detention Standards," www.ice.gov/detention-standards/2011.

[78]Caitlin Dickerson, "Trump Plan Would Curtail Protections for Detained Immigrants," *New York Times*, April 13, 2017, www.nytimes.com/2017/04/13/us/detained-immigrants-may-face-harsher-conditions-under-trump.html.

[79]Jeffrey Passel and D'Vera Cohn, "As Mexican Share Declined, U.S. Unauthorized Immigrant Population Fell in 2015 Below Recession Level," Pew Research Center, April 25, 2017, www.pewresearch.org/fact-tank/2017/04/25/as-mexican-share-declined-u-s-unauthorized-immigrant-population-fell-in-2015-below-recession-level.

[80]"United States Border Patrol Sector Profile—FY2016," US Customs and Border Protection, January 2017, www.cbp.gov/sites/default/files/assets/documents/2017-Jan/USBP%20Stats%20FY2016%20sector%20profile.pdf.

[81]"U.S. Border Patrol Southwest Border Apprehensions by Sector," US Customs and Border Protection, November 3, 2017, www.cbp.gov/newsroom/stats/usbp-sw-border-apprehensions.

[82]J. Weston Phippen, "Asians Now Outpace Mexicans In Terms of Undocumented Growth," *Atlantic*, August 20, 2015, www.theatlantic.com/politics/archive/2015/08/asians-now-outpace-mexicans-in-terms-of-undocumented-growth/432603.

[83]Ibid.

[84]Arturo Sarukhán, "Leading the Way 2017," National Immigration Forum, October 5, 2017, https://youtu.be/Dthj23LVMzk.

[85]M. Daniel Carroll R., *Christians at the Border: Immigration, the Church, and the Bible* (Grand Rapids: Baker Academic, 2008), 92.

[86]Leith Anderson, "'Comprehensive' Immigration Reform Means No Stop-Gap Solution," *New York Times*, December 9, 2012, www.nytimes.com/roomfordebate/2012/12/09/understanding-immigration-reform/comprehensive-immigration-reform-means-no-stop-gap-solutions.

[87]"Amnesty," *Merriam-Webster*, accessed December 18, 2017, www.merriam-webster.com/dictionary/amnesty.

[88]"Evangelical Statement of Principles for Immigration Reform," Evangelical Immigration Table, June 15, 2012, www.evangelicalimmigrationtable.com/sign-the-principles.

[89]John McCain, quoted in Dana Farrington, "Senator McCain Calls for Compromise in Return to the Senate Floor," NPR, July 25, 2017, www.npr.org/2017/07/25/539323689/watch-sen-mccain-calls-for-compromise-in-return-to-senate-floor.

[90]Drew Westen, "Immigrating from Facts to Values: Political Rhetoric in the US Immigration Debate," Migration Policy Institute Transatlantic Council on Migration, October 2009, www.migrationpolicy.org/research/immigrating-facts-values-political-rhetoric-us-immigration-debate.

[91]Ibid.

[92]Ibid.

[93]Peter Wehner, "Evangelicals, Trump and the Politics of Redemption," Religion News Service, August 11, 2017, http://religionnews.com/2017/08/11/evangelicals-trump-and-the-politics-of-redemption.

[94]Martin Luther King Jr., "A Knock at Midnight," June 11, 1967, http://kingencyclopedia.stanford.edu/encyclopedia/documentsentry/doc_a_knock_at_midnight.1.html.

CHAPTER 9: IMMIGRATION AND THE CHURCH TODAY

[1]Michael Lynch, "Serving Immigrants Saved Our Church," *Leadership Journal*, fall 2014, www.christianitytoday.com/pastors/2014/fall/serving-immigrants-saved-our-church.html.

[2]Ibid.

[3]Ibid.

[4]"Religious Landscape Study," Pew Research Center, 2015, www.pewforum.org/religious-landscape-study.

[5]Sarah Pulliam Bailey, "Christianity Faces Sharp Decline as Americans Are Becoming Even Less Affiliated with Religion," *Washington Post*, May 12, 2015, www.washingtonpost.com/news/acts-of-faith/wp/2015/05/12/christianity-faces-sharp-decline-as-americans-are-becoming-even-less-affiliated-with-religion.

[6]Michael Lipka, "5 Key Findings About the Changing U.S. Religious Landscape," Pew Research Center, May 12, 2015, www.pewresearch.org/fact-tank/2015/05/12/5 -key-findings-u-s-religious-landscape.

[7]"Religious Landscape Study: Evangelical Protestants," Pew Research Center, 2015, www.pewforum.org/religious-landscape-study/religious-tradition/evangelical -protestant.

[8]"Religious Landscape Study: Catholics," Pew Research Center, 2015, www.pewforum .org/religious-landscape-study/religious-tradition/catholic.

[9]"US Denominations Growth Rate, 1970–2015," ed. Todd M. Johnson and Gina A. Zurlo, World Christian Database, accessed September 2017, http://worldchristian database.org/wcd/home.asp. The World Christian Database is an online database accessible only to subscribers.

[10]Matthew Soerens, "The Church and the Huddled Masses," *Christianity Today*, October 2016, www.christianitytoday.com/pastors/2016/october-web-exclusives/ church-and-refugees.html.

[11]"Statistics," Assemblies of God (USA), accessed October 3, 2017, https://ag.org/ About/Statistics.

[12]Darrin Rodgers, "Assemblies of God 2015 Statistics Released, Growth Spurred by Ethnic Transformation," Flower Pentecostal History Center, June 24, 2016, https:// ifphc.wordpress.com/2016/06/24/assemblies-of-god-2015-statistics-released -growth-spurred-by-ethnic-transformation.

[13]Carol Pipes, "Southern Baptists Report More Churches in 2016; Baptisms, Membership Decline," LifeWay Christian Resources, June 8, 2017, http://blog .lifeway.com/newsroom/2017/06/08/southern-baptists-report-more-churches -in-2016-baptisms-membership-decline.

[14]"Resolution on Racial Reconciliation on the 150th Anniversary of the Southern Baptist Convention," Southern Baptist Convention, Atlanta, GA, 1995, www.sbc .net/resolutions/899/resolution-on-racial-reconciliation-on-the-150th-anniversary -of-the-southern-baptist-convention; "On the Anti-Gospel of Alt-Right White Supremacy," Southern Baptist Convention, Phoenix, AZ, 2017, www.sbc.net/ resolutions/2283/on-the-antigospel-of-altright-white-supremacy; "On Refugee Ministry," Southern Baptist Convention, St. Louis, MO, 2016, www.sbc.net/ resolutions/2273/on-refugee-ministry; "On Immigration and the Gospel," Southern Baptist Convention, Phoenix, AZ, 2011, www.sbc.net/resolutions/1213; "Fast Facts About the SBC," Southern Baptist Convention, accessed November 3, 2017, www.sbc.net/BecomingSouthernBaptist/FastFacts.asp.

[15]Ed Stetzer, "The Future of the SBC—Is Not White," *Christianity Today*, June 23, 2016, www.christianitytoday.com/edstetzer/2016/june/our-future-is-not-white.html.

[16]Wesley Granberg-Michaelson, "Commentary: The Hidden Immigration Impact on American Churches," *Washington Post*, September 23, 2013, www.washingtonpost

.com/national/on-faith/commentary-the-hidden-immigration-impact-on-american
-churches/2013/09/23/0bd53b74-2484-11e3-9372-92606241ae9c_story.html.

[17]Martin Luther King, Jr., "Meet the Press," NBC News, April 17, 1960.

[18]Leith Anderson, quoted in in Leah Fabel, "Credo: Leith Anderson," *Washington Examiner*, October 11, 2009, www.washingtonexaminer.com/credo-leith-anderson/article/22079.

[19]Soong-Chan Rah, *The Next Evangelicalism: Releasing the Church from Western Cultural Captivity* (Downers Grove, IL: InterVarsity Press, 2009).

[20]Soong-Chan Rah, *Many Colors: Cultural Intelligence for a Changing Church* (Chicago: Moody Publishers, 2010), 175.

[21]Scholars John Berry, Joseph Trimble, and Esteban Olmedo identify at least four distinct models of immigrant acculturation (assimilation, marginalization, separation, and integration), each defined by whether immigrants want (and are allowed by the receiving community) to be relationally connected to other groups and whether they want (and are allowed) to maintain their cultural identity and characteristics ("Assessment of Acculturation," in *Field Methods in Cross-Cultural Research*, ed. Walter Lonner and John Berry [Beverly Hills, CA: Sage, 1986]). At World Relief, we believe that integration—when immigrants both seek and are allowed to simultaneously maintain their cultural identity and become a part of the whole—is the most effective, biblical model, both for immigrants joining a new country and, for those who are or become Christ-followers, the church.

[22]Sandra Maria Van Opstal, *The Next Worship: Glorifying God in a Diverse World* (Downers Grove, IL: InterVarsity Press, 2016), 35.

[23]Ibid., 38-39.

[24]Justo González, quoted in Miriam Adeney, "A Wake-Up Call to Become Global Christians," *Christianity Today*, September 1, 2001, www.christianitytoday.com/ct/2001/septemberweb-only/9-10-35.0.html?start=4.

[25]Bob Smietana, "Evangelicals Say It Is Time for Congress to Tackle Immigration," LifeWay Research, March 11, 2015, http://lifewayresearch.com/2015/03/11/evangelicals-say-it-is-time-for-congress-to-tackle-immigration.

[26]J. D. Payne, *Pressure Points: Twelve Global Issues Shaping the Face of the Church* (Nashville: Thomas Nelson, 2013), 69.

[27]Andy Olsen, "Immigrants Are Reshaping American Missions," *Christianity Today*, June 21, 2017, www.christianitytoday.com/ct/2017/july-august/immigrants-are-reshaping-american-missions.html.

[28]Ibid.

[29]In many Spanish-speaking countries, a *notario* has earned a credential *beyond* that of an attorney, but a notary public in the United States is merely authorized to verify signatures on legal documents, not to give legal advice. Unfortunately, many indi-

viduals who are not authorized to practice law have exploited this false cognate to present themselves as a credible source for immigration legal advice, sometimes with disastrous effects.

[30]Zach Szmara, quoted in Matthew Soerens, "A Clear and Present Mission," *Christianity Today*, November 2014, www.christianitytoday.com/pastors/2014/november-online-only/clear-and-present-mission.html.

[31]Zach Szmara, quoted in in Noel Castellanos and David Drury, "Are You the People That Help Immigrants?," National Association of Evangelicals, Spring 2014, www.nae.net/are-you-the-people-that-help-immigrants.

[32]"Aurora, Illinois: Language Spoken at Home," American Fact Finder: US Census Bureau, 2015, https://factfinder.census.gov.

[33]Bryant Wright, "Reaching Refugees—Reaching the Nations," International Mission Board, October 24, 2017, www.imb.org/2017/10/24/reaching-refugees-reaching-the-nations.

[34]Alice Su, "As German Police Attempt to Deport Refugees, Hundreds of Churches Are Trying to Shelter Them," *Washington Post*, September 6, 2017, www.washingtonpost.com/world/europe/in-germany-churches-offer-unofficial-asylum-for-muslim-refugees/2017/09/05/1c068b68-88e6-11e7-96a7-d178cf3524eb_story.html.

[35]German pastor, quoted in Sam George, "Is God Reviving Europe Through Refugees?," *Lausanne Global Analysis*, May 2017, www.lausanne.org/content/lga/2017-05/god-reviving-europe-refugees.

[36]Sam George, quoted in ibid.

[37]Bryan Hanson, quoted in in Margaret Colson, "Former SBC President on '60 Minutes,' Addresses Refugee Crisis," *Baptist Press*, October 19, 2016, www.bpnews.net/47747/former-sbc-pres-on-60-minutes-addresses-refugee-crisis.

[38]Bryant Wright, quoted in in Bill Whitaker, "Finding Refuge," *60 Minutes*, October 16, 2016, www.cbsnews.com/news/60-minutes-syrian-refugee-crisis-immigration.

[39]Ibid; Jonathan Serrie, "Popular Georgia Evangelical Pastor Criticizes Anti-Refugee Politics," Fox News, December 21, 2015, www.foxnews.com/us/2015/12/21/popular-georgia-evangelical-pastor-criticizes-anti-refugee-politics.html.

[40]Whitaker, "Finding Refuge."

[41]"Evangelical Leaders from All 50 States Urge President Trump to Reconsider Reduction in Refugee Resettlement," World Relief, February 8, 2017, www.worldrelief.org/press-releases/evangelical-leaders-from-all-50-states-urge-president-trump-to-reconsider-reduction-in-refugee-resettlment.

[42]Luis Cortes, "An Open Letter to Evangelical Leaders on Comprehensive Immigration Reform," *Esperanza*, accessed January 30, 2008, www.esperanza.us/atf/cf/percent7bB793CA9C- D2B9-4E02-886B-E6DE52E04944 percent7d/Open percent 20Letter percent20to percent 20Evangelicals.pdf.

[43]Samuel Rodriguez, quoted in Tim Stafford, "The Call of Samuel," *Christianity Today*,

September 1, 2006, www.christianitytoday.com/ct/2006/september/31.82.html.

[44]"Immigration," Resolution of the National Association of Evangelicals, October 2009, www.nae.net/immigration-2009.

[45]"On Immigration and the Gospel," Southern Baptist Convention, Phoenix, 2011, www.sbc.net/resolutions/1213.

[46]"Resolution on Immigration," Evangelical Covenant Church, 2014, www.covchurch. org/wp-content/uploads/sites/65/2013/03/2014-Resolution-on-Immigration -FINAL-without-Resource.pdf; David Roller and Bruce Cromwell, "The Free Methodist Position on Immigration," *Free Methodist Conversations*, 2013, http:// fmcusa.org/conversations/the-free-methodist-position-on-immigration.

[47]Jim Wallis, *The (Un)Common Good: How the Gospel Brings Hope to a World Divided* (Grand Rapids: Brazos Press, 2013), 84.

[48]Lindsey Graham, quoted in Mary Orndorff Troyan, "Spartanburg Baptist Minister Lobbies for Immigration Reform," *The State*, June 13, 2013, www.thestate.com/ living/religion/article14434268.html.

[49]"Evangelical Views on Immigration," LifeWay Research, February 2015, http:// lifewayresearch.com/wp-content/uploads/2015/03/Evangelical-Views-on -Immigration-Report.pdf.

[50]Ibid.

[51]Alan Cross, "Why Evangelicals Should Care About the Immigrants in Our Midst," *Christianity Today*, October 21, 2015, www.christianitytoday.com/edstetzer/2015/ october/why-evangelicals-should-care-about-immigrants-in-our-midst.html.

[52]Alan's book, *When Heaven and Earth Collide: Racism, Southern Evangelicals, and the Better Way of Jesus* (Montgomery, AL: NewSouth Books, 2014), explores the ways that many white evangelical Christians allowed culture and economic interests to trump their theology, with devastating consequences for African Americans.

[53]Bill Hybels, Willow Creek Community Church, April 13, 2014, https://willow creek.tv/sermons/south-barrington/2014/04/week-3.

CHAPTER 10: A CHRISTIAN RESPONSE TO THE IMMIGRATION DILEMMA

[1]Dietrich Bonhoeffer, *The Cost of Discipleship* (New York: Touchstone, 1995), 58.

[2]Henri Nouwen, Donald McNeill, and Douglas Morrison, *Compassion: Reflections on the Christian Life* (New York: Doubleday, 1982), 104, 116.

[3]Ibid., 104.

[4]Ibid., 109.

[5]Mary Pipher, *The Middle of Everywhere: The World's Refugees Come to Our Town* (New York: Harcourt, 2002), 331.

[6]For those who would like to delve deeper into understanding immigrants and immigration, we have provided a list of additional resources in appendix four.

[7]"Evangelical Views on Immigration," LifeWay Research, February 2015, http://
lifewayresearch.com/wp-content/uploads/2015/03/Evangelical-Views-on
-Immigration-Report.pdf.

[8]Ibid.

[9]"Discovering and Living God's Heart for Immigrants: A Guide to Welcoming the
Stranger" is available as a free download at www.welcomingthestranger.com.

[10]Charles Spurgeon, quoted in Nigel Rees, *Brewer's Famous Quotations: 5000 Quotations and the Stories Behind Them* (London: Weidenfeld & Nicolson, 2006), 119.

[11]"For the Health of the Nation: An Evangelical Call to Civic Responsibility,"
National Association of Evangelicals, accessed January 21, 2008, http://nae.net/
wp-content/uploads/2015/06/For-the-Health-of-the-Nation.pdf, 2-3.